D0754371

V.S. NAIPAUL

V. S. NAIPAUL

A Critical Introduction

LANDEG WHITE

First published 1975 by
THE MACMILLAN PRESS LTD
London and Basingstoke
Associated companies in New York
Dublin Melbourne Johannesburg and Madras

SBN 333 17320 1

Photoset, printed and bound
in Great Britain by
REDWOOD BURN LIMITED
Trowbridge & Esher

CONTENTS

ACKNOWLEDGEMENTS

The author and publisher wish to thank the following for their permission to reproduce copyright material:

V. S. Naipaul and André Deutsch Ltd., for the extracts from *The Mystic Masseur, The Suffrage of Elvira, Miguel Street, A House for Mr Biswas, The Middle Passage, Mr Stone and the Knights Companion, An Area of Darkness, The Mimic Men, A Flag on the Island, The Loss of El Dorado, In a Free State*, and *The Overcrowded Barracoon*; Alfred Knopf Inc., for the extracts from the copyrighted works of V. S. Naipaul: *The Loss of El Dorado, In a Free State*, and *The Overcrowded Barracoon*; Macmillan Publishing Co. Inc., for the extracts from *An Area of Darkness* (copyright © 1964 by V. S. Naipaul) and *The Mimic Men* (copyright © 1967 by V. S. Naipaul); Mrs D. Naipaul for the quotations from *Gurudeva and Other Indian Tales* by Seepersad Naipaul; the Vanguard Press Inc., for the extracts from *Miguel Street* (copyright © 1959 by V. S. Naipaul).

CHAPTER ONE

What is it that we look for when we go to the work of a favourite writer? It is, I feel, a peculiar type of adventure – an adventure with a mind, a sensibility, that appeals to us. A certain way of looking and feeling, which we think amusing or illuminating. We do not go for characters or for language so much as for the writer himself. A writer stands or falls by his sensibility and our assessment of his work depends on our response to his sensibility.[1]

I

This book is a study of the development of a writer who is still in his early forties. Yet it needs no justification. Since 1957, V.S. Naipaul has published twelve books. They include two travelogues, a collection of articles, a substantial history, and eight works of fiction, two of which – *A House for Mr Biswas* and *The Mimic Men* – are acknowledged to be masterpieces. He has won five major literary prizes, plus a grant from the Phoenix Trust and bursaries from the Trinidad Government and the British Arts Council. His works have begun to appear in a special uniform edition. Already, however, there is a clear need to bring his achievement into focus. A writer who has been blamed by West Indian critics for racial arrogance and by their English counterparts for contenting himself with being charming; who produces a book almost every year yet whose favourite words are 'absurdity' and 'exhaustion'; who has created a range of characters of Dickensian memorability yet who admits to a constant struggle against contempt; whose technical accomplishment and elegance of style are unquestioned yet who is often visibly at odds with the novel form; who recreates his backgrounds in infectiously loving detail yet who ends every book with a celebration of escape: a writer whose achievement turns on such apparent contradictions clearly merits careful attention.

Yet despite the paradoxes in which Naipaul constitutionally

I

deals, the critic's task is in one sense fairly straightforward. Naipaul has no severer judge than himself, and we shall find repeatedly that the most stringent comment on each book is its immediate successor. When his books are read in the order in which they were written (which is not always the order of publication), four points emerge which form the substance of this present study. The first is that although the books vary considerably in merit, there is none that is irrelevant to his total achievement. *A House for Mr Biswas* was the first to reveal his full abilities. Yet it could not have been written without the 'apprenticeship', as Naipaul calls it, of the early Trinidad novels. Similarly, *Mr Stone and the Knights Companion* and the long story 'A Flag on the Island' (both of which draw extensively on *The Middle Passage* and *An Area of Darkness*) are essential preliminaries to the writing of *The Mimic Men*. The second point is that within this framework of two masterpieces preceded by less ambitious, preparatory works, there is a steady broadening of scope. In *The Mystic Masseur* he is little more than a regional writer reporting on the East Indian minority in colonial Trinidad. In his latest fiction *In a Free State* he handles a thoroughly international cast against the backgrounds of Egypt, New York, London and independent Africa. The themes may seem similar – all Naipaul's important ideas have been present in embryo from the start – but their relevance has steadily widened. The third point is a consistent development in sheer ability. Naipaul has never been interested in experiment for its own sake, insisting that technique 'ought not to be noticeable except to the practitioner or the percipient critic'. [2] But it will be clear as we move from one book to the next not only that he has reflected deeply on the skills he must acquire to achieve effects appropriate to his themes, but also that he is far more aware than those writers who can take a literary tradition for granted of the implications for his material of the form to which he is shaping it.

Fourthly, however, and most important, are the ways in which his whole career is centred on the uncertainties of his own position. A Brahmin from Trinidad who sets up house in London – the cultural ambiguities implicit in such a background are the pivot of his work. Naipaul rejects the phrase 'the search for identity' as a piece of camouflage, an attempt to pretend that writer, peasant and politician in ex-colonial territories can make common cause. But some equivalent phrase is necessary if we are to recognise the extent to which the struggle against the effects of displacement lies at the heart of his work. It is not just that his writing seems to spring from the need to define his position in the world. It is his awareness of the gap between his Hindu background and the assumptions inherent in the novel form that keeps him asking himself *why* he is setting all these imaginary characters in motion. It is his recurring scepticism about the relevance of the form he is using to the disturbance which is his subject that makes each novel a new attempt at truth, a fresh qualification of its predecessors. It is his recognition that he is writing about societies to which he cannot belong that governs his approach to the problem of placing himself, as author or narrator, accurately and honestly in relation to his material. It is his deepening understanding of his own displacement that makes possible the broadening of scope. From frivolity to despair, from homelessness as the affliction of East Indians in Trinidad to homelessness as a universal condition — the gap is measured by his own gradual emergence from the security of colonialism.

2

Vidiahar Surajprasad Naipaul was born at Chaguanas in central Trinidad on 17 August 1932. Four months earlier, the local correspondent of the *Trinidad Guardian* had described Chaguanas as 'the peasants' paradise', adding that a village of 438 rateable buildings and 1452 inhabitants 'couldn't be called dull'.[3] The *Guardian* welcomed such jauntiness. But the correspondent was Naipaul's father, Seepersad Naipaul, who did not own one of the 438 buildings. V.S. Naipaul was born in the Lion House, home of the powerful Capildeo family whose seventh daughter, Bropatie, Mr Naipaul had married in 1929. The Lion House, reproduced almost exactly in *A House for Mr Biswas* as Hanuman House, still dominates the older section of a town still largely dependent on the surrounding sugar estates.

In the same book, in the character of Anand, we have by and

large an account of Naipaul's own childhood. Naturally, there are changes; the novel is not an autobiography. Anand is keen to be initiated as a Brahmin though Naipaul declined to undergo the exotic ceremony. Anand, like Naipaul, has three sisters, one two years older than himself, but there is no reference in the novel to Shiva Naipaul, born in 1945 (though it is amusing to note the Tulsi sisters' prophecy, 'One day you will get a brother, and he will cut off your nose': Shiva Naipaul with *Fireflies* and *The Chip-chip Gatherers* has quickly established himself as a rival talent). Naturally, too, the main emphasis in the novel is on Anand's close relationship with his father. But the broad outlines of Anand's career are taken from life. Naipaul spent just under two years at Chaguanas Government School which, in its days as the Canadian Mission School, his father had attended twenty-odd years earlier. In 1938, following his father's transfer to Port of Spain, he moved to Tranquility Boys School where he distinguished himself sufficiently to be put in the exhibition examination class under the 'legendary' teacher Mr O.E. Romilly. In 1942, when Tranquility boys won seven out of the twenty-one exhibitions offered, Naipaul came third in the Island and gained a free place at Queens Royal College. He attended Q.R.C. from January 1943 to April 1949, eventually specialising in French and Spanish. Through some oversight he failed to comply with the regulations for an ordinary Island scholarship, but in view of his brilliance the Education Board created a special scholarship for him.

These five years at Q.R.C. together with the years the family spent shifting from one address to another (from Chaguanas to Port of Spain in 1938, to Diego Martin in 1940, back to the Capildeos' house in Port of Spain in 1941, and finally to a house of their own in Nepaul Street, St James, in 1947) are, as we shall see, extremely important as source material. The school features in three of the novels, but Naipaul seems to have left little impression there. The only record of his presence, apart from the usual registers and prize lists, is a contribution to the Q.R.C. *Chronicle* for 1948. The article is a discussion of Somerset Maugham's first novel *Liza of Lambeth*. It is not difficult to see why Naipaul should have been drawn to the novel. Liza's fate turns on the clash between her desire for beauty and romance, and the sordid circumstances of her slum life – a theme of his own early work. Significantly, however, his initial interest seems to have been in 'how the author of *Of Human Bondage* and *Cakes and Ale* began his literary career':

> The faults in this work are obvious; but it is full of promise. Most young writers will take a little comfort from reading it. [4]

Apart from this clear declaration that he sees himself as a young writer, the article contains sentences which suggest that he has already reflected on problems which are to concern him in *Miguel Street*, his own first book:

> But what, I suppose, has rescued the novel from obscurity and has made it at least fit to be included in collected editions is the study of slum life. Maugham describes the slum people with a detachment that is not without humour. His novel is free from the social realism that has imposed itself upon modern literature. The women, especially, are interesting. For them life is a messy monotony of motherhood and maulings ('It won't seem so bad after yer gits used to it; it's a bit disappointin' at fust, but yer gits not to mind it.'). The women accept blows as a normal part of their existence. 'We come from a very prodigal family, we do,' Mrs Kemp tells Liza. 'We've all run into double figures, except your Aunt May.' [5]

Naipaul returned to Queens Royal College in January 1950 as a student teacher, but left after six months to take up his place at University College, Oxford.

Eight years later, summarising his experiences in England, he writes:

> After eight years here I find I have, without effort, achieved the Buddhist ideal of non-attachment. I am never disturbed by national or international issues. I do not sign petitions. I do not vote. I do not march. And I never cease to feel that this lack of interest is all wrong. [6]

It seems an extraordinary comment on what would appear to be eight extremely active years. By August 1958, Naipaul had published *The Mystic Masseur*, which became a Book Society choice and won him the John Llewellyn Rhys Memorial Prize, and *The Suffrage of Elvira*, reviewed in the *Sunday Times* as 'a perfect novel'. *Miguel Street*, which was written in 1955, was in the press awaiting publication, and he was well advanced with *A House for Mr Biswas*, his first attempt at a major work. Add to this an Oxford degree in English, experience as editor of the B.B.C. 'Caribbean Voices' programme and as a reviewer with the *New Statesman*, marriage in 1955 to an English girl – all in all it seems no bad record of successful involvement in English life, the fulfilment of every young immigrant's dream. But Naipaul is continuing to think of himself as a young writer, anxious to leap 'the regional barrier' but lacking the necessary experience. The same article concludes, 'I fear that living here will eventually lead to my own sterility', and a feeling has been defined which is to deepen in intensity over the following years. He suggests the solution might lie 'in travel – to Trinidad, to India'. But by 1964, after seven months in the West Indies and a year in India, he knows better. The visits are productive, not only in the accounts of his travels in *The Middle Passage* and *An Area of Darkness*, but also in the material which he eventually incorporates into 'A Flag on the Island' (written in 1965) and *The Mimic Men*. Once again, he would appear to be enjoying considerable success. *A House for Mr Biswas* won him immense acclaim and *Mr Stone and the Knights Companion*, his first novel about London, brought him a Hawthornden Prize. But his own position has darkened. By 1964, he sees himself as a person utterly displaced, connected by birth and education with three different societies yet unable to establish living contact with any of them.

The full record of homelessness is, of course, the novels themselves, and the different stances Naipaul adopts and the perceptions defined through them will be discussed in my succeeding chapters. Nevertheless, one wonders at times whether Naipaul the writer could ever fit into any existing society, whether a longing for other places, other circumstances, is not his strongest creative urge. By the date of his first departure from Trinidad, he seems to have developed the feeling that his talent must be protected from the corruption of any kind of commitment. Such is his intense desire for privacy, such his fear of 'violation', that when confronted with one society he seems to take a delight in retreating to that aspect of his persona which rejects it. As a Brahmin in Trinidad, he was always able to operate between two worlds. In the opening chapter of *An Area of Darkness*, he examines what 'India' meant to him as a boy, contrasting the irrelevant India which lay about him in the form of string beds, straw mats, brass vessels, a broken harmonium, with the India within which led him to refuse to suck a pipette in the chemistry class after other boys had used it, and which remained a virgin world of the imagination powerful enough to deny him any real sense of participation in Trinidad. But he returns to Trinidad in 1960 not as a Hindu but as a product of Q.R.C. and Oxford University. The record of his visit in *The Middle Passage* is a tirade against the second-rate in the accents of Trollope and Froude.

Two years later in India he is more open and responsive. He recognises in Indian life elements of himself, a detachment, a denial of concern, that matches his own existence in London. But he remains an outsider. His visit to the village of his grandfather, though briefly enchanting, arouses problems over language, fears about the food and water, demands for money, and concludes with Naipaul's angry refusal to give a relative a lift into town. There is no home for him in India; his assumptions are too much of the West. Yet just as it was in London that he wrote the Trinidad novels, viewing his background from the security of escape, so it is in Kashmir that he writes *Mr Stone and the Knights Companion*, projecting on to his English hero a strong Hindu sense of the world as illusion. Returning to Europe, he is no longer able to believe in the places in which he has lived and worked. A Brahmin-cum-Englishman in Trinidad, a European in India, an Indian in London: one wonders whether such detachment, such seizing of the opportunities for retreat, is less a source of regret to him than a precondition of his writing life.

Describing his return from India, in the closing paragraphs of *An Area of Darkness*, he redefines his 1958 statement with a finer, more poignant insight:

Some days later in London, facing as for the first time a culture whose point, going by the advertisements and the shop-windows, appeared to be homemaking, the creation of separate warm cells; walking down streets of such cells past gardens left derelict by the hard winter and trying, in vain, to summon up a positive response to this city where I had lived and worked; facing my own emptiness, my feeling of being physically lost, I had a dream.

An oblong of stiff new cloth lay before me, and I had the knowledge that if only out of this I could cut a smaller oblong of specific measurements, a specific section of this cloth, then the cloth would begin to unravel of itself, and the unravelling would spread from the cloth to the table to the house to all matter, *until the whole trick was undone*. Those were the words that were with me as I flattened the cloth and studied it for the clues which I knew existed, which I desired above everything else to find, but which I knew I never would.[7]

The fear has deepened. Naipaul sees himself no longer as the poised writer, anxious only about losing his audience or running short of material, but as a man threatened by desolation, driven deep within himself, reduced by homelessness to 'a smaller world than I had ever known . . . my flat, my desk, my name'. Yet surely it is an attractive despair – the romantic recluse with the world at his disposal, the universal seer, uncorrupted by nationalism, campaigning for no cause but bearing the full weight of a lonely quest for truth. Newspaper photographs at this time show Naipaul tormented and dishevelled, his collar rumpled, his luxuriant hair falling across furrowed evasive eyes. The accompanying texts emphasise his disturbance, his exhaustion, his appalled irony.

The pose contains its truth. It produced some brilliant writing, culminating in 1967 with *The Mimic Men*. Yet it was a relief to see, in *The Times* of 13 May 1971, a three-quarter page advertisement placed by Action Bangla Desh, calling on the British Government to suspend aid to West Pakistan and to launch a massive relief operation, and containing under the caption 'The life and death of millions is everyone's problem' two hundred and four signatures including the name V.S. Naipaul. At the age of thirty-eight and after nearly twenty-one years in England, Naipaul had at last announced a commitment by signing a petition. In August 1971, an interview in the *Times Literary Supplement* confirmed this crucial change of emphasis. Questioned by Ian Hamilton about his 1958 'Buddhist non-attachment' piece, Naipaul completely repudiated his earlier position:

I think what happened is that I've begun to understand the world a lot better than I did when I wrote that piece. When I came to England in 1950 I was a thorough colonial. Now, to be a colonial is, in a way, to know a total kind of security. It is to have all decisions about major issues taken out of one's hands. It is to feel that one's political status has been settled so finally that there is very little one can do in the world. I think this is the background to a lot of my thinking at that time. I was eighteen when I came here and in a way I have grown up here. I've had a second childhood, a second becoming aware of the world. I've grown out of one attitude and begun to understand the world from another point of view, in my maturity. How much of this is England and how much is just age and how much is the act of writing I don't know. But I remain quite astonished at my political indifference. Things like Mau Mau in Kenya passed over me completely. Suez: these things always came to me a few years late. Vietnam: at the beginning, people asked me to sign a petition in 1965. I didn't know what they were talking about, I really didn't know. This is, I think, the complete colonial attitude.

What I find very interesting is that one has ceased to be a colonial. One no longer enjoys this great security. In fact, when something like Bengal comes along, I am aware of a new difference between me and people in England. I am aware that I am the insecure person and that people here are the totally secure. The cartoonists here have taken up the Oxfam Rich West — Poor East attitude. They've missed the point, which to me is that the people in Bengal are being killed by Chinese and American weapons.[8]

Naipaul continues by championing West Indian blacks in London who are 'without representation' anywhere and by attacking government expediency on moral issues such as arms sales – unfamiliar sentiments from our Brahmin-Buddhist but confirming what already seemed to be the trend of his more recent work. For if *A House for Mr Biswas* is the climax of the first phase of Naipaul's career, a phase in which he writes almost exclusively about the society he has escaped, *The Mimic Men* clearly marks the end of a second phase, the end of an absorption with his personal homelessness, a final release from what his narrator Kripalsingh calls 'a barren cycle of events'.

The first product of this new freedom was *The Loss of El Dorado*, a historical study of Trinidad built round the two short periods of history when Trinidad was important to Europe, as a base for El Dorado expeditions and as a centre for revolution in Spanish America. Naipaul's irony is as active as ever and there is no preaching. But he never lets us forget that the cruelty and greed, the hypocrisy and confusion of motives which his irony so exactly exposes, have as their anonymous victims the slaughtered Amerindians and the Negro slaves. His account rouses in the reader more passion and disgust than many more obviously polemical writings. More recently, with *In a Free State*, he expresses through a group of linked stories his new realisation of 'how much one's concerns in the world are founded on one's political assumptions about the world'. [9]His subject is again homelessness, but not now the homelessness of West Indians. Homelessness is seen as a universal feature of the modern world, afflicting all races, even the former colonial rulers, even those who inhabit 'the capital of the world'. The book closes with an extract from one of Naipaul's journals, a record of the kind of experience out of which the stories arose. He is in Luxor having lunch at the rest house, watching the attempts of the child beggars to dodge the guard with the camel whip and invade the restaurant for scraps of food left by the tourists. Some Italians toss sandwiches and apples in order to film the scrambling children and the flailing whip, and Naipaul is outraged. He leaps shouting from the terrace, seizes the whip, and astounds the guard by threatening, 'I will report this to Cairo'.

3

Naipaul's development, then, can in a sense be measured by the gap between the closing chapter of *Miguel Street*, with his narrator totally self-preoccupied watching his dancing shadow as he walks towards his plane, and the closing section of *In a Free State*, with Naipaul intervening to prevent an exploitation which appals him. But if such a development seems desirable, one must be very careful in stating how and why. Naipaul's belated recognition that politics is an integral part of one's view of the world must not be used to invalidate the perceptions based on his earlier attitudes. His work has from the beginning been subjected to criticism more political than literary in its terms of reference, and it has not always been clear how much the resentment he has left in his wake arises from irritation with the man or from the feeling that his novels are a depressing recipe for independence. Writing about the former colonies for an audience in Britain, he has never identified himself with nationalist aspirations. He has never taken the line that it is his job to defend his culture against British misrepresentations – it is impossible to imagine him doing as Chinua Achebe, countering such productions as 'The Pacification of the Primitive Tribes of the Lower Niger' with a novel like *Things Fall Apart*. Naipaul's first novel, by contrast with Achebe's, is a deliberate act of satiric detachment, an attempt to get his bearings in a larger world. Describing himself only as a writer who happens to be from Trinidad, he has consistently rejected any idea of his belonging to a West Indian school. He has good grounds for the rejection – 'I have nothing in common with the people from Jamaica', he said retrospectively in 1968, 'or the other islands for that matter. I don't understand them.'[10] But to many West Indians especially, reading his early novels at a time of nationalist fervour, at a time when the West Indian Federation was still in existence, this refusal to identify with local currents of strong feeling seemed like a betrayal. Thus to the Trinidadian poet Eric Roach he is 'a cold and sneering prophet'; to the Jamaican novelist John Hearne he is 'a West Indian snob'; to the Guyanese critic Gordon Rohleur his work shows 'a contemptuous rejection of all things West Indian'.[11]

The issue here is not, as Naipaul has suggested, that 'the inse-

cure wish to be heroically portrayed'.[12] The standard most frequently invoked is not that of national dignity but of compassion.
To many West Indian critics, as well as to English counterparts
like Gerald Moore, novels which set out to expose the inadequacies of a society whose history is one of slavery and exploitation are acceptable only if the prevailing tone shows sympathy
and understanding. George Lamming's extraordinarily bitter criticism of Naipaul's first two novels follows this line:

> His books can't move beyond a castrated satire; and although
> satire may be a useful element in fiction, no important work,
> comparable to Selvon's can rest safely on satire alone. When
> such a writer is a colonial, ashamed of his cultural background
> and striving like mad to prove himself through promotion to the
> peaks of a 'superior' culture whose values are gravely in doubt,
> then satire, like the charge of philistinism, is for me nothing
> more than a refuge. And it is too small a refuge for a writer who
> wishes to be taken seriously.[13]

Lamming had reasons for launching what in its context is a very
personal attack. Naipaul had reviewed his *Of Age and Innocence* in
the *New Statesman* in terms which even today seem patronising. At
the time, in 1958, this fellow West Indian novelist was Naipaul's
senior not only in years and reputation but also, with *In the Castle
of my Skin*, in achievement. But it would be wrong to dismiss
Lamming's remarks as professional pique. What is at stake here is a
fundamental *literary* problem, faced by every writer, ex-colonial
or not, who tries to apply the assumptions and resources of English
literature to non-European societies.

It is hard to feel that Naipaul is really guilty of the charges laid
against him. Except possibly in the story 'My Aunt Gold Teeth'
and in the ending of *The Suffrage of Elvira*, his detachment is always
genial, verging towards irony and acceptance rather than towards
satire and contempt. William Walsh, in fact, suggests that
Naipaul's real fault is that his rejection is not rigorous enough, that
he relies far too much on 'charm'.[14] Moreover, there can be little
doubt that his early insistence that he was committed to nothing
but writing has for all its dangers been beneficial in the long run.

He argues revealingly in *The Middle Passage* that West Indian writers as a whole have failed their society by failing in detachment. His particular complaint that 'by accepting and promoting the unimpressive race-and-colour values of his group' the West Indian writer 'has not only failed to diagnose the sickness of his society but has aggravated it'[15] may be less than fair to Salkey, Lamming and Selvon, the nucleus of the group under attack. But its assumption that the irony which springs from a wider viewpoint will ultimately be more productive explains a good deal about his own work. It is no accident that of all those budding West Indian writers who travelled to London in the decade after the war, Naipaul has shown the most consistently developing power.

Nevertheless, Lamming's attack does take us to the heart of what I believe to be the major problem faced by all writers in Naipaul's position, namely, the problem of taking account in literary terms of the fact that the language and the form one is using embody judgements and assumptions which may be utterly at odds with those of the people of whom one is writing, and in terms of which they may be cruelly vulnerable. In his article 'London' Naipaul offers one kind of answer:

> It isn't easy for the exotic writer to get his work accepted as being more than something exotic, something to be judged on its merits. The very originality of the material makes the work suspect. And the exotic humorous writer is in a particularly delicate position. Consider this comment on my first novel in a weekly paper, now justly defunct: 'His whole purpose is to show how funny Trinidad Indians are'. The *Daily Telegraph* says I look down a long Oxford nose at the land of my birth. The *Evening Standard*, however, thinks that I write of my native land with warm affection. None of these comments would have been made about a comic French or American novel. They are not literary judgments at all. Imagine a critic in Trinidad writing of *Vile Bodies*: 'Mr Evelyn Waugh's whole purpose is to show how funny English people are. He looks down his nose at the land of his birth. We hope that in future he writes of his native land with warm affection.'[16]

Plausible as this sounds as a means of dismissing one type of rather silly comment, it hardly amounts to an adequate statement. We have seen already in the conclusion of the same article Naipaul's fear that living in London will 'eventually lead to my own sterility'. What is this but an acknowledgement of the ultimate barrenness of trying to detach aesthetic standards from political and social assumptions? 'A writer stands or falls by his sensibility', says Naipaul in the quotation with which I headed this chapter, 'and our assessment of his work depends on our response to his sensibility.' What is this but the perception that, however trivialised they may seem, the questions raised by the *Daily Telegraph* and the *Evening Standard* do in the end involve literary judgements?

In 'A Flag on the Island' Naipaul makes great play with Mr B. White's *I Hate You*, a racial tract which is published with the assistance of an American foundation and bought mainly by the tourists it abuses. But one can point to similar contradictions about his own work. *The Mystic Masseur* has a foreword in which the size and population of Trinidad are explained with reference to Lancashire and Nottingham, and all his novels carry translations of local idioms for the uninitiated. Whatever loyalties Naipaul rejects, however much he denies being a spokesman for his region, he is still a writer from the West Indies writing largely about the West Indies for an audience abroad. He cannot avoid being regarded to some extent as the interpreter of one region to another, and his political and social attitudes cannot be dismissed as irrelevant – the same foreword to *The Mystic Masseur*, for instance, includes a jibe at local politicians. Nor is it any use suggesting that Naipaul's Trinidad is only a setting against which he works out ideas of universal significance, for the problems are intensified by his subject matter. Naipaul writes of homelessness, of cultural confusion, of characters fighting to retain their dignity in surroundings which disown them. Yet in *The Mystic Masseur* and *The Suffrage of Elvira*, the novels Lamming has in mind, the style is impeccable, the narrator tremendously assured. Even if we forgive the author for not being more charitable, we are still entitled to ask what makes him so different, what has released him from the absurdities in which his characters are trapped, why homelessness holds no terrors for

himself. These are literary questions because they turn on the relation between form and content, between style and subject
matter. Could it be, for example, that it is only in the context of
this highly sophisticated, imported form of which Naipaul has
made himself master that Trinidad seems so anarchic and Trinidadians so bizarre? We shall see in my subsequent chapters that the
weakest parts of the early novels (and also, significantly, of *Mr
Stone and the Knights Companion*, the first non-Trinidadian novel)
are the endings. What can be maintained as a stylish pose may well
be much more difficult to clinch thematically.

I am writing, of course, as though Naipaul had never advanced
from his early novels, as though he had never come to appreciate
that displacement has a personal dimension and disorder a political
source, both of which need to be examined. The publication of *A
House for Mr Biswas* quickly made Lamming's attack look very
much off target. Yet the attack is worth attention, partly because it
is still current (critics now tend to make exceptions of *Miguel Street*
and *A House for Mr Biswas*), and partly because there is another
whole side to the question which has never been examined. Naipaul is not just a West Indian living in London. He is also an East
Indian from Trinidad, and his refusal to be no more than a spokesman for the West Indies is initially only an extension of his refusal
to limit himself to being the spokesman of Ganesh and Beharry,
Baksh and Chittaranjan. While his early critics were protesting
that metropolitan standards could not fairly be applied to the slave
society, Naipaul was busy exploring the relevance of the novel
form to the close-knit Hindu world in which he grew up and of
which he was writing. *The Mystic Masseur*, for example, is offered
to the reader as a substitute for Ganesh's autobiography 'The
Years of Guilt', which was suppressed in its year of publication.
The point becomes clear when the narrator quotes passages from
the autobiography in contrast with what in fact 'happened'.
Ganesh believes in predestination, the narrator in the interaction
of characters with their environment. Ganesh attributes his success
to God, the narrator to that accident in time which saved him
from becoming 'a mediocre pundit' or 'a dangerous doctor'.
Ganesh's sense of Fate becomes for the narrator simply his oppor-

tunism. As the joke develops, a gap is opened up between the assumptions of the people of whom Naipaul is writing and the assumptions appropriate to a novel.

In *The Suffrage of Elvira*, the joke continues as a running contrast between the characters (mainly East Indians) who see the election as complicated by witchcraft, and the author who sees it as simplified by money and race. In *A House for Mr Biswas*, however, the discussion becomes more serious. Mr Biswas's birth is surrounded by bad omens – he will have an unlucky sneeze, he will turn out to be a spendthrift and a lecher, and he must be kept away from trees and water. But one of Naipaul's major concerns is to do justice to the Hindu world into which Mr Biswas is born and to emphasise the coherence and intimacy which he leaves behind forever at Pagotes. Naipaul is forced, in other words, to take the horoscope seriously. Mr Biswas is indeed involved in a sequence of events including water whose climax is the death of his father; and when at the age of twelve he is sent to be trained as a pundit, he does indeed defile Jairam's oleander tree. So long as he attempts to stay in the Hindu world, the predictions are fulfilled. It is only later in creole Trinidad that his horoscope becomes an irrelevancy, a subject for ridicule. By then we can recognise his loss, for the horoscope – however irrational and however unlucky – did represent a type of order no longer available to him, a system of belief in terms of which his life could have made sense. But it is hard to see how this Hindu doctrine of *karma*, this belief that character is determined by events in a previous life, could be sustained throughout a full-length novel.

Naipaul's first books, then, are not only attempts to give a coherent picture of the society he has escaped. They are also attempts to clarify the assumptions inherent in the form he is using – and, in the case of the first chapter of *A House for Mr Biswas*, to protect his characters from them. Discussing the same topic in *An Area of Darkness*, Naipaul is quite clear about the type of commitment involved in writing novels:

Indian attempts at the novel further reveal the Indian confusion. The novel is of the West. It is part of that Western concern with the condition of men, a response to the here and now. In India thoughtful men have preferred to turn their backs on the here and now and to satisfy what President Radhakrishnan calls 'the basic human hunger for the unseen'. It is not a good qualification for the writing or reading of novels.[17]

The emphasis is given point by Naipaul's comments on the failings of Indian intellectual life – the reduction of man to his caste, the smothering of the imagination by ritual, the sweetness and sentimentality with their parody of concern, the mimicry of European forms of expression coupled with an 'underlying, unwitting rejection of the values implied'. He reinforced his argument with a literary example. *The Princes* by Manohar Malgonkar is a novel about an Indian prince of medieval grandeur who falls from power at independence and kills himself by going out unarmed after a wounded tiger. The narrator is the prince's son, an English-educated army officer, who in the post-independence era finds himself identifying more and more with his father's values. Naipaul's point is that the novel by its very form contradicts those values. The plot involves an 'untouchable' boy whom the narrator initially admires for playing the traditional role of underdog with dignity and gratitude. But the boy grows up to be a left-wing politician, a 'malevolent revolutionary', and we are to consider him as having lapsed morally by denying his caste, by refusing to accept the humiliations imposed on him by his birth. The novel form, which allows all characters equal importance as human beings, resists such a judgement. The narrator describes the poverty of India as 'quivering', and Naipaul dwells on the word, seeing it as 'a concession to a convention of feeling' in which the real India is dismissed. But the novel form with its awareness and concern will not allow poverty to be relegated to a picturesque backdrop.

It will be appreciated not only that Naipaul's standards for the novel are extremely rigorous but that he regards them as totally opposed to the standards of the Hindu community in which he grew up. One whole aspect of *A House for Mr Biswas* is the hero's journey from a world ruled by religious myth to a world which he tries to comprehend through his journalism, his paintings and his short stories. Not until *The Mimic Men*, arguably the most 'Hindu' of the novels, does Naipaul qualify this antithesis. The Hinduism of *A House for Mr Biswas*, after Chapter 1, involves little more than a general fastidiousness about food – when Mr Biswas dedicates his new house at Green Vale he shares a bottle of rum with Mr Maclean and Edgar: it is Naipaul the Hindu who notices that Edgar drank 'without wiping the bottle'. But the Hinduism of *The Mimic Men* is on an altogether different level. It is an attempt (following on the somewhat similar *Mr Stone and the Knights Companion*) to give imaginative expression to that deep sense of the world as illusion, that 'total Indian negation', which Naipaul describes at the end of *An Area of Darkness*. One of the main themes of the novel is the close parallel between Kripalsingh's independence movement and his father Gurudeva's uprising in the mid-thirties. Naipaul continues the parallel into his conclusion. Gurudeva eventually finds release from his need for drama as a holy man, a Hindu ascetic making sense of his world in terms of religious myth. Kripalsingh finds peace in a suburban hotel, a recluse writing his memoirs, making sense of his world in terms of the central fact of his displacement. He reflects that by doing so he has fulfilled the fourfold division of life prescribed by his ancestors. Naipaul's equation between past and present myth-making is deliberate. The satisfying, liberating effects of a coherent vision of the world are now seen as more important than the means by which the pattern is grasped.

At the same time, however, *The Mimic Men* also represents the climax of Naipaul's attempts to resolve what for many of his readers is the more immediate problem of relating the form he is using to Trinidad as a whole. It was ironical that while Eric Roach in the *Trinidad Guardian* was accusing an Anglicised Naipaul of breaking his roots and opting for 'satire and disdain', the *Observer* should have been upset about his Hinduism, about the lack of 'some sense of position when all the ironies have had their say'.[18] Yet disagreements of this nature only point to the larger ambiguities of Naipaul's position and to say only that he is committed to a western form embodying western ways of looking at the world is hardly precise enough. Naipaul, of course, despite Lamming's criticism, is far from taken in by metropolitan values. The imperial myth that London is the centre of the world is precisely what is under attack in *The Mimic Men*, and it is not only the later novels which make the point. From the time of *Miguel Street* and *The Mystic Masseur*, a major theme of his work has been the irrelevance to life in Trinidad of the imported education conferred on his heroes. Elias studies 'litricher and poultry' at Titus Hoyt's academy and ends up driving a scavenger's cart. Ganesh teaches at a school whose function is to 'form, not inform'. Mr Biswas learns about oases and igloos, which equips him to understand Anand's essays about 'hampers – laden hampers'. Kripalsingh attends Isabella Imperial, a private world from which the island is excluded and where any mention in the classroom of local events draws satiric laughter. The point developed here is that the imported information, so far from offering solutions, only heightens the disorder. Furthermore, Naipaul has from the beginning been aware of the implications of this for his writing. From B. Wordsworth's line-a-month poem to Ganesh's weighty Victorian prose, from Mr Biswas's many versions of 'Escape' to Mr Stone's distrust of all creative activity, from Mr B. White's search for a local language to Kripalsingh's lengthy discussions of the actual form of his memoirs, there is a parallel line of reflection in which Naipaul keeps questioning the activity he is engaged in. We shall be following these developments in subsequent chapters, but there is one general comment which is relevant here. It concerns this difficult word 'detachment', for though frequently invoked both by Naipaul himself (as a virtue, a product of the broad vision) and by his critics (as an inadequacy, a sign of his lack of nourishing commitments), it is not at all clear that they are talking about the same thing.

The point can be illustrated neatly by a comparison between *The Middle Passage* and *An Area of Darkness*. I do not wish to exaggerate the contrast between the two books. They share a novelist's eye for character and revealing incident, an alert style and a marvellous sensitivity to landscape. They are governed by the same persona – patrician, hypersensitive, prone to exasperated generalisation: the man who can write 'Port of Spain is the noisiest city in the world' will drop easily into 'To be in Bombay was to be exhausted'. Yet they remain very different achievements, and the differences are instructive. This is Naipaul in British Guiana:

> Georgetown, most exquisite city in the British Caribbean, is for the visitor the most exasperating. Try getting a cup of coffee in the morning. The thing is impossible. Yesterday you expressed a dislike for lukewarm 'instant' coffee, particularly when the coffee is placed on the water and not the water on the coffee; so this morning your hotel offers you half a teaspoonful of last year's coffee grounds in a pint of lukewarm water, since in your folly you said that you 'used' ground coffee — 'use', revealingly, being the Guianese word for 'drink' or 'eat'. Protest is futile . . .
>
> After half an hour you rise, sweating, for the cafe is hot and unventilated, and you find yourself saying passionately but precisely, 'You Guianese are the slowest people I have ever met.' You alone are affected by these words; the waitresses simply stare and you go out into the white light trembling with anger, solacing yourself with the words of abuse which have just leapt into your mind.[19]

Compare it with Naipaul in Kashmir, refusing to eat a vegetable stew which he suspects has been made with meat:

> After some time there was a call from behind the curtained doorway. It was the *khansamah*. In one hand he held a frying pan, in another a fish slice. His face was flushed from the fire and ugly with anger and insult.
>
> 'Why you don't eat my vegetable stew?'
>
> As soon as he began to speak he lost control of himself. He stood over me and was almost screaming. 'Why you don't eat my vegetable stew?' I feared he was about to hit me with the frying pan, which he had raised, and in which I saw an omelette. Immediately after his violence, however, came his alarm, his recognition of his own weakness.
>
> I suffered with him. But the thought of egg and oil nauseated me further; and I was surprised by the rise within myself of that deep anger which unhinges judgement and almost physically limits vision.

'Aziz,' I said, 'will you ask this person to go?'

It was brutal; it was ludicrous; it was pointless and infantile. But the moment of anger is a moment of exalted, shrinking lucidity, from which recovery is slow and shattering.[20]

The difference here is not just that between abuse and potential sympathy. It is the difference between a man detaching himself on the spot from circumstances which infuriate him and a man distancing himself in time and place from an incident on which he has meditated.

The contrast points to overall differences in procedure. *The Middle Passage* is subtitled 'an impression of five societies', *An Area of Darkness* 'an experience of India'. The one is written up from a diary in which Naipaul's day-to-day 'impressions' are recorded, the other is composed after his return from India when the 'experience' is being digested as a whole. *The Middle Passage* retains something of a diary's shapelessness; apart from the balancing of the beginning (West Indians pouring into London) against the ending (Americans pouring into the Caribbean), there is little sign of organisation, ideas and topics recurring spontaneously as from day to day. But *An Area of Darkness* is polished and calculated, from the tact with which it channels its strongest criticisms through quotations from Gandhi to the thoroughness with which it balances specific encounters against general commentary, glimpses from a train against residence in Kashmir, the 'Indianness' in himself against the India he is rejecting. My point, however, is not just that *An Area of Darkness* is the better of the two books (which it is) but that the difference in quality is the direct consequence of the different stances Naipaul has adopted. Whereas in his study of India, Naipaul is reflecting on a total experience, recognising that even at his most appalled he is considering a situation in which he is involved and which reflects aspects of himself, *The Middle Passage* is the brusque response of a man who denies that he has anything to do with what has irritated him.

The consequences should be pursued, for in so detaching himself from the people among whom he grew up Naipaul falls into the very trap Lamming dug for him. I spoke earlier of Naipaul adopting the accents of English nineteenth-century travellers to the West Indies. In his own travelogue, Naipaul not only quotes Trollope continuously and with justifiable approval, but copies his actual style:

> 'But Demerara makes a little sugar,' I ventured to remark.
> 'It makes deuced little money, I know,' said A.
> 'Every inch of it is mortgaged,' said B.
> 'But their steam-engines,' said I.
> 'Look at their clearances,' said A.
> 'They have none,' said B.
> 'At any rate, they have got beyond windmills,' I remarked, with considerable courage.
> 'Because they have got no wind,' said A.[21]

In Martinique, Naipaul also offers a little agricultural advice:

> Couldn't they even make their own coconut oil for the margarine factory that employs seven people? Surely coconuts can grow in Martinique? 'Impossible,' says one. 'The man is mad. Pay no attention,' says another. And so the bickering goes on . . .[22]

The mimicry is presumably unconscious but, announcing his allegiance in this manner, he is not well placed to talk about Indians and Negroes 'each claiming to be whiter than the other'. It is hard not to feel that his comments on racial matters, and particularly his despair about future race relations, are not completely invalidated by the inflexibility of his own position, by his refusal to acknowledge that the obsessions he describes might be in control of his own cadences. It is hard, too, not to be a little pleased that he apparently finds the role so difficult to sustain — in Trinidad he shrinks from Carnival, in Martinique he is reduced to using a walking stick, in Jamaica he rushes to the bar for phensic.

The lesson of the two travel books, then, is that the insulated, too-knowing author is likely to be more than usually offensive when writing in Naipaul's position, when reporting on a society from which he has grown away or to which he is historically connected. The offense lies not only in the assumption of superiority, though this is irritating enough. It lies also in the fact that the pose largely determines the quality of what is seen. Anyone can visit the West Indies and see 'how deep in nearly every West Indian, high and low, were the prejudices of race'. But it requires an altogether different stance to report with sensibility on the Indian knack of operating between two worlds:

> And in India I was to see that so many of the things which the newer and now perhaps truer side of my nature kicked against — the smugness, as it seemed to me, the imperviousness to criticism, the refusal to *see*, the double-talk and double-think — had an answer in that side of myself which I had thought buried and which India revived as a faint memory. I understood better than I admitted.[23]

There is detachment here too, but it draws on different resources. The detachment of *The Middle Passage* takes the form of resistance to any circumstance which threatens Naipaul's composure. The author is at war with his subject, and the irony diminishes and is ultimately self-destructive. But the irony of *An Area of Darkness* is a kind of perspective. It allows for discovery, for a constant revelation of new dimensions. It returns constantly to that personal crisis which is at the heart of the experiences recorded. It depends on the fact of distancing in place and time.

In this distinction lies the answer to those who see Naipaul as lacking in compassion or in nationalist loyalties. In his best work there is no incompatibility between the distancing of which I am speaking and that openness to the total meaning of an experience which may end in compassion but may also end in rejection and flight. For the novels bear many resemblances to the book about India. The dependence on distancing in place and time is obviously significant. The first four books are set in Trinidad but were written in London, drawing on memories which by the time of *A House for Mr Biswas* were at least ten years old. Only in Kashmir in 1962 does Naipaul write about London in *Mr Stone and the Knights Companion*, and the novel which examines the joint experience of London and Trinidad was completed in Uganda. Naipaul's two least satisfactory fictions are in fact those written partly on the spot — *The Suffrage of Elvira* which was begun in Trinidad during the

1956 elections, and 'A Flag on the Island' which coincided with his visit in 1965.

Kripalsingh's aim in his memoirs is 'to impose order on my own history', and the words can usefully be applied to Naipaul's work as a whole. He is not flattered by references to the autobiographical or documentary nature of his novels and he insists, not surprisingly, on how much has come out of his imagination. Yet all his books have their feet firmly in his own experience. To those who know Trinidad well, his settings are instantly recognisable, his characters often disguised so thinly as to run the risk of libel (for critic as well as author). Time and time again the factual basis of incidents worked into the novels can be established from other sources. There are severe limits to the relevance of this kind of information; Naipaul is a novelist not a reporter. But it is fair to suggest that on the whole his is a shaping rather than an inventive imagination. He does consciously use the novel to define his position in the word, to 'give back the past', to 'impose order' on his history. The product remains fiction, but the discipline is not fundamentally opposed to that involved in writing *An Area of Darkness* and it is not surprising that Naipaul should have moved easily into the writing of history with *The Loss of El Dorado*.

For Naipaul, then, and I would suggest for other writers in his position, the problem of form becomes the problem of establishing the right perspective. Only by placing himself as author accurately in relation to his material can he convince the reader that his vision is complete, and that he is not taking the virtues of Westernisation for granted. What is forced on him by the special circumstances in which he became a writer is a quality of self-consciousness, a nagging awareness that:

> There's something absurd about the fictional form: it's an artificial activity, made-up people taking part in invented actions. The first thing for the writer is to understand *why* he's setting all these people in motion. Which leads to the second problem: I didn't know who I was.[24]

We have seen that as early as 1948 Naipaul described himself in the Q.R.C. *Chronicle* as 'a young writer'. Yet before he wrote the first story of *Miguel Street* 'without pausing' one afternoon in 1955, the seeming irrelevance of the novels he admired to his own 'inarticulate society' had set up inhibitions which cramped all successful fiction. Naipaul has recorded his joy that after two or three false starts he had at last 'discovered the trick of writing'.[25] His problem was that he had no tradition, no local examples of the 'distorting, distilling power of the writer's art'. Fortunately, there was an exception. In the summer of 1943 there was published a small volume called *Gurudeva and Other Indian Tales*. Naipaul's earliest debt is to the short stories of Seepersad Naipaul, his father.

CHAPTER TWO

'Father and blasted son'

I

*The writing that has mattered most to me is that of my father,
which has never been published. It taught me to look at things
that had never been written about before, and seemed dull in life,
yet when transformed to paper became very surprising. A great
deal of my vision of Trinidad has come straight from my father.
Other writers are aware that they are writing about rooted societies; his work showed me that one could write about another
kind of society.*[1]

Some of the funniest passages in *A House for Mr Biswas* deal with
Mr Biswas's attempts to become a writer. He begins as a sign-
painter, relishing the beauty of the letters of the alphabet but
knowing that the words they compose have no relevance to himself – his first job, after a week of idling, is to paint the notice
'Idlers Keep Out'. Later, he becomes a journalist, his head buzzing
with reporter's clichés, and writes facetious stories through which
his anxieties are expressed only obliquely: two of his earliest, semi-
fictional reports feature 'a wife and four kiddies' – the family he
has deserted. He buys a typewriter and takes a correspondence
course on How to Write Articles. But he cannot relate the hints
sent from London to the island he inhabits, and the only article he
submits contains the representative howler, 'We have gathered in
the corn which soon . . . we shall enjoy, roasted or boiled on the
cob'. He writes short stories about barren heroines, but is forced to
hide them from his wife's mockery, and eventually – after meeting
Bhandat's barren mistress – he flushes them down the W.C. Only
very occasionally does his writing bring him any satisfaction – in
his letter rebuking the doctor who insulted his mother's body, in

the prose poem idealising his mother's welcome home after his ex-
pulsion from Pundit Jairam's, perhaps in the letters of comfort he
addresses to Anand shortly before his death. But writing is important to him. At every stage of his adult life, it is present in one form
or another. It is part of his attempt to come to terms with the new
world.

To separate Mr Biswas from Naipaul's father is not easy. Naipaul has drawn so directly on his father's experience in writing *A
House for Mr Biswas* that one sometimes forgets he is writing fiction.
So many incidents in the novel are drawn from life and are corrob-
orated by other sources that one feels a certain naive surprise,
amounting almost to disappointment, to discover in Seepersad
Naipaul's career a pattern often very different from that which his
son has imposed on it. Yet it is essential to distinguish the real from
the fictional father, not only to understand more fully how the material is shaped in the novel, but also to appreciate just how much
Naipaul owes to his father's attempts to define his society and his
own position in it.

Seepersad Naipaul was born in Longdenville in Central Trinidad in 1906, afterwards guessing his birthday as 6 April. He was an
infant when his father, who was a pundit, died and at about the age
of six he moved with his mother to Tunapuna, a town ten miles
east of Port of Spain. There he lived as a poor dependent of his
mother's sister, the wife of a local 'millionaire' who owned a
garage, a rum shop, a fleet of thirty buses, and a chain of stores
throughout the east of the island. He attended different church
schools and then, after working for his uncle, achieved a precarious independence as a sign-painter. Sign-painting took him to
the Lion House, Chaguanas, where he met Bropatie Capildeo
whom he married in 1929. Shortly after his marriage, he submitted
some articles to Gault McGowan, editor of the *Trinidad Guardian*
for which he had already painted advertisements, and was taken on
as a reporter. He lived in various parts of north Trinidad, including
Port of Spain, before becoming the paper's Chaguanas correspondent early in 1932. His four children, of whom V.S. Naipaul
was the second, were all born in the Lion House, though Seepersad
Naipaul preferred to live a short distance away at Montrose in a

wooden house he had built for himself. There, in 1934, he suffered
a nervous breakdown, which seems to have coincided with a quarrel with his wife's family over his support for the Arya Samaj, a
reformist Hindu movement inspired by missionaries from India,
and with his resignation from the *Guardian* after McGowan's dismissal in an official change of policy. Refusing ever afterwards to
re-enter the Montrose house, he became an overseer on one of the
estates attached to the Lion House, and then a shopkeeper in Chase
Village, such activities having apparently been recommended by
his doctor as a 'cure'. In 1938, however, following another change
of editor, he rejoined the *Guardian* staff and returned to Port of
Spain where, after some ten years in houses belonging to the
Capildeos, he eventually acquired a house of his own in Nepaul
Street in the suburb of Woodbrook. He became the *Guardian's*
expert on social welfare and, in 1945, joined the government's new
Department of Social Welfare, spending six months in Jamaica on
a training course. The department collapsed in 1948 and although
he could have continued as a probation officer he chose to return
once more to the *Guardian*, in spite of losing his seniority and his
pension rights. He died of a heart attack in October 1953 at the age
of forty-seven.

The relevance of these events to *A House for Mr Biswas* will be
discussed in a later chapter. What concerns me now are Seepersad
Naipaul's publications, both as a journalist and as a writer of short
stories. The first articles which can definitely be ascribed to him
appeared in the *Guardian* in March 1932, when correspondents
were first named, but it is clear he was working for the paper earlier than this. His first signed stories are a series of interviews with
amusing or remarkable characters – a Hindu ascetic doing elaborate penance by a river, a blind violinist concealing his handicap to
get a job, a one-hundred-and-twelve year-old Negro woman who
remembers slavery – but he is also responsible for reporting court
and road board proceedings in Chaguanas which provide him
with a rich source of drama. His reports are written with real zest,
the daily incidents of a death or of a court-room clash being recon-
structed in a manner which must owe a great deal to his imagination. All the characters are idealised – husbands love their wives

dearly, lawyers are quietly brilliant, bereaved sweethearts have a pallid beauty – and all express themselves in perfect English. But in spite of the frequent improbability of his reports they make better reading than the rest of the paper. Flamboyance, pathos, and stoicism are what appeal to him most. He is not above occasional irony at the expense of his profession ('I told him I was a reporter sent in the sacred cause of publicity'), but it is obvious that McGowan, who came to the *Guardian* in 1929 and quickly doubled its circulation, found in Seepersad Naipaul a journalist after his own heart. In July 1932, for instance, he was assaulted for reporting manoeuvres in connection with the coming elections and for a few days became the paper's hero. Eleven months later, he achieved notoriety. Following a feature exposing the 'superstitious practices resorted to by Hindus to combat the spread of rabies', he was threatened with death unless he sacrificed a goat to the goddess Kali whom he was alleged to have insulted. For a week he appears on the front page, with every aspect of the story – the earnest, the comic, the macabre – exploited to the full. At first, he refuses to make the sacrifice, describing the threat as 'bunkum', and dismissing the cruel Kali myths as superstition. He is removed from Chaguanas and put under police protection. Then comes an interview with his wife, entreating him to appease the goddess: 'ju-ju,' she is reported as saying, 'is shrouded in mystery, and it is not for us to try to fathom that mystery'. Mr Naipaul responds by describing the conflict in his mind – 'orthodox Hindus condemn me, the modern ones commend me' – and recounting various little incidents which well-wishers interpret as bad omens. Insurance companies are asked whether they are willing to cover his life: two accept, but two refuse. After five days, he agrees to make the sacrifice – 'I am thinking of my two children. I must live for them'. The ritual takes place with a *Guardian* reporter to describe it in all its sweetness and horror, and Mr Naipaul himself contributes a very earnest account of his feelings during the ceremony, developing his thoughts into a broad statement of his beliefs:

But nothing so fogs and bewilders one's moral judgments, nothing so blurs the boundaries of right and wrong, nothing so cuts the nerve of effort, nothing so enervates and enfeebles character as the teaching of polytheistic Hinduism.

And that is why I rather believe in a single God, than a thousand Kalis.

And now that I have said all this, Kali may again threaten my life, but I am certain I will never again make a sacrifice.

I know my faith now.[2]

The incident seems to have established him as a national character, and all the major stories of the next few months – the hurricane in south Trinidad, the Port of Spain floods – carry his signature. But the story ends, as it began, in sheer comedy. On the Sunday he was destined to die, a short signed feature announces, 'Good morning everybody. As you behold, Kali has not got me yet. I was still alive late last night.'

Inevitably, one reads these reports with Mr Biswas very much in mind. When Seepersad Naipaul writes about artists who have overcome crippling handicaps, businessmen who have progressed from nothing in true Samuel Smiles manner, young men who have forfeited all for love, octogenerians who impress him with their philosophy of survival, it is impossible not to reflect on how such subjects would have appealed to Mr Biswas. In September 1932, he was the centre of a 'mysterious stranger' publicity stunt which obviously inspires the 'scarlet pimpernel' episodes of the novel. Rejoining the *Guardian* staff in 1938, he was put in charge of the Neediest Cases Fund, and spent a month each Christmas for the next seven years visiting the destitute and writing a column of case histories – as does Mr Biswas all the year round. Other details, such as his flippant reporting of two 'neediest cases' after learning his son has been awarded an exhibition, or his features on the Belmont Orphanage, the Belmont Crèche, and the Chacachacare Leper Settlement, or an article on the problems of school transport from Diego Martin (the 'Shorthills' of the novel) where the Naipauls lived in 1940, are so close to the novel that one gets a sense of reading passages which have somehow been misplaced. And it is, of course, a sheer delight to find a report beginning, 'Extraordinary scenes were witnessed . . .'

Fascinating as these stories are as source material, they do however have a broader importance. Even in Seepersad Naipaul's
journalism, one recognises qualities shared by his son. There is the
same appreciation of eccentric characters: Daniel Martin, the
'Robinson Crusoe' of Chaguanas, sets out to discover the overland
route to Tobago – when told Tobago is an island, he replies that
people laughed at Columbus too. There is the same enjoyment of
inconsistency, especially that between profession and practice: a
pundit convenes a large meeting to form a temperance society and
finds, after he has secured overwhelming support, that only four of
his new members are actual abstainers. Or consider such a report as
the following, betraying in every calculated cadence a delight in
sheer farce:

> In one of the secret recesses of the notorious Ravine Sable river
> in Longdenville, a Shouter 'High Priest' who led his flock to
> celebrate their annual devotion, narrowly escaped drowning
> when he attempted to fathom the basin in which he had to
> christen new members:
>
> The bedecked High Priest wearing a robe of purple and white
> and followed by members who wore pure white garments,
> carrying lighted candles, crucifixes, and a silver-like bell,
> reached the river at dawn on Friday:
>
> The ceremony began with loud singing and clapping of hands
> punctuated by intermittent ringing of bells:
>
> As they chanted their songs their bodies shivered and swayed
> in wild contortions:
>
> All went well until the baptismal ceremonies began:
>
> The High Priest, to instil confidence and faith in the new con-
> verts, entered the water:
>
> The basin was deeper than expected and he was covered:
>
> He came to the surface and with flashing eyes and stretching
> arms, he tried to regain the bank, but missed and for a second
> time was lost beneath the water:
>
> Helpers rushed to his aid and brought him to the bank:
>
> Excitement reigned amid cries of 'Hallelujah! he is delivered:'

After reviving, the High Priest denounced their action for saving him:
He said it was a test of their 'faith by the Master,' and consequently he could not proceed with the baptism.
The party then abruptly left the river sadly disappointed.[3]

The young V.S. Naipaul must have learned a great deal from his father about how to shape a story.

But the jokes have their serious side. I have already quoted part of Mr Naipaul's very earnest summary of his own position with regard to the goat sacrifice, and it is typical of him that he should wish to make such a statement. The words could stand as a commentary on one whole aspect of *The Mystic Masseur*. The same applies to his reporting of the 1933 elections to the Legislative Council:

Three or four of the leading supporters of Mr Robinson – the men behind the recent Hindu-Muslim revolt – have split following a clash at a religious meeting of Hindus in Chaguanas recently.

One of them has actually joined the ranks of Mr Teelucksingh's supporters and at a meeting of the Indian Congress on Sunday was elected a member of the Executive Committee of that Body.

He is now a staunch convert to the cause of Mr Teelucksingh.

Another has withdrawn his pledge of support to Mr Robinson and is now neutral.

At the meeting in the Hindu-Muslim school, he was accused of being non-Hindu.

Differences of opinion over one word brought about the clash. The word was Nameste – a Hindu form of greeting.

Mr Sirriran Maraj said that most Hindus used the wrong form of greeting. It should be 'Nameste', meaning 'God protect you'.

The Pundit teacher and other Pundits held otherwise – a meeting was held to decide what it should be.

Piles of books on Hinduism did not, however, settle the dispute and the whole affair ended in chaos.[4]

Mr Naipaul's accounts of the battle of slogans ('Vote for Teeluck-singh and down with traitors'), the swift changes of allegiance, the precarious Hindu-Muslim alliance, the deep-rooted racialism, the inevitable climax of violence, are extremely entertaining. But taken together, they make up the same intelligent, despairing analysis that entertains us in *The Suffrage of Elvira*. V.S. Naipaul was, of course, only an infant when these reports appeared – the sacking of McGowan in 1934 ensured that his father would never again write for the paper with such zest. What emerges most strongly is a similarity of temperament. 'To me it appeared amus-ing at first', says Seepersad Naipaul reporting flood damage in Port of Spain, 'but then I realised the tragedy of it'; 'If through the comedy you can't see the central tragedy, then the comedy isn't very good', says his son in another Trinidad paper some thirty years later.[5] The latter statement is obviously more general, obvi-ously more sophisticated and literary. Both hint at personalities for whom laughter is a reflex, an ineffectual shield against the impact of suffering.

2

It is when we turn to the short stories, however, that we can begin to measure the real extent of Seepersad Naipaul's influence. *Guru-deva and Other Indian Tales* was issued by Trinidad Publications in the summer of 1943 (V.S. Naipaul is never so much his father's son as when he describes publication in Trinidad as 'never been pub-lished'), and though other stories exist [6] there can be little doubt that this volume represents his best work. It contains a critical introduction by Charles Espinet, news editor with the *Trinidad Guardian*, a foreword by Seepersad Naipaul, and seven stories: 'Gurudeva', 'Panchayat', 'Sonya's Luck', 'Obeah', 'Gopi', 'The Wedding Came But – ' and 'Dookhni and Mungal'.

'Gurudeva', the title story and the longest, relates in a series of episodes the progress of an Indian youth from mission school to prison. 'Had other things been equal', we are told, Gurudeva 'might have risen to the distinction of a legislator; he might have been a doctor or a lawyer or an electrical engineer; for his father was wealthy as well as indulgent.' But his father is a staunch Hindu, and he removes Gurudeva from school at the age of fourteen to marry Ratni, the twelve year old daughter of Pundit Sookhlal. Gurudeva's story becomes one of frustrated ambition as he tries to assert himself, first at the expense of Ratni whom he beats brutally, and then in the only other way he can in this displaced Indian community from which, lacking education, he has no escape. Inspired by village stories of famous stick-fighters, he becomes a 'badjohn' himself. He forms a band of fighters in preparation for Hosey, the Moslem festival, but on the day of the celebrations, shirking the real fighting, he attacks an old man and then a policeman, and is sent to jail as a hero. 'Is orright, Bap', he tells his proud father. 'I is a man.'

'Panchayat', by contrast, is a pastoral idyll, a simple nostalgic account of the traditional Indian method of settling disputes — in this case, a quarrel between a girl and her husband — by bringing them before a council of village elders. It is the girl's mother who has summoned the *Panchayat*, but the daughter insists, against her mother's wishes, on returning to her erring husband, and the oldest man present approves whole-heartedly.

'Sonya's Luck' is the story of a Hindu girl who, the night before her wedding to a man she has never met, elopes with Nirmal the man she secretly loves. But meeting him at night under the appointed tree, she finds he too is dressed for marriage — he is the man her parents have chosen for her.

'Obeah' is a brief comic anecdote, told completely in dialect, about a boy who asks the obeahman for a love potion. The fee is paid and the ceremony carried through to the point where he has to reveal the name of the girl he wishes to seduce. It turns out to be the obeahman's married daughter.

'Gopi', to which we must return in detail, is a study of the disturbance raised in Gopi's mind by his brief glimpse in a railway carriage of a young Indian girl.

'The Wedding Came But — ' returns to the situation of 'Sonya's Luck'. Leela is afraid her Hindu father will marry her off to a man of his choice before Ganpat whom she loves can intervene. But again the story ends happily, not this time by coincidence but because Ganpat persuades the father of Leela's prospective husband to accept his own sister instead with a larger dowry than Leela's father can afford, and then offers to repair the wrong he has done by marrying Leela himself.

Finally, 'Dookhni and Mungal' relates with great tenderness an incident in a happy marriage. Dookhni is insulted by her mother-in-law because she is childless five years after her wedding. But Mungal takes her side by offering, against the custom, to send her home to her parents. Rejoicing in his loyal anger, Dookhni calms him down with food and then, that night, reveals she is with child.

Again, inevitably, one begins by noticing all that V.S. Naipaul has borrowed. His evocation in the opening chapter of *A House for Mr Biswas* of the pastoral world of the original indentured labourers, with their submission to Fate, their talk of the coming Black Age, their tales and memories of the India to which they intend shortly to return, draws extensively on 'Gurudeva'. The long account of Gurudeva's preparations for stick-fighting – the roasting of the poui sticks, the soaking with coconut oil in bamboo cylinders, the 'mounting' with the spirit of a dead Spaniard – is worked into Mr Biswas's experiences at The Chase, while Gurudeva himself provides the model for Mungroo the stick-fighter whom Mr Biswas is prosecuted for slandering. Running through the other stories is the same sense of threat as traditional customs decay: the same fear that mission education will lead to short skirts and love letters, the same resistance to Western-style marriages, the same nostalgia for the sweetness and security of the past balanced by awareness of its growing irrelevance. A few names are appropriated (Jairam, Dinnoo, Kamla, Leela, Sumintra); the use of standard English to represent Hindi as opposed to dialect English is imitated in *A House for Mr Biswas*; and occasionally phrases are echoed – Mungal's growing love for Dookhni is described in the same cadences ('without knowing it he had come to love . . .') and with the same inhibitions ('such things were simply not done') as Ganesh's unacknowledged love for Leela. At times, too, it is hard to dismiss the feeling that one is handling Mr Biswas's own work. Most of the illustrations, for instance, are by the Trinidad artist Alf Codallo, but one signed S.N. with its winding road and wide treeless landscape is exactly like those with which Mr Biswas consoles himself at The Chase and Green Vale. Many of the judgements, as we shall see, are exactly what we might expect of Mr Biswas. And most important of all, there is 'Gopi'.

'Gopi' is set in a railway carriage. The hero, 'short, shrunken, spare-framed', boards the train and is immediately attracted to a girl of about seventeen, 'a piece of raw, unspoilt femininity', who is already seated. Staring at her face and her 'virginal curves', he remembers with disappointment that he is married, 'and not only married but the father of two children'. He reflects on the circumstances of his marriage, a stupid 'cat-in-bag' affair with a girl he had never seen and with whom he still has nothing in common:

> But Kamla – well, Kamla was like nobody if she was not like herself. Good. That one word summed her up. But too good; more good than intelligent. Sympathetic without sparkle. A drudge, and not minding being a drudge, the philosophy that stood her in hard moments was the philosophy of surrender – but not the cheap surrender of a coward or a weakling, but a calm co-operation with life and with all that life brought her. Good. That was it – too distressingly good. Just like a nun. Well chuck it; one didn't relish always living in a monastery; one wanted to live like a normal human being – go to the pictures, to dances, parties, picnics. Pictures and dances! Well, he would like to see the person who could induce Kamla to go to a dance. One might succeed, perhaps, in carrying her to a picture, even to a picnic, but to a dance? – no; She'd be martyred first. That was it. She was the very embodiment of a martyr, and he, Gopi, so often felt *he* was the tyrant.[7]

The urge to rebel becomes irresistable. After all, he is only thirty-three, and smoking has left him with a veneer of boyishness. He goes to sit beside the girl but, his courage failing at the last moment he sits on the next seat with his back to her. Ashamed of his cowardice, he tries to think of an excuse for shifting his position ('By George! This place is over-run with ants'), and gets up to go to the window, intending to sit beside her when he returns. But suddenly, she leaves her seat. Gopi returns to where she was sitting, and persuades himself he is keeping her place for her. But she never comes back and, arriving at his own station, he is forced to accept that he will never see her again:

> He bent his steps homeward. 'How strange,' he mused, 'that in a whole lifetime two persons may look into each other's eyes but once, and may never, ever do so again. Well, anyway, she will make someone happy . . . books, companionship, children.'[8]

Mr Biswas writes many versions of this story, all beginning with the phrase 'At the age of thirty-three, when he was already the father of four children'. All the versions are called 'Escape', and they are quoted as a symptom of his frustration during his years in the Tulsis' house in Port of Spain. In the final version, the one intended for but never actually read to the judge's literary group, the hero becomes 'Gopi, a country shopkeeper, small, spare and shrunken'. Yet V.S. Naipaul has drawn more from this story than just a few phrases and a touching obsession. It is not too much to claim that in the characters of Gopi and Kamla we have the beginnings of Mr Biswas and Shama, sketches by the father for the full-scale portraits by the son. Gopi's smallness, illustrated by his clothes, his sense of being trapped by his 'cat-in-bag' marriage and his Indian background, his longing for romance and for books, his sense of being cut off from important events, all find an echo in Mr Biswas; while the description of Kamla quoted above is translated point by point if not word for word into Shama's passiveness:

> For Shama and her sisters and women like them, ambition, if the word could be used, was a series of negatives: not to be unmarried, not to be childless, not to be an undutiful daughter, sister, wife, mother, widow.[9]

This would scarcely be the case if Seepersad Naipaul's story were no more than the private fantasy it becomes in *A House for Mr Biswas*. Nowhere in the novel are we given the impression that Mr Biswas could write stories of the quality of those in *Gurudeva and Other Indian Tales*. Inevitably, as I have said, one reads them with V.S. Naipaul's work in mind, but to see them only as source material would be to underestimate their real importance. It is, in fact, only when we appreciate their independent merit as early attempts to define Trinidad in fictional terms that we can understand fully what V.S. Naipaul is saying in the quotation with which I began this chapter.

Seepersad Naipaul's own foreword is as unpretentious as the rest of the volume. 'I don't know whether these stories are any good', he begins, 'I wrote what I saw – what, in fact, I see every day, and what I know.' Later, he speaks of 'Gurudeva' and 'Gopi' as 'quite undisciplined writings, nothing more than a succession of pictures, and as such, perhaps, rather crudely drawn'. The modesty of this should not blind us to the claims he is making, albeit obliquely. These stories are written straight out of experience. Local traditions of 'fine writing' are set aside. There is little attempt to dignify his subject, none of the engaging pretence of his early journalism, no concern to follow the rules of How to Write Short Stories. Beginning with his own circumstances, he provides us with a simple and direct vision of the life of East Indians in Trinidad. Occasionally, his characters are embalmed in cliché – one is 'a dapper little man', another's voice is 'heavy and mellow with the wisdom of the ages'. But one can sense Mr Naipaul feeling his way towards accuracy. Ratni's father, for instance, is described as 'a portly person in dusty unlaced shoes'; the 'portly' may be Dickensian, but the 'dusty unlaced shoes' are straight from life. Relationships are sometimes badly done – the hero of 'Sonya's Luck' waxes gallant, and embraces the heroine in 'a sudden mad impulse'. But even these embarrassments are understandable in terms of the contradictions inherent in his subject, as I shall try to show in a moment; and he can be both tender and convincing:

Mungal bounded for the house to find his mother, but quickly she clung on to him. 'No,' she pleaded, 'No! Do not make a row tonight. Come . . . come, Man, and eat your food.'

He suffered himself to be led to his food, and piloting him gently upon the bag-spread, she pressed him gently. 'Sit down, Man. Sit down and eat. You are not vexed with your food, are you?'

He grunted, and began to eat, eating with his bare hands, eating – well, not ravenously, but with relish and gusto, – head down, minding nobody and nothing but his food. His long strong fingers ploughed through the rice, took in dahl, mixed in chutni. He ate and ate. And Dookhni sat against the wall, facing him, hands clasped against one up-turned dungaree-covered knee, watching him, waiting for whatever he might want in the way of a second or third helping.

He would not have to call. She had developed a sixth sense that told her exactly when he wanted more rice, more dahl, or more of anything or everything that was to be had.

The rice heap dwindled, the dahl lessened, the chutni vanished. He belched. Then he straightened up and stayed his hand and mouth a while for rest. He took up the lotah with the hand hitherto unemployed, and drank in large, telling gulps . . . glut-glut-gluck, glut; glut-gluck; glut-glut-gluck. Like that. And he set down the lotah and belched again – the full free belch of repletion. Over-come for the moment by the sheer process of eating and drinking, as it were, he rested his head against the wall, his hand on his lap and his eyes on Dookhni's face. Then he began to eat once more, slowly now, almost leisurely.[10]

To have made such an obviously accurate description the means of dramatising tenderness is, I think, a real achievement. Similar passages in V.S. Naipaul's novels invariably carry overtones of disgust.

The most impressive feature of these stories, however, is the dialogue, for it is when they speak that the characters are most alive. My example, from 'Gurudeva', happens to be in dialect, but even the conversations in the somewhat biblical English Mr Naipaul uses to represent Hindi are surprisingly effective. The subject is once again food, food being the only topic on which husbands and wives converse – another of Gopi's complaints against Kamla:

It was in the fifth year of her marriage, however, when she was nearly seventeen, that Ratni got her worst mauling. That day Gurudeva was really angry. Ratni was in the kitchen, preparing the midday food, when he came rushing in.

'Ei,' he called, 'What about me food?' He jammed his hands

against his waist, pressed his teeth on his lower lip and waited ominously for answer.

Ratni grew pale. She sensed trouble. She had not yet finished cooking the midday food.

'Come on, I waitin'!' thundered Gurudeva.

Long spoon in hand, Ratni turned from the pot and faced him, trembling in every limb. She said:

'I – I was washing clothes today. There was plenty to wash. I will give you food jus' now . . . Two minute . . . the bhart finish, the dahl finish too; the bhaji cookin'.'

'Bhaji! W'at bhaji?' roared Gurudeva.

'Pumpkin vine wid sal'fish.'

'Pumpkin vine! Who tell you to cook pumpkin vine?'

'But you always eat. I thought . . .'

'Back answer, eh!' spluttered Gurudeva. 'I will show you . . .'[11]

The timing is right and the characters well distinguished. Each of Gurudeva's speeches carries two menancing stresses, at the beginning and the end; Ratni's stresses come in the middle, and she begins and ends hesitantly – the melodramatic stage directions 'thundered', 'roared', 'spluttered' are quite unnecessary, adding nothing to what we can hear for ourselves. Mr Naipaul's ear for dialogue is as finely attuned as his son's, and his transcription of dialect is, in fact, rather more accurate, possibly because he does not have to make allowances for an English audience.

The first really important point about these stories, then, is that they are good enough to succeed in making the local scene interesting, and interesting in direct proportion to their truth of presentation. 'I wrote what I saw', says Mr Naipaul, and life in Trinidad suddenly becomes not dull and second-rate but absorbing and important. The full significance of this is discussed by V.S. Naipaul himself in an article called 'Jasmine'.[12] He describes what literature meant to him as a boy in Trinidad – 'To open a book', he says, 'was to make an instant adjustment'. Books were valuable only in so far as they could be translated into the local situation. Reading Dickens, for instance, he gave the characters 'the faces and voices of people I knew and set them in buildings and streets I knew'. Anything that could not be so transposed, such as the illustrations to Dickens or the fog and snow, or Jane Austen's assumption of social distinctions more complex than those between rich and poor, anything that did not suggest an equivalent in Trinidad, was more than irrelevant; it was embarrassing and excluding, making nonsense of what was essentially an exercise in fantasy. It was natural, then, he argues, that a love of literature should focus on a love of language for its own sake (Naipaul's main subjects in the Sixth Form at Queens Royal College were French and Spanish), just as for Mr Biswas reading develops into a love of lettering.

When it came to writing about Trinidad, however, English literature was of very little use:

> Something of more pertinent virtue was needed, and this was provided by some local short stories. These stories, perhaps a dozen in all, never published outside Trinidad, converted what I saw into 'writing'. It was through them that I began to appreciate the distorting, distilling power of the writer's art. Where I had seen a drab haphazardness they found order; where I would have attempted to romanticise, to render my subject equal with what I had read, they accepted. They provided a starting point for further observation; they did not trigger off fantasy.[13]

V.S. Naipaul does not refer specifically here to his father's stories, but there can be no doubt that these (together possibly with one or two others by such writers as Mendes, Gomes and C.L.R. James) are what he has in mind. To a young writer, for whom the gap between literature and experience was four thousand miles of ocean, this demonstration that the life and people he knew best were worth writing about, that the problems of his own society could be analysed effectively in fiction, that fantasy was unnecessary when the realities could be made so meaningful, this demonstration in his own home must have been of crucial importance.

These stories, then, are valuable partly as source material but more profoundly as local examples of the power of good writing to interpret and transform. They become, as V.S. Naipaul acknowledges, his substitute for 'a tradition'. Yet, as always with Naipaul, the statement involves its opposite. For while his father's stories taught him one kind of acceptance, they also bring home as a more immediate message the urgency of the need to escape.

Seepersad Naipaul's characters are all East Indians. Other races are scarcely mentioned, yet the pressures of their presence are felt in every story. We are aware all the time of two distinct worlds, the Indian and the Creole, whose customs and judgements are mutually opposed. In three of the stories, he attempts to reconcile the conflicting claims of East and West. 'Panchayat', his account of the traditional Indian method of settling disputes, is essentially an act of piety, an acknowledgement of the quality of the past. Yet even here, at his most exclusive and most nostalgic, Mr Naipaul has to admit that the sanctions invoked by the *panchayat* are irrelevant 'in this hotch-potch island of many races and many creeds. Trinidad was not India.' In 'Sonya's Luck', in which Hindu and Western attitudes to marriage come into collision, the two worlds meet when Sonya's lover and the husband chosen for her turn out to be the same person. But in attempting to present her as a Western-style heroine, he succeeds only in creating a pastiche of romance, the unreality testifying to his inability to see such a figure genuinely existing in such a situation, and the solution is really no more than a lucky coincidence. In 'The Wedding Came But − ', the best story of these three, Leela's traditionally minded father is presented with considerable dignity:

> At thirty he married, in the middle of his indentureship on the plantation to which he had come, a Trinidad-born Hindu girl. She died when Leela, the only child, was six. Not wishing to inflict a stepmother on the child, he had not married a second time. He had taken good care of Leela and she had not disappointed him. At seventeen years of age, he was sure she was all that any Hindu girl should be. In keeping with the prevailing custom, not one day had he sent her to the Mission School in the village.

His conservatism rebelled against sending girl-children to school. He was sure they came to no good. In the first place, they learned to write love letters, then again, they wore knee-length frocks, and — the most shameful thing of all — many of them chose their own husbands! He was glad and proud he had saved Leela from all this.[14]

Yet Mr Naipaul's sympathies are entirely with Leela in her desire to marry not the man her father chooses but the man she loves. Ganpat is clever enough to cope with the situation. By offering his sister with a large dowry to Leela's prospective husband, and then offering to marry Leela himself for a nominal fee, he seems to have reconciled Hindu customs with romance. But the reconciliation is no more than a trick, a trick which serves to illustrate once more how irreconcileable the two worlds really are. Everyone is satisfied, but only by an expedient of limited relevance — and we cannot help wondering what Ganpat's sister must have felt about this casual disposal of her.

With a foot in both worlds, Mr Naipaul finds it impossible to bring the two together. His failure is not surprising, for while by birth and insights he may belong to the one, by temperament and judgements he is wholly committed to the other. In such a passage as the following, his position is absolutely clear. Pundit Sookhlal is reflecting on the significance of the beating his daughter Ratni has just received at Gurudeva's hands. Mr Naipaul obviously knows this point of view from the inside, but the bitter irony with which he records it leaves us in no doubt as to his own opinions:

'Ari! Ari!' he said, 'the more I ponder over the suffering of Ratni, the clearer I see — as in a mirror — that whatever befalls the girl — whether of woe or weal — it is neither the doings of Guru-deva, nor mine, nor anybody's but Ratni's herself. She is simply reaping what she had sown in a previous life; just as how I and you, and Jokhoo here, are each reaping whatever we had sown. Only a fool will try to stop the workings of karma.'

Pundit Sookhlal thoughtfully fingered the bowl of his chee-lum. 'Yet, against all the dark menacing clouds of her life,' he said, 'I see one gleaming thing that makes me almost happy —

certainly proud: it is fine how Ratni is putting up with everything. Thank God for that. It says a lot for the exemplary upbringings I have bequeathed her.'

And the Pundit once more pulled heroically at the cheelum which now seemed dead. 'Bring me another lump of fire,' he said. 'This stupid cheelum has gone cold again.'[15]

The difference here, of course, is not simply between those who care and those who do not. It is the difference between the Hindu doctrine of *karma* and the belief fundamental to the writing of fiction that what has happened to Ratni *is* 'the doings of Gurudeva' and the rest of the family. By the very act of writing, Mr Naipaul has stepped outside the world which is his subject. My point is exactly that discussed in Chapter 1, except that instead of making horoscopes a subject for comedy, as does his son, Seepersad Naipaul, being closer to the situation, is unable to conceal his anger and his fear.

The word 'fear' is no exaggeration. Mr Naipaul knows well the consequences of failure to bring the two worlds together, and it is impossible for him to regard the clash with the amused detachment of *The Mystic Masseur*. In 'Gurudeva' and 'Gopi', he presents us with two victims of the situation. Gurudeva remains in the Indian world. Removed from school at the age of fourteen to be married to a child bride, he is condemned to assert himself in a decaying peasant society too limited and moribund to satisfy his ambitions; like the village heroes of the past, he becomes a hooligan and ends up in jail. Gopi is Westernised. His dream is not of stick-fighting but of 'books, companionship, children'. He yearns for the outside world where important events happen, and he cherishes the newspapers which keep him in touch. He is the only character in these stories who could possibly have written any of them. When he complains 'Kamla was no companion for a man whose urge was to transcend present limitations', it is clear that the limitations are all Indian. He is no snob, but he blames his 'cat-in-bag' marriage to a woman of little education for his failure to achieve the kind of life he longs for. She cannot share his interests and she will not meet his friends. Gopi sees himself as trapped by a world he denies but whose traditionally limited relationships still claim him, and he lacks the ability of Ganpat – or later of Ganesh Ramsumair – to play off one world against the other to his own advantage.

A shrinking, decaying peasant community fights a rearguard action against its more sophisticated surroundings. It maintains both dignity and sweetness, but its sanctions are no longer important and its rituals are only imperfectly understood, and for the young trapped within it or only partially released its traditions can still cripple. The vision of Trinidad that emerges from these stories, then, is of a place where custom and ambition, opportunity and talent, ritual and imagination, are in direct conflict; a place where ability is squandered for the sake of ancient prejudices, and where romance is finally accommodated in dreams of escape. The ultimate effect of these stories on V.S. Naipaul was, as I have said, to demonstrate the value of the material at hand. Their immediate influence, and of the personality behind them, was to teach him the urgency of getting away:

> When I was in the fourth form I wrote a vow on the endpaper of my Kennedy's *Revised Latin Primer* to leave within five years. I left after six; and for many years afterwards in England, falling asleep in bedsitters with the electric fire on, I had been awakened by the nightmare that I was back in tropical Trinidad.[16]

Naipaul entered Form 4a at Queen's Royal College in January 1944, some six months after the publication of *Gurudeva and Other Indian Tales*.

3

By the time V.S. Naipaul comes to turn his father into Mr Biswas, he has moved away from this simple vision. Even in his second book *The Mystic Masseur* he has ceased to think in his father's terms and has formulated his own theories of the 'picaroon' society. *A House for Mr Biswas* makes the divergences clear. The belief in an outside world of romance and opportunity remains – it is not until *The Mimic Men* that Naipaul examines this colonial myth – but the quarrel between East and West is not so clear cut. Naipaul lacks conviction that the new is necessarily better than the old. He accepts the inevitable, but his father's truths are modified. It is interesting, for instance, to compare Mr Sohun, the schoolmaster in 'Gurudeva', with Lal, the presbyterian teacher at Pagotes. Mr Sohun remonstrates with Gurudeva's father when he removes his son from school. He becomes the spokesman of the enlightened West who 'couldn't possibly put right all the wrong things in the world, but . . . could at least give a warning' — a warning which the story amply justifies. Lal, by contrast, is a semi-literate snob whose rudimentary mission-school education has taught him only to despise other Indians, whom he refuses to address in Hindi preferring his own pidgin English. Nowhere, in fact, in Seepersad Naipaul's work do we get the impression, overwhelming in *A House for Mr Biswas*, that the new world is a slum too, and that much of what he says of the Indian community applies to the island as a whole. Another simple contrast which illustrates the profound difference in attitude is the device by which Hindi is represented by standard English to distinguish it from dialect. In *Gurudeva and Other Indian Tales* it is no more than a device, made necessary by the presence of characters who speak both languages. In *A House for Mr Biswas*, it becomes, as we shall see later, one of Naipaul's most subtle means of distinguishing between the two worlds, of indicating their essential qualities, of making us feel how much is lost when the old is superseded and what a violation of personality is involved in stepping from one to the other.

In *Miguel Street*, however, Seepersad Naipaul's influence is pervasive and strong. Although not published until 1959, *Miguel Street* was written in 1955, before *The Mystic Masseur* and *The Suffrage of Elvira*. Two earlier stories, 'The Mourners' and 'My Aunt Gold Teeth', have been collected in *A Flag on the Island*, and Naipaul in various interviews has made enigmatic and not entirely consistent references to two earlier books written while he was still an undergraduate, and to a third begun shortly after he had left Oxford. But it is clear he regards *Miguel Street* as his first serious work, the book in which he discovered 'the trick of writing':

There's a building near the B.B.C. called the Langham Hotel, where characters in Sherlock Holmes used to stay, and Room 235 was reserved for freelance writers. There was a very old typewriter in it. I remember, late one afternoon, putting in a bit of paper, setting it at single space, and without pausing writing the first story of *Miguel Street*.[17]

The result is 'Bogart'. Bogart models himself on the star of the film *Casablanca*, and when he explains a long absence in terms of smuggling and brothel-keeping in British Guiana, he becomes the 'most feared man in the street'. Eventually, he is jailed for bigamy and it turns out his absences have no more melodramatic an explanation than that he has been trying to produce a child. But the men of the street do not laugh; they understand his desire 'to be a man, among we men'. This ending is a direct echo of the closing words of 'Gurudeva' ('Is orright, Bap. I is a man'), and Bogart himself is none other than Gurudeva in modern dress. His inspiration comes from a different source – he wants to be not the badjohn of village tales but the tough guy of movieland – but the essential and defining idea, that manhood is achieved by romantically defying the law, is exactly the same. The second story, 'The Thing Without a Name', makes a similar point. Popo is a lovable poetical character who enjoys rum and sunshine and works hard at objects which are never named or completed. The street despises him as 'not a proper man'. His wife leaves him. He begins to drink heavily, goes to court for beating up her lover, and is immortalised in a calypso – and so finds himself accepted. But his new character takes a perverse turn. He works hard to regain his wife – he acquires new furniture, paints the house and, seemingly respectable, forfeits the admiration his court appearance had brought him. But when it is learned he has stolen everything and is sent to jail, he becomes the street's new hero, 'a better man than either Hat or Bogart', and his wife never leaves him again.

In the third story, however, the badjohn hero is re-examined. George has all the features one might expect Miguel Street to admire – he gets drunk, beats his wife, despises beauty, is cruel and insulting, and finally runs a brothel. But this time the street sides with his wife and children. Dolly puts flowers in the front room, Elias is well-dressed and serious-minded, but neither is mocked. 'That man George giving the street a bad name', says Hat, and his words make us aware of standards more human and flexible than those of the first two stories. The badjohn can go too far, the pose can become too serious, sympathy can swing from the hero to his victims.

From this point on, the tone of the book changes. Gurudeva is left behind and it is Gopi, the man with the urge 'to transcend present limitations', who is remoulded into the next few characters. Naipaul presents us with a series of people who one way or another are dissatisfied with life in Miguel Street. Elias, George's son, wants to become a doctor. When he fails his exams, modifies his ambitions, fails again, and becomes a dust-cart driver, the street's attitude is protective, for it has been recognised he wants to escape from his father's world. Man-Man tries hard to relate to his own circumstances an alien language and religion. The words he writes on the pavement correspond strangely in time to the activities they describe, and eventually he seeks crucifixion as his ultimate identification with the word he preaches – but with the first stone reality breaks in and his dream collapses in 'a cry of agony'. B. Wordsworth is an artist, the spiritual brother of the English poet. His pose is not ridiculous for his sense of wonder is genuine and his excitement over simple actions communicates itself to the narrator. But there is no poetry in Miguel Street, apart from the calypso which cannot contain his yearnings, and the dreams by which he has lived are only dreams. By the time we reach the seventh story, even the badjohn has become a victim. Big Foot's fearsome appearance and his sulky manner set him apart from the other men. He knows himself to be a coward. But the role of fighter is forced upon him, and when he is beaten he breaks down and weeps publicly. This time, significantly, the men of the street *do* laugh. Failure as a badjohn is the one failure they cannot forgive.

Miguel Street is not a community without standards, but the standards are not the sort that can promote achievement by giving shape to ambition, and in the end they amount to little more than a good-natured tolerance of eccentricity and failure. The lack of sanctimoniousness is superficially attractive, but even this is basically no more than a lack of real concern. Occasionally, someone is moved to protest. Hat is contemptuous when Morgan puts his family on trial as a joke. Even Bogart is angry about George's behaviour, and Nathaniel, Laura's seventh lover who comes from east Port of Spain where 'they aint have any culture', goes too far when he laughs at Miss Ricaud who 'was too fat to be laughed at and ought instead to be pitied'. But no one actually helps anyone else, and sympathy is limited to this occasional suspension of laughter. Only one character is healed by the community's protectiveness, when Eddoes finds the child which he has to support but which can't possibly be his is accepted by the street as his own. Of the other fifteen characters, two end up in jail and one in an asylum, two die and the daughter of a third drowns herself, two move elsewhere in Trinidad and two (excluding the narrator) seek anonymity abroad. Miguel Street may tolerate, but it cannot rescue or satisfy. The stories thus become up-to-date and extended versions of *Gurudeva and Other Indian Tales*. Instead of a shrinking peasant community we have a city street, instead of a clash between East and West, a contrast between a small unimportant island and a world of opportunity abroad. But the antitheses remain the same. Ambition and opportunity are in direct conflict, talent is squandered in eccentricity, romance lies only in escape. 'What else anybody can do here except drink?' asks the narrator immediately before his own departure. Even Laura, who with her laughter and her eight children by seven men, seems of all people to be adjusted to life in the street, even Laura cannot accept the same life for her daughter. When Lorna admits she is pregnant, Laura cried 'all the cry she had saved up since she was born', and Hat beats Boyee for not understanding why.

Yet such a summary badly misrepresents the book. *Miguel Street* (unlike *Gurudeva and Other Indian Tales*) is, after all, exceedingly funny, and while one can abstract from it a message of frustration the overall impression is not of bitterness but of relish and an infectious nostalgia. In the last story but one, Hat the street philosopher is sent to jail. By the time he is released three years later, the narrator has changed:

I offered Hat a cigarette and he took it mechanically.

Then he shouted, 'But, eh-eh what is this? You come a big man now! When I leave you wasn't smoking. Was a long time now, though.'

I said, 'Yes. Was a long time.'

A long time. But it was just three years, three years in which I had grown up and looked critically at the people around me. I no longer wanted to be like Eddoes. He was so weak and thin, and I hadn't realised he was so small. Titus Hoyt was stupid and boring, and not funny at all. Everything had changed.

When Hat went to jail, part of me had died.[18]

This contrast between a child's acceptance and an adult's critical detachment is extremely important. Whatever larger conclusions about Trinidad one may have to draw from the book, Naipaul's first concern is to recreate the world in which he grew up, to do justice to characters he once admired. It is significant that much of the material in *Miguel Street* is based on anecdotes which are still widely current in Trinidad. I myself, for instance, had heard the adventures ascribed to Bolo many times before I read *Miguel Street*, and 'Man-Man' exists in other versions. It is retold, rather feebly, in Samuel Selvon's *The Lonely Londoners* as a typical piece of lovable eccentricity, and it is also the subject of the final verse of a splendid calypso by The Mighty Wonder:

> We had a preacher by de name of Nosegay
> Who say he wan' to die so as to wash our sins away;
> He say don' nail but tie me to de cross
> But don' use no big stone, pebble or force;
> Well! Peter hit him with a poui;
> He bawl out, Man, have some sympathy!
> Help! Take me down;
> Help! I ain' do no wrong.
> Every niggerman go bear livin'
> I ain' dyin' again.[19]

Dolphus, the little boy in Michael Anthony's *The Games Were*

Coming, lies in bed listening to the steelband practising this calyp-so.[20] Its conclusion, that even for a 'niggerman' life is better than death, seems to me at least as good as Naipaul's.

Reviewers have suggested that Naipaul owes a considerable debt to John Steinbeck's *Cannery Row*. It is true that a number of Steinbeck's characters would be very much at home in *Miguel Street* – Hazel, for instance, so named because after having seven children in eight years his mother was too exhausted to see he was a boy; or Henry who has been building a boat for seven years but is too frightened of the sea to be able to finish it; or Mr and Mrs Sam Malloy who live in a disused boiler and quarrel because although the boiler has no windows Mrs Malloy wants some curtains. But *Cannery Row* can have given Naipaul little help with his first and most basic problem, namely, how to do justice to a society one has by choice left behind, how to write about people so vulnerable that any assessment seems patronising. Steinbeck's method is to be fiercely partisan, and he defends his misfits by repeated and some-what apocalyptic assaults on the standards of those who are pre-sumably his readers. But sooner or later he has to illustrate imaginatively the plea he is making, and his solution gives him away. He concentrates on 'The Doc', an educated misfit who hap-pens to live in the area, and he proves the goodheartedness of his characters by their muddled efforts to thank the Doc for all he has done for them. The effect is disturbing. The Doc becomes the author's representative, surrounded by a crowd of troublesome but lovable children who are shown to be basically good because they respond gratefully to his appreciation of them.

Obviously, such a solution is of no use to Naipaul. Instead, he goes back to childhood, returning to that state of innocency when he could share Miguel Street's view of itself because he was as much a part of it as anyone else. Perhaps I should make it clear that Miguel Street does not actually exist – the 'autobiographical' details are misleading. But the return to childhood is the factor which governs the book's tone. We meet the characters at a time when Eddoes is still a hero and Titus Hoyt has not yet come to seem stupid and boring. We meet them not only before the author has escaped but before he has defined to himself the need to escape.

If anyone is patronised, it is the author's younger self.

In practice, however, we are never quite sure about the child's position. 'The Pyrotechnist' begins with perhaps the clearest statement in the whole book of his commitment:

> A stranger could drive through Miguel Street and just say 'Slum' because he could see no more. But we, who lived there, saw our street as a world, where everybody was quite different from everybody else.[21]

But later in the same story, when Morgan's house catches fire and everyone turns out at night to watch, we are told 'I never slept in pyjamas. I wasn't in that class', betraying some degree of surrender to the stranger's point of view. There is, in fact, more than one voice in *Miguel Street*, not simply because the author frequently intrudes with what is obviously an adult comment, but because the child too varies from story to story. In 'Bogart', which contains such innocencies as 'Popo had a wife who . . . ended up by becoming the friend of many men', the child is no more than the source of the information, and all the characters are distanced through an irony inherited from Seepersad Naipaul – it is Hat who makes the final speech 'To be a man. Among we men'. In the second story, however, we see the beginnings of a divergence between the street's and the child's views. The child likes Popo ('I thought he was a poetical man') and he rejects as unreasonable Hat's criticism 'Popo too conceited, you hear'. When Popo, after his jail sentence, is established as 'a bigger man than any of us', the child feels only a sense of loss – Popo, the badjohn hero, has ceased to be a poet. By the time we reach 'B. Wordsworth' and 'The Coward', the gap between the child's and the street's judgements has become absolute:

> And all of us from Miguel Street laughed at Big Foot. All except me.[22]

However, in the very next story, 'The Pyrotechnist', and perhaps as a reaction against this indulgence, the child is reduced again to an observer, patronised by the author over his lack of pyjamas or his delight at seeing his picture in the paper, but credited with no unusual insight. The burden of comment again falls on Hat whose remarks are quoted with such additions as 'I don't think any of us understood what Hat meant'.

The trouble is that however much Naipaul tries to lay aside his adult impatience, to return to a state of childhood delight, he is still deeply committed to his father's vision of Trinidad. Having chosen a boy as his narrator, he has made the boy see a succession of Gurudevas and Gopis. So long as this vision coincides with the street's or with Hat's views there is no difficulty – the child remains a child, the point of contact, the source of the information, and his acceptance and relish can be shared by the reader. But when Naipaul's sympathy for the street's most Gopi-like victims makes it necessary for him to impose a special lonely insight on the child, the result is embarrassing – the end of the much anthologised 'B. Wordsworth' is surely the most mawkish thing Naipaul has ever published.

But then, in 'The Mechanical Genius' and 'Caution', Stories 13 and 14, there is a new development:

It was not until 1947 that Bolo believed that the war was over. Up till then he used to say, 'Is only a lot of propaganda. Just lies for black people.'

In 1947 the Americans began pulling down their camp in the George V Park and many people were getting sad.

I went to see Bolo one Sunday and while he was cutting my hair he said, 'I hear the war over.'

I said, 'So I hear too. But I still have my doubts.'

Bolo said, 'I know what you mean. These people is master of propaganda, but the way I look at it is this. If they was still fighting they woulda want to keep the camp.'

'But they not keeping the camp,' I said.

Bolo said, 'Exactly. Put two and two together and what you get? Tell me, what you get?'

I said, 'Four.'

He clipped my hair thoughtfully for a few moments.

He said, 'Well, I glad the war over.'

When I paid for my trim I said, 'What you think we should

do now, Mr Bolo? You think we should celebrate?'
He said, 'Gimme time, man. Gimme time. This is a big thing. I
have to think it over.'
And there the matter rested.[23]

This is no longer the boy of the earlier stories. It is the voice of the
narrator of *The Mystic Masseur*, intelligent and ironical, half
belonging and half detached, relishing his companion's eccentricities and playing along with them to see how far they will be
carried. After a dozen experiments, Naipaul has at last hit on a
means of exploring his society in his own rather than in his father's
terms. For it is no accident that this development coincides with
another. I claimed earlier that between the third and fourth stories,
Naipaul lays aside the Gurudeva model and presents us instead
with various versions of Gopi. Now at last the Gopi prototype is
also laid aside, and we are given the first version of theories which
are to find their fullest expression in *The Mystic Masseur* and *The
Suffrage of Elvira*, the two subsequent novels. Through the disasters
that befall Bolo (the housing scandal, the abortive Venezuela trip)
we are introduced to what Naipaul in *The Middle Passage* calls the
'picaroon' society – a society in which the hero is not the badjohn
but the 'smart man', the trickster whose exploits are appreciated
even by his victims. The full implications of this thesis will be discussed in my next chapter, but it is significant that it first appears in
the last few stories of *Miguel Street*, and moreover that Naipaul
owes nothing of them to his father. The influence which has per-
vaded the whole book so far is laid aside, and Naipaul at last discovers a vision and a voice of his own.

There is one curious detail which throws light on this conclusion. Naipaul gives the narrator a mother who, of all the characters in the book, seems best adapted to life in Miguel Street. She
is practical and competent, but rather humourless and impatient of
ambition and of imaginative impulses of any kind. 'You like your
mother?' asks B. Wordsworth. 'When she not beating me', replies
the boy, and this answer sums up their relationship – though it is
important to add that it is she who arranges for his departure at the
end. But where is his father? One entirely suitable answer would

be that children in Miguel Street do not have 'fathers' and, if they are like George and Nathaniel, do not want them. The fatherless family is fairly common in Trinidad, and Laura's eight children by seven men is exceptional only in scale. In, for example, *The Year in San Fernando* and *Green Days by the River*,[24] marvellously sensitive and accurate novels by the Trinidadian Michael Anthony, we again have boy narrators. In the first case the father is dead, in the second a permanent invalid; as in *Miguel Street*, the strongest masculine influences come from outside the family. But another, rather different answer is hinted at in *Miguel Street*. In 'The Blue Cart', the mother refers to 'this boy's father' who was 'always painting scenaries', and in the next story 'Love, Love, Love Alone', she adds enigmatically, 'When I uses to go to the room where he was he uses to jump out of the bed and run away bawling – run away screaming.' This sounds very like the behaviour of Mr Biswas at Green Vale shortly before his breakdown. Otherwise we hear nothing of him. References to him are always in the past tense but his absence from the book is unexplained. Viewed from the vantage point of later books, however, it would seem that we have the first hint here of the Biswas-Shama relationship, with a Biswas-type figure being kept well in the background.

This suspicion is confirmed by the story 'The Enemy', first published in *Vogue* (of all places), and now collected in *A Flag on the Island*, where Naipaul describes it in the preface as having been 'written as part of my book *Miguel Street*'. The events precede the boy's arrival in Port of Spain, and the situation is almost exactly that described in the Green Vale section of *A House for Mr Biswas*. His father is an overseer on a sugar estate, and is being threatened by some of the labourers. Intimidated by noises outside at night and by the killing of Tarzan the puppy, his mother decides to leave. The boy, like Anand, is faced with a choice between accompanying her and staying with his father who has offered him some crayons. He stays, and a relationship develops in which there are the same discussions about gravity and God and the blending of colours as take place between Mr Biswas and Anand. But the father's terrors grow. There is a violent storm, but whereas in *A House for Mr Biswas* Anand feels only abandoned and betrayed, in

'The Enemy' the father actually dies of fright. The boy rejoins his mother, and the remainder of the story concerns his relationship with her. She is the enemy, 'someone from whom I was going to escape as soon as I grew big enough', but the episodes trace the same kind of indirect love as later grows between Mr Biswas and his children, and again the material is similar – like Savi, the boy cannot tie his shoelaces and is beaten for it; like Anand he writes a brilliant essay on his escape from drowning and is beaten again for refusing to read it to his mother.

It is not hard to see why Naipaul decided to omit the story. By the time *Miguel Street* was eventually published in 1959, he was well advanced with *A House for Mr Biswas*. He would scarcely have wished to anticipate some of his best scenes. Moreover, the story is not really a success. Naipaul is writing about childhood feelings of injustice (it is impossible to believe in the fictional narrator here), but he writes with a cynical lightness which seems a direct denial of the emotions involved. We are left with a sense that something is being evaded, a feeling that all these details have for the author a much deeper significance than is brought out by the story itself. Yet it is interesting to be able to read it now, not least because it il-lustrates the enormous advance in Naipaul's art in the years be-tween the two versions. This is how Naipaul describes Anand's decision to stay with Mr Biswas:

> Shama said, 'Anand, do you want to come with me, or do you want to stay with your father?'
>
> Mr Biswas, the stick in his hand, looked at Anand.
>
> Anand continued to stroke Tarzan, whose head was now upturned, his eyes partly closed.
>
> Mr Biswas ran to the green table and awkwardly pulled out the drawer. He took the long box of crayons he used for his pla-cards and held it to Anand. He shook the box; the crayons rat-tled.
>
> Savi said, 'Come, Anand boy. Go and get your clothes.'
>
> Still stroking Tarzan, Anand said, 'I staying with Pa.' His voice was low and irritable.
>
> 'Anand!' Savi said.

'Don't beg him,' Shama said, in control of herself again. 'He is a man and knows what he is doing.'

'Boy,' Dookhnee said. 'Your mother.'

Anand said nothing.

Shama got up and the circle of women around her widened. She took Myna, Savi took the suitcase, and they walked along the path, muddy between sparse and stubborn grass, to the road, scattering the hens and chickens before them. Tarzan followed, and was diverted by the chickens. When he was pecked by an angry hen he looked for Shama and Savi and Myna. They had disappeared. He trotted back to the barracks and Anand.

Mr Biswas opened the box and showed Anand the sharpened crayons. 'Take them. They are yours. You can do what you like with them.'

Anand shook his head.

'You don't want them?'

Tarzan, between Anand's legs, held up his head to be stroked, closing his eyes in anticipation.

'What do you want then?'

Anand shook his head. Tarzan shook his.

'Why did you stay then?'

Anand looked exasperated.

'Why?'

'Because — ' The word came out thin, explosive, charged with anger, at himself and his father. 'Because they were going to leave you alone.'

For the rest of that day they hardly spoke.[25]

Compared to this, the version given in 'The Enemy' seems tightly buttoned-up and stilted in its cynicism:

My mother had decided to leave my father, and she wanted to take me to her mother.

I refused to go.

My father was ill, and in bed. Besides, he had promised that if I stayed with him I was to have a whole box of crayons.

I chose the crayons and my father.[26]

The difference here is not simply that Naipaul has learned to mount a big scene – though his sensitivity to every nuance of everybody's feelings (Mr Biswas is not humiliated into actually voicing his bribe; Anand makes his reply not to his mother but to Savi), the clarity of the details (the green table, rattling crayons, the muddy path and sparse, stubborn grass), the use of Tarzan (towards whom Anand's attention is diverted but who remains supremely indifferent to what is going on), and the long suspense before we learn Anand's real reason for staying – a decision that is crucial to his future relationship with his father; all these obviously work together to make the later version far superior. Nevertheless, the real difference between them is that Naipaul, confident now in his abilities as a writer, sure of his own vision and no longer threatened by his father's influence, is free to release a quality of emotion which at the time of *Miguel Street* he deliberately suppresses.

Seen in the light of 'The Enemy', the choice of a fatherless child as the narrator of *Miguel Street* takes on a new significance. The father is killed off, remaining killed off through *The Mystic Masseur* and *The Suffrage of Elvira*, in which there are no comparable figures, until his resurrection in the opening pages of *A House for Mr Biswas*. Naipaul clearly feels he can explore his society in his own terms only by eliminating his father from the Trinidad scene. Yet as we have seen, it is not until after a dozen stories of *Miguel Street* that the device pays dividend, and it is not until he has had three books published and has established the beginnings of a considerable reputation that he can explore with confidence and detachment a depth of experience which is suppressed in his early writing.

I do not mean to suggest that there is nothing original in *Miguel Street*, nothing until the last few stories that is not derived directly from *Gurudeva and Other Indian Tales*. Seen once again from the vantage point of later books, it is surprising how much is anticipated in these stories. In the film star dialogues of Hat and Bogart are the beginnings of *The Mimic Men*; in B. Wordsworth and Titus Hoyt, artists whose dreams are mocked by their surroundings, we see something of Mr Biswas; in Morgan the pyrotechnist who is broken by achievement and in Edward the practical joker whose contentment is ruined when the Americans make him ambitious, there is a hint of 'A Flag on the Island'. The seeds of later books are scattered through *Miguel Street*. But it remains an apprentice work. Naipaul begins his career with a salute to the world of his childhood – it is not surprising that this, of all his books, is the most popular in Trinidad. But despite the humour and the splendidly funny dialogue, he has to struggle to find a voice of his own. Only towards the end are the ghosts of his father's heroes finally laid, and by then it is inevitable that his father's attitude, and his own Fourth Form vow to escape, should be written into the ending. By then it is inevitable that the book should conclude with a chapter, 'How I Left Miguel Street'. No one could stay in the situation he has described and hope to complete anything.

CHAPTER THREE

'Trinidad full of crazy people'

I

The spirit of Ganesh Ramsumair dominates Naipaul's early work. He features twice in *Miguel Street*, in 'Man-Man' where he sets the fashion for seeing God and in the final chapter where he is bribed into giving the narrator a scholarship to 'go study drugs' in London. He is mentioned again in *The Suffrage of Elvira* as the island's greatest mystic – before, regrettably, he took up politics. And he is, of course, the hero of *The Mystic Masseur*. 'Who is this Ganesh?' runs the advertisement in the *Trinidad Sentinel*, and the answer is, in a way, the subject of these first three books. The quack doctor, the phoney mystic, the corrupt politician who is nevertheless 'a hero of the people', Ganesh seems to stand in Naipaul's mind for all those contradictory features of Trinidad life he is trying to pin down. His first attempt at a novel, completed at Oxford 'in twenty hours', contained 'the beginnings of *The Mystic Masseur*',[1] and it is not until his fourth book that he at last ventures beyond the problems Ganesh personifies.

We first meet Pundit Ganesh the year before *Miguel Street* in the story 'My Aunt Gold Teeth', written in 1954 and now collected in the volume *A Flag on the Island*. Gold Teeth is the rich but childless wife of Pundit Ramprasad, and Ganesh is called in when Ramprasad falls ill. The district medical officer calls it diabetes, but Gold Teeth knows his illness has been caused by the Christian prayers she has been offering in secret to release her from the curse of childlessness. Ganesh reassures her ('God is pleased if you pray at all') and prescribes something which hastens Ramprasad's death – though, charitably, he refuses payment. The night before her husband dies, Gold Teeth becomes possessed, and is deeply respected by her family for the quality of her double religious commitment.

But the death changes everything. Gold Teeth is suddenly to blame; her 'trafficking with Christianity' has killed her husband; it is her own fault she has no children to support her.

The story contains several features which are to be developed in succeeding novels — Pundit Ganesh himself, the packed Port of Spain house, the 'venerable' grandmother who is to become Mrs Tulsi, the moral claustrophobia, the maddening self-deceptions. What is striking, however, is the extreme detachment of the narrator. Nowhere else (except in the ending of *The Suffrage of Elvira*) does Naipaul pretend to be so utterly untouched by the events he describes. Nowhere else does he come so close to deserving the criticism that he writes as an Oxford snob. His style surrenders completely to the artificial rhythms of mock-heroic prose:

> She was living at the time in a country village called Cunupia, in County Caroni. Here the Canadian Mission had long waged war against the Indian heathen, and saved many. But Gold Teeth stood firm. The Minister of Cunupia expended his Presbyterian piety on her; so did the headmaster of the Mission school. But all in vain. At no time was Gold Teeth persuaded even to think about being converted. . . She was willing to select, modify, and incorporate alien eccentricities into her worship; but to abjure her own faith — never![2]

One can hear in every calculated cadence the terribly arch B.B.C. voice required to read the passage aloud. The eccentricities of later stories suffocate in this atmosphere. Humour lies not in what the characters say and do but in the narrator's stylish comments — Gold Teeth entering the churchyard feels 'like an explorer in a land of cannibals'. It is all amiable enough, but the impression is created, however unintentionally, that although Naipaul chooses to write about these people he is not to be thought of as one of them. Afterwards, when Gold Teeth throws her fit, we are told 'I was rather ashamed at the exhibition'. Later narrators are equally sceptical, but never again does Naipaul use such a phrase.

Inevitably, the character who suffers most is Pundit Ganesh. Who is *this* Ganesh? Certainly not the stylish eccentric who is to amuse and intrigue us later. The charge of hypocrisy is direct and unambiguous – when Gold Teeth breaks down, Ganesh 'filled his eyes with charity and love'. He is in no sense a victim. He doesn't even speak dialect unless (though Naipaul does not make this clear) his polished English is meant to stand for Hindi. Ganesh here is a smooth professional, a Hindu P.R.O. man who has 'exploited the commodiousness of Hinduism' to gain for himself 'many satisfied clients'. There is no hint of his potential as a representative hero, a symbol of the island's contradictions. When we do eventually meet such a Ganesh in The Mystic Masseur, we do so in a context which specifically rejects the mock-heroic approach. Gamesh's rival is Indarsingh, who returns from the Oxford Union to try 'talking to peasants' and is repeatedly outwitted by the hero. Naipaul qualifies the portrait by making it quite clear that Indarsingh is what he is long before he leaves Trinidad and by permitting him to be Ganesh's final critic and successor. But the main intention is obviously to dramatise the irrelevance of seeing Trinidad through borrowed Oxford spectacles. At no stage does Indarsingh influence events, and while it is perfectly understandable that Naipaul should enjoy ridiculing such a standard character, one wonders whether he has not invented Indarsingh partly as a reminder of the pitfalls to be avoided, a self-conscious insurance against charges that he has gone the same way himself.

Between 'My Aunt Gold Teeth' and The Mystic Masseur comes Miguel Street, containing an encounter with Ganesh in the final chapter. This time, of course, Ganesh is seen through the eyes of the child narrator – by now a lively, ironical boy with a taste for oddity, but still sufficiently involved with his friends to view from within their own environment. The contrast with the earlier story is a measure of how much fairer – and more intriguing – such an approach is likely to be. We meet Ganesh as a man expecting to be bribed, and his duel of tears with the boy's mother is obvious playacting. Yet the bribe and the tears are now seen as accepted rituals which in no way compromise the characters' opinions of each other, and they both fulfil the roles expected of them with such sincere self-deception that the earlier charges of hypocrisy are made to look beside the point.

It is hardly surprising, then, that Naipaul's spokesman in The

Mystic Masseur should again be a Trinidadian boy who grows up to be a student in England, and the first problem in finding a firm track through the book's ambiguities is to be clear about the narrator's role. Does he speak as a child, or as a reminiscing adult, or are the voices mixed? Is he genuinely Naipaul's representative? Or are we to take him as just another character in the story, deluded by Ganesh like everyone else?

> You never felt that he was a fake and you couldn't deny his literacy or learning – not with all those books. And he hadn't only book learning. He could talk on almost any subject. For instance, he had views about Hitler and knew how the war could be ended in two weeks. 'One way,' he used to say. 'Only one. And in fourteen days, even thirteen – bam! – no more war.' But he kept the way a secret.[3]

This summary of Ganesh's methods might suggest that the child narrator is just another admirer, with no more insight or detachment than, say, Beharry. We know that Ganesh's possession of 'all those books' does not mean he is learned – only that his clients are impressed by appearances. We know that Ganesh is talking nonsense about the war – and that this is why he keeps his solution a secret. But is the narrator taken in? The paragraph continues:

> And he could discuss religion sensibly as well. He was no bigot. He took as much interest in Christianity and Islam as in Hinduism. In the shrine, the old bedroom, he had pictures of Mary and Jesus next to Krishna and Vishnu; a crescent and star represented iconoclastic Islam. 'All the same God,' he said. Christians liked him, Muslims liked him, and Hindus, willing as ever to risk prayers to new gods, didn't object.[4]

Now it is the narrator who underlines the irony – he, for instance, who comments objectively on Hinduism, he who draws our attention to the fact that along with the images of other religions Ganesh has hung on his wall the symbol of 'iconoclastic Islam'.

This passage is typical of the whole novel. Naipaul is exploiting to the full the methods we saw him evolving in the thirteenth and fourteenth stories of *Miguel Street*, where the themes developed in

The Mystic Masseur first appear. The narrator is an intelligent observer who understands very well what is happening. If he frequently appears to be going along with the accepted view of Ganesh, this is not because he is taken in but because he is delighted and intrigued and because it is only by talking with his tongue in his cheek that he can explore the whole situation and at the same time convey the full flavour of his delight. It is the pose of a man who relishes the contradictions he is exposing. His first reaction, meeting Ganesh as a boy, is to be amused and puzzled, and though the boy grows up ('Thinking now about that visit I made to Ganesh as a boy, I am struck only by my egotism'), this early fascination is never repudiated. 'The day go come', his mother insists, 'when you go be proud to tell people that you did know Ganesh', and though in the course of the novel Ganesh is thoroughly exposed, the narrator's final 'shout of joy' when he meets Ganesh on the station seems wholly appropriate. In this most Trinidadian of his novels, Naipaul manages to make us feel that, faced with such a disarmingly successful enigma, condemnation is the dullest of responses.

Ganesa, the elephant god, is the Hindu god of success. In the novel's opening sentence, Ganesh's career is defined as a success story – he begins as 'a struggling masseur' and rises to occupy the highest position his society can offer, 'famous and honoured . . . a hero of the people . . . a British representative at Lake Success'. The contrast with the poignant failures of *Miguel Street* is like a breath of fresh air. But Ganesh does not triumph by accident. 'The history of Ganesh', the narrator tells us in his apology for the book, 'is in a way the history of our times.' His success defines and illuminates the society which makes him its hero. An image from *Miguel Street* is relevant here. In the earlier book only Eddoes, the sagaboy, achieves real status. Outside the street he is vulnerable – his story ends with him having to accept responsibility for a baby which cannot be his. But on his own ground he is an impressive figure, worshipped by the boys of the street for the panache with which he drives his dust cart. The hero rides proudly on a cartload of rubbish. The image is a foretaste of Ganesh and his society.

When Ramlogan is trying to persuade Ganesh to marry his

daughter Leela, he buys a new glass case for the counter of his shop:

> 'Is really Leela idea,' Ramlogan said. 'It does keep out the flies from the cakes and it more modern.'
> The flies now congregated inside the case. Presently a pane was broken and patched up again with brown paper. The glass case now belonged.[5]

Later it is patched again with part of the cover of *The Illustrated London News*, and this picture of fly-blown decay is repeated throughout the book. The Trinidad of the tourist brochures – a vibrant meeting-point of different races and cultures – becomes in *The Mystic Masseur* a centre of dereliction. Beharry's shop, its 'decaying distemper flaking off the walls', its roof 'warped and rusting', contains his books – the *Napoleon Book of Fate, Eothen* with both covers missing, the *Gita*, the *Ramayana*, and three issues of Booker's *Almanac*. Ganesh's paper *The Dharma* is modelled on the *New Statesman* and *Time* magazine and dedicated to Gandhi, but the result is of a piece with the Chinese calendars, the American booklets, the pictures of Indian filmstars, the portrait of George V – the detritus of three continents littering the island. The details are significant, for the dereliction extends to the people. Naipaul sees his characters as abandoned on the rubbish heap, struggling confusedly to come to terms with it while their original identity disintegrates. The picture is deliberately two-dimensional. Naipaul is clearly trying to bring the indulgences of *Miguel Street* under much firmer intellectual control, and it is not until *A House for Mr Biswas* that he discusses the displacement with the depth of historical perspective. For the time being he contents himself with specific pictures – Ganesh's father cursing Port of Spain in eloquent Hindi, Mr Stewart the eccentric Englishman dressed as a mendicant, the Negro woman with white powder on her face, the American servicemen dispensing gum to the children of Fuente Grove where they have come for 'spiritual advice', Leela's fridge packed with coca-cola and visible from the road – pictures which, taken together, dramatise the confusion of origins and loyalties, customs and aspirations, which is the setting of Ganesh's success.

The whole displaced society is summed up neatly in the dinner at Government House for newly elected members of the Legislative Council. The scene has been much criticised on the grounds that Naipaul, secure in the achievement of having dined at Oxford, thinks it funny to ridicule West Indian table manners. If this were the point, it would indeed be a very cheap triumph. But Naipaul's purpose is to complete his picture of the society of which Ganesh is the hero, and to show that what has been true of the peasants is true also of the new élite. Such are the varieties of displacement that it is impossible for the new legislators to sit down at table together without the most elementary problems arising – problems of culture and principle, and only superficially of table manners. Ganesh himself, for instance, accustomed to eating with his fingers, consults a friend about knives and forks, and turns up wearing dhoti, koortah and turban. Other guests wear dinner jackets, jodhpurs, a khaki suit and sun helmet, or ('adhering for the moment to his pre-election principles') shorts and an open shirt. Mr Primrose, the blackest Negro, comes in a blue suit with yellow gloves, and is racially aggressive about his monocle. He brings his second wife, a teetotaller, by contrast with the Indian Christian who, never having been married, brings his four year old daughter – with whom he shares the meat soup that Ganesh, the Hindu, rejects in disgust. The hostess is the governor's wife, who is surely included in the irony as she presides 'with assurance and determination' over an occasion unfamiliar to everyone except herself.

An assortment of displaced individuals inhabits a landscape not lushly tropical but 'flat, treeless, hot'. The picture, as I have said, is two-dimensional, for *The Mystic Masseur* is a novel written primarily to illustrate a thesis, with the characters chosen to support a comic but intellectual framework. If, however, such scenes as the governor's dinner should seem unnecessarily cruel, it is fair to add that there are balancing moments, occasions when Naipaul all but steps outside his self-imposed terms of reference. He is too sensitive to the contradictions in which his characters are trapped, too alert for the paradox within the paradox, to turn his back entirely on the mood of *Miguel Street*. In the following passage, for instance, Ganesh is unable to give Bissoon a job as a salesman and offers noney instead:

> To his surprise Bissoon rose, very much like the old Bissoon, dusted his coat, and straightened his hat. 'You think I come to beg you for charity, Ganesh? I was a big big man when you was wetting your diaper, and you want now to give me *charity*?'
> And he walked away.
> It was the last Ganesh saw of him. For a long time no one, not even The Great Belcher, knew what became of him, until Beharry brought the news one Sunday morning that Suruj Mooma thought she had glimpsed him in a blue uniform in the ground of the Poor House on the Western Main Road in Port of Spain.[6]

In this image of Bissoon refusing help from a friend only to be forced into accepting the anonymous and humiliating charity of the state, there is little hint of satire; only a sense of dignity struggling against hopeless odds. The point is worth noticing for there are occasions when Ganesh too almost takes on the extra dimension which would make him a comparable figure to Mr Biswas — when, for instance, he stands by his father's body in the silence punctuated by the dripping ice, or when after Leela has left him he bursts into a temper because she can't have 'a small tiny little thing like a baby'. Such moments of poignancy are not typical of the book as a whole, but they do remind us that Ganesh, too, is to some extent a victim and that his success must be seen in the context of circumstances not dissimilar to those which trap Mr Biswas.

Naipaul emphasises this point by setting the second and third chapters in careful contrast. In Chapter 2, we meet Ganesh as a boy travelling from his home to Port of Spain, from a world where the prospect of secondary education confers real status, to one where his Indian peasant background makes him quaint and ridiculous. At Queens Royal College, he changes his name to Gareth (a foretaste of the ending) and even plays football, but his accent, his country habits, and the sensational appearance of his bald head after his initiation as a Brahmin, mark him out as alien and somewhat absurd. Yet education has its effects. The two worlds clash in a single sentence when Ganesh's father congratulates him on his school certificate and tells him to come home to get married. Ganesh's refusal ('If Ganesh didn't want to get married, he mus consider himself an orphan') is a clear break with his background Yet he remains dissatisfied and out of place. He drifts into teaching but when one final taunt about being 'up from the cane-field' co incides with news of his father's death, he turns his back on Port o Spain for the next dozen years. Back in Fourways in Chapter 3 however, he is equally out of place. At his father's funeral he feel only that 'ritual had replaced grief', and he cannot recognise his re lations. His education earns him the title 'sahib' and the oil royal ties free him from the need to work, so he plays no part in the life of the village, seeing in his detachment the proof that he is set apart for something big. Naipaul does not, of course, analyse the dis placement with the sympathy and insight he devotes to Mr Biswas, but the situations are in some respects similar. By the time he is twenty-one, circumstances have combined to make Ganesh an alien in both worlds.

The difference between him and Mr Biswas is that Ganesh learns how to handle things, how to play off one world against the other to his own advantage. We first see him in action in Chapter 4 when he gets married – an event which for Mr Biswas marks the closing of the trap. Ramlogan persuades Ganesh, after one of those sessions of piously oblique bargaining that Naipaul handles so well, that twelve thousand dollars would make a respectable father-in-law. The match is agreed, and tradition is honoured in the pretence that Ganesh and Leela have never met. Ramlogan, however, rejects traditional methods of invitation in favour of cards with R.S.V.P. on them, Ganesh being a 'modern' man, and we begin to appreciate his thinking when he pretends he has been robbed and that a dowry is not 'modern' either. Ganesh sympa thises, but refuses to violate tradition by skipping the kedgeree eating ceremony. Perhaps it is not until he discovers Ramlogan is cheating him over the wedding expenses that he decides to act, but when it comes to the eating of the kedgeree he forces a small for tune out of his father-in-law. This is the first time we see him in action, exploiting to his own advantage the sanctions of Indian so ciety – though it is significant that he is responding in kind to

Ramlogan's attempts to select from the past only what does not cost too much. But Ganesh is getting the knack, by contrast with Mr Biswas who, having written a 'modern' love-letter, is trapped into a 'modern' marriage with no dowry. It is in the sequel, however, that Ganesh's real skill emerges. Something has to be done to square Ramlogan. By demanding from Leela a photo of her father, Ganesh first terrorises him with the threat of witchcraft and then thrills him with his picture in the *Sentinel* under the heading 'Benefactor Endows Cultural Institute'. Ganesh's education has paid off. It has taught him what Ramlogan does not know – the sanctions of modernity.

By the end of Chapter 4, the pattern is established. Throughout the rest of his career, Ganesh reveals the same alertness to the demands of both worlds, the same wit and political skill in manipulating them to his own advantage. His first book, for instance, is an educational primer to 'bring the people up', but it deals with questions on Hinduism. The sign outside his house is bilingual, offering spiritual consolation in Hindi but warning away beggars in English. His *Guide to Trinidad* is aimed mainly at American servicement, but advertises a genuine Hindu temple in Fuente Grove 'well worth a visit for spiritual and artistic reasons'. He is furious with Ramlogan for running 'blessed' taxis at five shillings a trip, so takes them over to run at four shillings instead. Even his political campaign is climaxed by a seven-day prayer meeting, to which he invites Indarsingh who 'stupidly, talked about politics'. It is difficult to discuss such alertness without giving the impression that as well as being exceptionally clever he is also exceptionally dishonest. One is tempted to fall back on a sentence from *The Middle Passage* as a summary of Ganesh's career:

> Trinidad has always admired the 'sharp character' who, like the sixteenth-century picaroon of Spanish literature, survives and triumphs by his wits in a place where it is felt that all eminence is arrived at by crookedness.[7]

Yet the statement needs qualifying before it is applied to *The Mystic Masseur*. Ganesh is not just a trickster hero, clever enough and unscrupulous enough to turn his back on all moral standards.

He is also a man who, had he been born ten years earlier or later, might have become 'a mediocre pundit' or 'a dangerous doctor'. The accident in time which supplements his Indianness with half an education is crucial. His whole career is shaped by his relationships, not just because they limit his opportunities but because he depends on their inspiration. It is Mr Stewart, for instance, who sets Ganesh on the road to mysticism. Ganesh's Hinduism at this time amounts to little more than nausea at having to bite into Mr Stewart's sandwiches, but he is enchanted to hear Hindus described as the 'only people pursuing the indefinite' and to have his own loafing called 'meditation'. By contrast, it is The Great Belcher, a delightful creation and our one glimpse in the novel of an older Indian way of life dominated by the family rituals of weddings and funerals, who supplies the stimulus and the sacred texts for Ganesh to become a spiritual healer. And always in the background, there is the negative influence of Ramlogan, only once getting the better of Ganesh (over the 'cure' of Leela's foot), but providing a version of pious materialism which disgusts him even as it gives shape to his own schemes – marriage, the cultural centre, the taxis, journalism, politics.

He is not even 'dishonest' in any straightforward sense. People are impressed by his holiness, and his religiosity is clearly a pose. Yet Ganesh believes his own pretence. Moments of detachment such as occurs after he has cured the boy of the black cloud are balanced by surprise 'at the extent of his own powers'. Beharry and Ramlogan assume he is acting, and both are driven to exasperated complaint ('all this flashy talk' and 'this damn mystical nonsense') when they find he means what he says. The same applies to his books. Piles of them are displayed on all possible occasions and with striking effect. Yet Ganesh too is impressed by them. He genuinely loves his *Everyman* library. He feels all the authority and compulsion of print, and even such a detail as the description of Narayan in an English newspaper as 'chain smoking, balding and a veteran journalist' can irritate him into action. His own book is a triumph. He is thrilled to show it to Beharry and Leela, and Naipaul (perhaps remembering *Gurudeva and Other Indian Tales*) enters into his feelings so openly ('so the process began, the thrilling,

tedious, discouraging, exhilarating process of making a book') that
it is impossible for us not to share them.

Two incidents are especially instructive in this connection. The
first is the basis of his reputation, when he cures the boy tormented
by his brother's death. Ganesh has been waiting for a long time to
prove himself, and he plans his defeat of the 'black cloud' meticu-
lously. He uses all the paraphernalia of Hinduism – flowing gar-
ments, sacred pictures, incense in a darkened room, Hindi chants
with long-haired Leela interpreting – to heighten the impression
that he has supernatural powers; and a friend in the oilfields (education 'have it uses sometimes') shows him how to produce a black
cloud. The whole set-up is obviously fraudulent. Yet there is no
mistaking the genuineness of Ganesh's sympathy for the little boy,
and his real anxiety to help him as well as make his own reputation.
The point is driven home by Leela's change of heart after she has
seen the misery of the boy's mother, and by the contrast with the
brutal priest who has told the boy he must pay for the sin of wanting his brother to die. Most important of all, Ganesh really does
cure him. 'Is like watching a theatre show', he tells Leela, 'and
then finding out afterwards they was really killing people on the
stage'; and if it is a little difficult to imagine him saying such a
thing, the words do justify his methods. Where does the pose end
and sincerity begin? How should we react to his final instruction,
that the boy's parents should pay him only what they can afford?
He knows – and we know – he will get more that way. But would
we prefer him to have a fixed scale of charges? Naipaul's irony –
realistically detached, yet acknowledging Ganesh's qualities –
defines our only possible response.

If this incident supports the impression that Ganesh is after all
only a clever trickster, fortunate enough to be fulfilling a social
need, the second is even more revealing. An industrialist in India
offers thirty thousand dollars for the cultural uplift of Trinidad
Hindus, and Ganesh decides it is time for him to supplant Narayan
as leader of the Hindu community. By secretly forming his own
branches of the Hindu Association while publicly launching the
Hindu League, he gets control of Narayan's A.G.M. It is a brilliant
manoeuvre for which this time there seems no justification –

except, perhaps, that Ganesh seems likely to handle the money no worse than his opponent. But Naipaul dismisses such moral considerations. Narayan, recognising defeat, makes a retiring speech in which he pleads for forgiveness and insists on the need for unity. The delegates respond to his clichés, and the boy is worried:

'A diplomatic son of a bitch, pundit,' the boy said.
But Ganesh was wiping away a tear.[8]

Indarsingh protests 'in impeccable English' when the constitution is suspended. The bearded Negro calls the Hindus corrupt and threatens to become a Muslim. But faced with such success and such pious self-deception, both Oxford decency and simple outrage seem more than irrelevant. They are absurd.

The point is that Ganesh is perfectly attuned to his times. He is a hero because the contradictions of his society are expressed and heightened in himself. The 'smart man' is the hero, but the 'smart man' is also a product of his society. Indignation at his activities is tempered by recognition that he too is a victim of displacement, and gives way to relish that in such a limited society he should have been able to display so many and such attractive human qualities. Naipaul has made this point so well in *The Middle Passage* that his words should be quoted. He prints a *Trinidad Guardian* report that Valmond Jones, secretary of the Sam Cooke fan club, has absconded with the ticket money for concerts for which Sam Cooke, despite the advertisements, was apparently never booked:

Three youths were talking about this affair one afternoon around a coconut-cart near the Savannah.
The Indian said, 'I don't see how anybody could vex with the man. *That* is brains.'
'Is what my aunt say,' one of the Negro boys said. 'She ain't feel she get rob. She feel she pay the two dollars for the *intelligence*.'

She feel she pay the two dollars for the intelligence. And at once analysis is made ridiculous. For here is a natural sophistication and tolerance which has been produced by the picaroon society. How could one wish it otherwise? To condemn the picaroon society out of hand is to ignore its important quality. And this is not only its ability to beguile and enchant. For if such a society breeds cynicism, it also breeds tolerance, not the tolerance between castes and creeds and so on — which does not exist in Trinidad anyway — but something more profound: tolerance for every human activity and affection for every demonstration of wit and style.[9]

The episode had a sequel which Naipaul omits. 'Fatman' Jones returned to Trinidad and became the subject of a calypso. He protested; his mother, he said, was upset. Surely in Naipaul's comments we have the key to his irony in *The Mystic Masseur* — a tolerance, an affection for wit and style which, while it does not rule out assessment, definitely rejects contempt or indignation.

There remains, however, the ending to contend with. Ganesh becomes respectable, is recognised (once he has lost all influence) as 'an important political leader', is sent as a delegate to Lake Success where he defends British colonial rule, and is awarded the M.B.E. There is nothing inappropriate about this. It is an axiom that the élite of a colonial society have a vested interest in colonialism, and Ganesh is only defending the system under which he has prospered. Yet the defence involves him in repudiation — we last see him 'impeccably dressed', coldly insisting his name is G. Ramsey Muir. Unable to make that jump in thinking which would allow him to see his society and his career in true perspective, he joins the rulers and accepts his responsibilities as a member of empire. In *Miguel Street*, escape was necessary for the sake of personal fulfilment. Now, even for those who succeed within the system, the natural progression is still towards rejection. Under colonialism, to fail is to dream of escape; to achieve is to repudiate, to join the alien élite. The alternative is to change the system, and the only man in the novel who wants that is Indarsingh, the least adjusted of all. I am not suggesting that *The Mystic Masseur* is in any way written as self-justification — as a first novel it is deliberately un-autobiographical, an exercise in definition. But the implication is unavoidable. Even tolerance and affection cannot alter the inevitability of Naipaul's exile.

2

'At the moment', said the *Times Literary Supplement* in an otherwise complimentary review of *The Mystic Masseur*, 'Naipaul's strength seems to lie in the presentation of individual episodes and scenes, and not to be entirely equal to the strain of a full-length novel.'[10] Such a criticism must have had all the more force for a young writer who had a volume of short stories tucked away in a drawer. But the reviewer was not being unfair. There are signs of strain, especially in the ending. The last two chapters cover an immense amount – Ganesh's election to the Legislative Council, his humiliation at the Governor's dinner and his vow to 'show them', his move to Port of Spain, his temporary alliance with Indarsingh, his career as an agitator, his intervention in the strike, and his abrupt change of loyalties when he finds where his real interests lie. These are important chapters, not just because a lot happens but because they represent a broadening of the issues as we are shown that what worked in an obscure Indian village works too in the new politics of Port of Spain. Yet they are cramped into less pages than Naipaul devotes to, say, the launching of Ganesh's newspaper. The thesis remains intact, but the presentation is skimped – Ganesh's failure as an anti-colonial agitator (which, in some ways, would seem an appropriate climax to his career) is explained away feebly as 'Ganesh missed his cue'. Another detail to which a more assiduous Naipaul might have paid more attention is the new house Ganesh builds at Fuente Grove. Much of his career is represented symbolically – the fridge visible from the road, the temple to which American servicemen are invited, the musical toilet-paper rack, the sculptures of Ganesa facing different directions – the traditional and the modern combined in a structure which seems to Ganesh's friends not showy and eccentric but a rival to Government House. Yet reading backwards from the immensely complex house-metaphors of the later novels, one is struck by how little is made of the scene.

Naipaul seems to have been influenced by such considerations, and to have recognised the need to transcend the episodic: 'I wrote *The Suffrage of Elvira* to prove to myself that I could invent, invent a story constructed around a given incident.'[11] An election campaign is, of course, a perfect subject for this kind of experiment, containing as it must a natural beginning, a good deal of intrigue, and a climax which resolves the issues, but whatever one says about the novel must take account of the limitations suggested by this statement. If *The Mystic Masseur* was written to illustrate a thesis, in *The Suffrage of Elvira* everything is subordinated to the demands of the story. This is first evident in the Prologue. We approach Elvira by road, meeting first the Witnesses and the black bitch. These two 'signs' become, for two thirds of the novel, the main complications in Harbans' election campaign. We pass a group of key voters, the Spanish Negroes of Cordoba who are to be the centre of the Witnesses' activities, and a key scene in the cocoa house from which Tiger, one of the bitch's six puppies, is to exercise his own influence on events. The road itself is in very bad condition which pleases the candidate – he is a contractor, and he owns the gravel pit. In other words, we are back in the picaroon society with a candidate who is obviously standing in his own interests. Finally, we learn about Baksh and Chittaranjan, the 'powers of Elvira', whom Harbans is on his way to placate. Clearly, this is the prologue to a story – unlike, say, the prologue to *A House for Mr Biswas* in which Naipaul kills suspense, focuses our attention on the characters, and lays down standards for success and failure in the novel, by telling us right at the start that Mr Biswas is to die in his irretrievably mortgaged house at the age of forty-six.

Similarly with Chapters 1 and 2. Baksh and Chittaranjan, the leaders of the Muslim and Hindu communities, have been bribed into a temporary alliance against the Negro candidate. They are to pull most of the strings of the election, controlling as they do some five-eighths of the vote, so it is appropriate we should meet them and their families immediately. The bribes are re-negotiated (a loudspeaker van for Baksh, and Harbans' son for Chittaranjan's daughter), and the campaign is ready to begin – with two more neatly-balanced chapters, one dealing with the Witnesses who have persuaded the Spanish Negroes not to vote (and ending with 'What about the dog?'), the other concerning Tiger and the fears of witchcraft. A third pair of chapters describes a series of encounters, none taking up more than four pages but each important later – Loorkhoor warns Mr Cuffy about 'obeah', Mahadeo makes inquiries about sick Negroes, Baksh tells everyone about Tiger, Foam arranges to pass Tiger on to Nelly, and so on. Incidents which in *The Mystic Masseur* were loosely strung together around Ganesh's rise to fame become in *The Suffrage of Elvira* the carefully woven threads of a story. Suspense in *The Mystic Masseur* lay in the contrast between Ganesh's and the reader's interpretation of inconsequential events – Ganesh's autobiography was reviewed as 'spiritual thriller'; suspense in *The Suffrage of Elvira* becomes a genuine curiosity about events – the woman seen with Loorkhoor in Chapter 6 is a mystery not to be resolved for over one hundred pages. When Ganesh is nauseated to bite into Mr Stewart's sandwiches, we are being told something about Hinduism; when Harbans is reluctant to bite into Mrs Baksh's rock cakes, the point is to introduce Herbert's strictly functional 'gas'.

Inevitably, however, something has to be sacrificed. Naipaul achieves his aim of inventing a tightly knit story but only by resorting to a good deal of caricature. What do we make, for example, of Tiger's triumphal procession from Chittaranjan's cellar to Baksh's yard? Even as we laugh we recognise this is fantasy – not comic analysis but comic-strip:

> The news ran through Elvira. Baksh's puppy, the *obeah*-dog, the one that had been sent away, was back.
> Tiger limped on. Schoolchildren and labourers stood silently at the verge to let him pass. Faces appeared behind raised curtains. People ran up from the traces to watch . . .
> Mr Cuffy saw and was afraid . . .
> Tiger walked on . . .
> 'Shut up the shop,' Baksh ordered . . .
> Foam sucked his teeth . . .
> Mrs Baksh beat her bosom . . .
> Christians, Hindus and Muslims crossed themselves. To make sure, some Hindus muttered *Rama, Rama* as well.[12]

Then again, how well does the character of Chittaranjan hang together? He is introduced as 'easily the most important person in Elvira', and he is probably the cleverest. He alone suggests a solution to the obeah problem which he views with all the detachment of scepticism. He sees what Baksh is after long before anyone else does. He knows immediately Foam is responsible for making the cross of five puppies in Cordoba, and is able to inform Harbans he has won. Yet Chittaranjan alone in Elvira fails to see Harbans is cheating him over the question of Nelly's marriage, and he is genuinely frightened when Tiger turns up in his own cellar. His running argument with Ramlogan is childish, but his quarrel with Baksh, deliberately engineered to dispel rumours about Foam and Nelly, is a masterpiece of diplomacy. One hesitates to accuse Naipaul of inconsistency. His technique depends so much on the juxtaposition of incongruities that he can get away with a great deal. It is arguable that Chittaranjan is misled only when his own interests are at stake. Yet it is also arguable that he is forced into postures demanded by the story — that he is clever when Naipaul requires someone to redirect the intrigue, and blind when too much insight would interrupt the course of events.

None of this is surprising in a novel which deals with the public life of a small community and deals with it lightheartedly. It is to be expected that characters will be defined by the exigencies of the plot — that Haq, for instance, should be a drunken Muslim because his alchoholic fanaticism will turn events at a crucial moment; it is to be expected that only those at the fringe of events like Ramlogan should be permitted the free display of eccentricity we saw in *The Mystic Masseur*. The trouble is that such methods raise real problems of interpretation. Naipaul's overriding desire to prove he can construct a story affects not only character and events but also the quality of his conclusions, and he does not seem to have quite made up his mind whether he is writing a farce about the Trinidad elections or whether he is saying the Trinidad elections are a farce. In the prologue we are warned that Naparoni is 'the smallest, most isolated and most neglected of the nine counties of Trinidad', implying that what follows is not to be taken too seriously as social comment. Yet in the final chapter he jokes about official statistics and about the filming of a documentary on political progress in the colonies, implying that what he has described is the truth behind the flattering official reports.

We are back, as the prologue made clear, in the picaroon society where the 'smart man' triumphs; but not quite back in the world of *The Mystic Masseur*. 'Democracy', we are told, 'had come to Elvira four years before in 1946, but it was not until 1950 . . . that people began to see the possibilities.' Instead of Ganesh riding easily to victory in the first elections (to be discredited by 1950), we have Harbans whose candidature makes him the butt of everyone else's attempts to be smart. Otherwise, the setting is familiar. There is the same delapidated landscape, the same tumble-down houses and mildewed interiors. Ramlogan's gate is made up of tin advertisements, and Ramlogan himself is much as he was earlier – less scheming, less worried about his 'sensa values' and translated now into a rum-shop owner, but as greasy, as lonely and as ready to weep as ever. There are the same superstitions. The people of Elvira have a strong respect for the supernatural, and Ganesh is still remembered as the greatest of mystics. Harichand builds a reputation on ghost stories and Baksh is frightened but pleased when he is granted a 'sign' of his own. Religious orthodoxy is irrelevant – Mahadeo's *puja* 'seemed in the most discouraging way to have nothing to do with what went on in Elvira'. It is the muddle of superstitions that belongs:

> Things were crazily mixed up in Elvira. Everybody, Hindus, Muslims and Christians, owned a Bible; the Hindus and Muslims looking on it, if anything, with greater awe. Hindus and Muslims celebrated the Hindu festival of lights. Someone had told them that Lakshmi, the goddess of prosperity, was being honoured; they placed small earthen lamps on their money-boxes and waited, as they said, for the money to breed. Everybody celebrated the Muslim festival of Hosein. In fact, when Elvira was done with religious festivals, there were few straight days left.[13]

East and West meet once again in the picture of King George V and Gandhi, in the Hindi and American campaign songs, in the names of Baksh's children (alternately Christian and Muslim as 'a concession to their environment'). And amid the decay and confusion, there is the same passion for modernity — Baksh's dream of a California-style house, Foam's ambition to broadcast from a loudspeaker van, Mrs Baksh's skirts, Nelly's lessons in shorthand, Chitteranjan's gadgets, the radio advertisements at Mr Cuffy's funeral, and above all the language and conduct of the election itself. Democracy is modern, and although the election will be won through bribery and prejudice, the candidates are expected to put on a display worthy of modernity — with committees, posters, slogans, campaign songs and a motorcade as climax. Preacher's house-to-house methods don't stand a chance.

Yet there is a real difference between *The Mystic Masseur* and *The Suffrage of Elvira*, a difference which transcends the author's comments about wanting to construct a good story. *The Mystic Masseur* began, as we saw, with two chapters describing Ganesh's displacement, and everything that was said about his career was said in the context of this displacement. The picture was two-dimensional, but acknowledgement was made that Ganesh and his contemporaries were caught between an Indian past and a Creole present, and that the newer values of wit and style had a real attraction of their own. Superficially, Elvira makes a similar appeal. 'This democracy is a damn funny thing', says Dhaniram when Harbans appears suddenly to be losing, and *The Suffrage of Elvira* is a damn funny novel. Rafiq's claim 'Is my top. I thief it from a boy at school', has the same effect of making analysis ridiculous as the Negro youth's comment on Valmond Jones. What could be more engaging than Chittaranjan's frank admission that Lorkhoor's accusations of bribery are not going to cost Harbans any votes — 'People like to know that they could get a man to do little things for them every now and then'? On the surface, Elvira seems a delightful place where nothing is predictable, where moral lapses are harmless, where different cultures have coalesced to form a richly individual community. But the working out of the story reveals something far less attractive. The election simplifies. A vote is taken and the contradictions are resolved. Wit and style are shown after all to be unimportant. Beneath the apparent complexities, Elvira recognises only the values of money and race.

The point is clear when we follow the individual destinies of some of the main characters. There is never any doubt about Harbans' reasons for standing. He makes one perfunctory effort to bring issues into the election, but only in an attempt to induce Baksh to lower his demands – and we have learned in the prologue about the roads:

'We want another stand-pipe in Elvira,' Harbans said.
'Elvira is a big place and it only have one school. And the roads!'
Foam said, 'Mr Harbans, Lorkhoor start loudspeaking against you, you know.'
'What! But I ain't do the boy or the boy family nothing at all. Why he turning against a old man like me?'[14]

Harbans' reply indicates how much he is banking on racial loyalties, how irrelevant the issues really are. What he achieves at the end is the power over others they have temporarily had over him. He spends the campaign signing cheques as his 'entrance fee', but his first action once he is sure of winning is to note the number of the taxi driver who caused trouble over the motorcade – 'We go fix him up, Goldsmith.' Meanwhile, although he was elected through a Hindu-Muslim alliance, he is glad to be handed a reason for breaking his promise to Chitteranjan – his son couldn't possibly marry a girl who walked out with Muslims. Baksh, too, is sufficiently free of racial feeling to be able to exploit it in others. When Harbans suggests Hindu-Muslim tension is out of place in 'the modern world', he answers, 'depending', and in a word sums up his philosophy. He demands a loudspeaker van before he will support Harbans, but when Chittaranjan offends him by saying even Negroes can be Muslims he seizes the racial opportunity to back Preacher instead. Harbans in panic has to bribe him again to stand as a Muslim candidate, and a third bribe – that he should stand down – is only averted by Mr Cuffy's death.

Dhaniram, by contrast, stands to gain little from Harbans' election, only some contracts for the tractor of which he is part-owner. No one in Elvira is more excited by the modernity of the election than he is – 'words like campaign, candidate, committee, constituency, legislative council, thrilled him especially.' But he is a broken man when the *doolahin* runs off with Lorkhoor. Modernity cannot compensate for the loss of a girl of the right caste to do his cooking and housework. Chittaranjan, too, is a good Hindu. He lives in a two-storey concrete house which proclaims his wealth, and he lets Nelly take lessons in shorthand and typing. Curiously, he has status too as a badjohn; his proudest boast is of his appearances in the Supreme Court for stick-fighting. But the effect of his alliance with the Muslims is to bring out his deepest prejudices. His three-year quarrel with Ramlogan ends abruptly as they trade tales of the ingratitude and laziness of Muslims and Negroes. Nor do Foam and Lorkhoor, the new generation, offer much contrast. Foam betrays no racial feeling and he is scornful about obeah. But he involves himself in the election for strictly private reasons – he wants his own back on Lorkhoor and Teacher Francis – and he sees democracy simply as a means of bribing oneself into a position where eventually one will be able to demand bribes. Lorkhoor preaches the unity of races and creeds in the modern age, but his object from the beginning is to sell out to Harbans a week before the election.

'Superficially, because of the multitude of races, Trinidad may seem complex, but to anyone who knows it, it is a simple colonial philistine society.'[15] Naipaul's comment appeared just four months after *The Suffrage of Elvira* was published, and it defines precisely what is revealed by the working out of the story – simple philistine values under a complex surface. He now seems to regard his earlier affection for wit and style as a sophistication. The delicate balance of assessment and fascination that made *The Mystic Masseur* such a satisfying and beguiling novel is now upset. Money and race are what count in Elvira. It is true the contradictions remain very funny – Dhaniram advises Harbans, 'You must try and feel that you giving to the people. After all, is the meaning of this democracy' – but despite such geniality, the final judgement is harsh and constitutes a much firmer rejection of his society than we find anywhere else in Naipaul's novels.

The love affair with Ganesh is over. Yet one queries the terms of the rejection. Penelope Mortimer reviewed *The Suffrage of*

Elvira as 'a perfect novel', thus giving Naipaul considerable encouragement with the opening chapters of *A House for Mr Biswas*. Eight months later in a review in the *New Statesman*, we find Naipaul applying to Samuel Selvon's *Turn Again Tiger* the criticism made earlier of himself – 'Mr Selvon is without the stamina for a full length novel'; Naipaul clearly feels he has passed his self-imposed examination. Yet *The Suffrage of Elvira* remains his least satisfying novel. Even the story, the mainspring of the book, is less than perfectly resolved. The two 'signs' of the prologue, the Witnesses and the dog, have cancelled each other out two thirds of the way through when Foam establishes that the Witnesses have been responsible for the witchcraft by arranging the five puppies in the form of a cross above the slogan 'Awake'. Ten pages later, Chittaranjan is able to assure Harbans he has won, and the real complications are now over. Tiger is used once more as a narrative link with the cocoa house, where Lorkhoor is caught with his girlfriend the *doolahin*, and then with Mr Cuffy who, Herbert prophesies, will die 'like a cockroach' for having kicked Tiger – and Mr Cuffy does indeed die. I suppose it is ironically appropriate that, having warned Mahadeo of the consequences if anyone is harmed by obeah before polling day, he should himself die among rumours of self-imposed witchcraft, but the scene is far from satisfactory. Earlier, in joking about supernatural interpretations of natural events, Naipaul was careful to avoid coincidence. The only point of the scene in which Foam compels Rafiq to surrender his top to Herbert is to make clear that Mrs Baksh knew all along who had brought Tiger into the house. Rafiq told her; we are not expected to believe that the trial by Bible and key actually does establish Herbert's guilt. But there can be no casual connection between Tiger and Mr Cuffy's death, and in allowing the accident to stand as a confirmation of Tiger's significance, Naipaul fails to be true to his design.

Having failed to find a satisfactory extension of the main comic threads into the latter third of the novel, Naipaul falls back more and more on a straightforward catalogue of absurdities. Everything becomes the reverse of what it should be, and without the comic unpredictability of Elvira's reactions to the Witnesses and the dog, the novel loses much of its delight. The description of the election itself is simply an exposé, as Naipaul provides a glimpse of the 'truth' behind the colonial-office film and the official statistics. Harbans pays for taxis to bring his voters to the poll while Preacher's have to walk in the rain, clerks have to be bribed, agents interfere with the voters, policemen are partial, there is no proper control over the ballot boxes. And the result is a foregone conclusion. In a largely Indian community where votes have to be bought, the penniless Negro stands not the slightest chance. This is, of course, the point at which Elvira resolves its contradictions into simple philistinism, but one feels a sense of betrayal that out of such joyful farce should come such despairing conclusions.

The problem is, as I said earlier, that Naipaul does not seem to have quite made up his mind whether he is writing a farce about the elections in Trinidad or whether he is saying the Trinidad elections are a farce. To begin with the aim of writing a tightly-knit story about such a loosely 'mixed-up' society is to raise the most basic questions about the relevance of the form to the content. Naipaul seems to have solved them by choosing to write about the elections which inevitably impose on any situation patterns appropriate to the shaping of a story – a beginning, a period of intrigue and a natural climax. But one of the points made most consistently in the novel is the irrelevance of British-style elections to such a community, and a good deal of the humour is located in the gap between language and reality as the characters try to give the imported words a local meaning. So long as it all remains on the level of farce, there is no problem. But when Naipaul begins to use the election as a means of exposing inadequacies in Elvira, as happens more and more during the last ninety pages, then one begins to wonder whether he has forgotten the lessons of his two previous books. Judging Elvira by its reactions to a farcially irrelevant 'democracy' is tantamount to setting the characters an English-style examination and then calling them ignorant because no one knows the date of the battle of Waterloo. Nor is it sufficient to object that such elections have, after all, taken place and that Naipaul is entitled to describe them. When he returns to West Indian politics in *The Mimic Men*, Naipaul's emphasis is quite different:

> The colonial politician is an easy object of satire. I wish to avoid
> satire; I will leave out the stories of illiteracy and social ignor-
> ance. Not that I wish to present him as grander or less flawed
> than he is. It is that his situation satirises itself, turns satire inside
> out, takes satire to a point where it touches pathos if not trag-
> edy.[16]

The situation 'satirises itself'. It is not enough to laugh at people
trapped in absurd postures by an unreal situation. But the ending
of *The Suffrage of Elvira* makes no concession to such insights. It
does not even reflect the insights of the earlier books in which the
subjects were approached sympathetically through the child narrators. Who makes these judgements with which the book concludes? What has released him from the absurdities in which his
characters are trapped? We are not permitted so much as a glimpse
of him.

Instead, we are offered two characters who seem to focus the
author's impatience and despair. One is Mr Cuffy, the Negro arti-
san. Negro Trinidadians play very little part in the early novels,
but Naipaul could scarcely avoid introducing a representative
figure here, and once introduced he is treated with a good deal of
affection and respect. His shop, the United African Pioneer Self-
Help Society, and his Friday evening prayer meeting with its small
gathering of disciples, though both described from the outside,
confer on him an integrity possessed by no other character in the
novel. There is nothing corrupt about his support for Preacher,
and his distrust of Lorkhoor is obviously justified. Even Foam feels
a tinge of pity for Preacher's agent on polling day – she is one of
Mr Cuffy's disciples. When his funeral is joyfully commandeered
by Harbans' election committee as a final and effective bribe to the
electorate, Naipaul's disgust is barely concealed. The juxtaposition
of the radio adverts, the expensive coffin and the general celebrations, with the description of Mr Cuffy's corpse and of the
white-robed women singing hymns but dispossessed of their
proper occasion, engages our sympathies in a manner which dis-
pels comedy. Anger is perhaps too strong a word, but there is no

mistaking the change of tone. Mr Cuffy suddenly becomes a martyr to what so far has seemed amusingly harmless.

The other casualty is Teacher Francis, a city Negro, transferred by the ministry to Elvira as a reprimand for parading his agnosticism in the classroom. He has his moments of pretentiousness – his dress, the debating club – and his main function in the novel is to provide Foam with a reason for taking part in the election. But he is also the only character who views events with an intelligent detachment. 'A little boy like Herbert ain't have no right to go out campaigning', he tells Mrs Baksh, 'election bringing out all sort of prejudice to the surface.' In the absence of a narrator, he is the nearest we get to a spokesman for Naipaul. But there is no room for him, not simply in Elvira which he has to leave because of his comments, but in the novel itself from which he is banished only half way through. Naipaul doesn't know what to do with him. We learn at the end that he 'degenerated rapidly' in Port of Spain, marrying well and renouncing all intellectual aspirations. The phrase is revealing. There is no place in the Trinidad of this novel for one who sees what is happening with any real clarity.

CHAPTER FOUR

'I don't have a story. I want a job.'

I

Towards the end of *A House for Mr Biswas*, after the final move to Sikkim Street and shortly before Anand disappears from the book, there occurs a most important paragraph:

> Soon it seemed to the children that they had never lived anywhere but in the tall square house in Sikkim Street. From now their lives would be ordered, their memories coherent. The mind, while it is sound, is merciful. And rapidly the memories of Hanuman House, The Chase, Green Vale, Shorthills, the Tulsi house in Port of Spain would become jumbled, blurred; events would be telescoped, many forgotten. Occasionally, a nerve of memory would be touched – a puddle reflecting the blue sky after rain, a pack of thumbed cards, the fumbling with a shoelace, the smell of a new car, the sound of a stiff wind through trees, the smells and colours of a toyshop, the taste of milk and prunes – and a fragment of forgotten experience would be dislodged, isolated, puzzling. In a northern land, in a time of new separations and yearnings, in a library grown suddenly dark, the hailstones beating against the windows, the marbled endpaper of a dusty leather-bound book would disturb: and it would be the hot noisy week before Christmas in the Tulsi store: the marbled patterns of oldfashioned balloons powdered with a rubbery dust in a shallow white box that was not to be touched. So later, and very slowly, in securer times of different stresses, when the memories had lost the power to hurt, with pain or joy, they would fall into place and give back the past.[1]

The subject is the children's memories of everything that has gone before, and one reason why the passage is so very moving is that the reader can identify all the images and relate them to their context. The 'puddle reflecting the blue sky after rain' refers to the morning after the storm at Green Vale, the 'pack of thumbed cards' to the time Owad slaps Anand's face, the 'fumbling with a shoelace' to the day Savi was beaten before going to school, the 'smell of a new car' to the family's first excursion in Mr Biswas's new Ford Prefect, the 'sound of a stiff wind through trees' to the brief, enchanting holiday at Toco, and so on. But which of the children has such memories? Of the four, only Savi and Anand are old enough to remember The Chase and Green Vale, and in fact only Anand is involved in everything mentioned – it is Anand, for instance, who is fed on milk and prunes to assist his studies. Naipaul speaks of the children, but it is Anand's memories that count. Five pages later we are told that he gets a scholarship to England and the references to 'a northern land' and 'a library grown suddenly dark' become specific. Anand is, of course, the author – not Anand as he appears in the book but Anand as he has since become, Anand who has grown up into V.S. Naipaul, and whose memories, at first puzzling and disturbing, have through time and distance lost the power to hurt and – as he writes – are falling into place and giving back the past.

There is, of course, nothing very startling in the discovery that Naipaul is drawing on memories of his father, but it is interesting that the point should be established, however obliquely, within the novel itself since it explains a good deal of how Mr Biswas's experiences come to assume the shape the novel imposes on them. In both *Miguel Street* and *The Mystic Masseur* we were offered versions of the narrator as a child – a child who, while to some extent subject to later assessments, was the origin of the information and the basis of the interest taken in the other characters. In both cases, however, the child was fatherless, and it seems to be a precondition of the version of Trinidad presented by Naipaul in his first books that his father's experience should be suppressed. Trinidad can be relished as an island of 'characters' only so long as the displacement is ultimately harmless – so long as one can escape as easily as the narrator has done. The issue is complicated by the fact that, as we saw in Chapter 2, Seepersad Naipaul was also a writer, and the suppression of his experience seems partly a result of the wish to escape his influence. But three books have now been published: Naipaul has served his apprenticeship: and what about Mr Biswas? What about this 'father' so conveniently killed off? What about the man who, lacking Ganesh's opportunism and his capacity for self-deception, becomes not the hero·of the displaced society but its victim? It is not surprising that such a subject should merit a quality of treatment which virtually repudiates the tone of Naipaul's work so far.

This is not to say the Trinidad of *A House for Mr Biswas* is a totally different place. Mr Biswas in his role as welfare officer finds himself 'dealing with a society that had no rules and patterns', and the arbitrariness which we saw in, for instance, the scene of the governor's dinner is illustrated again in, say, the architecture of the Maraval Road – 'the Scottish Baronial castle, the Moorish mansion, the semi-Oriental palace, the Bishop's Spanish-Colonial residence . . . the blue and red Italianate college'. We have ·already seen something of Mr Biswas in Pundit Ganesh, and it is worth noting that there are characters in *A House for Mr Biswas* who would fit without difficulty into the earlier books – W.C. Tuttle, for example, who decorates his room with Indian pictures and English watercolours, is making the same concession to his environment as Baksh who gives every second child a Christian name. Naipaul's subject is still the middle generation of Indians, that unique group displaced between a shrinking Indian past and a disordered Creole present. Then again, the picaroon delight in trickery is as strong as ever. Bribery is still taken for granted, and the story of Billy who 'sold' houses with an offer of free removal thrown in and then emigrated with the deposit money (after turning up with a lorry on the morning of his departure and abusing those who had mistrusted him) draws the same admiring laughter as do the antics of Ganesh or of Valmond Jones.

But this time the details are filled in. One of the most remarkable things about *A House for Mr Biswas*, compared to the earlier books, is its solidity and comprehensiveness. Mr Biswas is only forty-six when he dies, but by the end of the novel a whole history has passed before our eyes. Naipaul conveys the impression of decades elapsing, and not only by such obvious means as references to the world wars or to the coming of motor cars, cinemas, or to Americans. He notes the effects of economic change; Mr Biswas, returning as a reporter to his birthplace, sees only 'oil-derricks and grimy pumps'. He records the alterations in his characters as they age: from Mrs Tulsi the supreme monarch to Mrs Tulsi the cantankerous invalid, regretting that 'the old ways have become old-fashioned so quickly'. He chronicles the stages in the loss of India, the shift from country to town, from Hindi to English, from a preoccupation with Fate to a preoccupation with ambition, so that as we move from the world of Raghu to the world of Anand, we are dealing not only with the life of a man but also with the history of a culture. It is all done with a marvellous attentiveness to the smallest details. When Mr Biswas attends his mother's funeral he is 'oppressed by a sense . . . of something missed in the past'. He wishes to be alone to commune with this feeling, but Shama and the children 'call him away from that part of him which yet remained purely himself'. Naipaul calls the reader away too. The picture shifts to Anand and his sisters, city children dressed for the funeral, picking their way round their uncle Pratab's muddy yard. They disturb a hen and its brood — 'Girls and chickens fled in opposite directions, and the country children tittered'; an aspect of the change has been illustrated, unobtrusively but accurately.

Similarly, the physical background is described with a precision that takes us far beyond the rather perfunctory references to the 'flat, treeless, hot' landscapes of *The Mystic Masseur*. We now see the island as a whole with all its contrasting features; the mud houses and buffalo ponds of the Indian villages, the 'flat acres of sugar-cane and the muddy rice-fields' surrounding Arwakas, the 'tormented coconut trees and the deserted beaches' of the Atlantic coast, the immortelles and cocoa of the lush Northern range — a comprehensive setting for a comprehensive history. Some of the descriptions are magnificent:

> Towards the middle of the morning the sky lightened and lifted, the rain thinned to a drizzle, then stopped altogether. The clouds rolled back, the sky was suddenly blinding blue and there were

shadows on the water. Rapidly, their gurgling soon lost in the awakening everyday din, canals subsided, leaving a wash of twigs and dirt on the road. In yards, against fences, there were tidemarks of debris and pebbles which looked as though they had been washed and sifted; around stones dirt had been washed away; green leaves that had been torn down were partly buried in silt. Roads and roofs dried, steaming areas of dryness spreading out swiftly, like ink on a blotter. And presently roads and yards were dry, except for the depressions where water had collected. Heat nibbled at their edges, until even the depressions failed to reflect the blue sky. And the world was dry again, except for the mud in the shelter of trees.[2]

In isolation, this reads like an anthology piece. But the landscape is not described for the sake of description. We are always referred back to the people who inhabit it. The description of the Port of Spain slums which Mr Biswas visits daily in his capacity as Investigator of Deserving Destitutes is built up of phrases like 'suffocating, rotting wooden kennels', 'dark and sweaty concrete caves', 'scabbed and blistered facades', 'yards choked with flimsy cooking sheds' – the adjectives and verbs suggesting not simply their dreadful appearance but their suffocating,choking, disfiguring effect on the people who have to live there. And in its context, the description of the drying sunny morning carries implications of the restoration of sanity and calm after the disorder and collapse of the night before. One never suspected that Naipaul, whose talent hitherto seemed reductive and excluding, could be so sensitive to the meaning of history and landscape.

The basic difference between *A House for Mr Biswas* and the earlier books thus becomes a difference in the quality of the irony. So far, Naipaul has been mainly concerned with characters, to varying degrees of caricature, and the function of his tongue-in-cheek style was not so much to expose them as to allow them to expose themselves. Their oddities were then presented as typical of Trinidad as a whole, but apart from muted references in the opening chapters of *The Mystic Masseur*, little attempt was made to explain them. Working as we saw within a set of self-imposed limitations,

Naipaul was not yet prepared to acknowledge – and perhaps at times forgot – that the absurdities could be caused by the attempt to rise above an absurd situation, a disastrous comination of place and time. In *A House for Mr Biswas*, the emphasis shifts completely. The picaroon-type story of Billy's smartness is told to an audience which includes Mr Biswas, who desperately needs a house himself. When it is finished we are told 'the laughter broke, but Mr Biswas could take no part in it'. Nor can the reader. We have seen too much of the background, too much for instance of the Port of Spain slums, to be amused at the exploitation of homelessness, no matter how wittily or stylishly it is done.

But this sympathy is achieved not as in 'B. Wordsworth' or 'The Coward' (Stories 6 and 7 of *Miguel Street*) by suspending irony and wading in distress. The climax of Mr Biswas's despair comes in the epilogue:

> Then the *Sentinel* sacked him. It gave him three months' notice. And now Mr Biswas needed his son's interest and anger. In all the world there was no one else to whom he could complain. And at last, forgetting Anand's own pain, he wrote on the yellow typewriter a hysterical, complaining, despairing letter, with not a mention of the shade or the roses or the orchids or the anthurium lilies.[3]

But in the opening paragraph of the novel, where Anand is, as it were, at last acknowledging his father's letter, the same event was described very differently:

> Ten weeks before he died, Mr Mohun Biswas, a journalist of Sikkim Street, St James, Port of Spain, was sacked. He had been ill for some time. In less than a year he had spent more than nine weeks at the Colonial Hospital and convalesced at home for even longer. When the doctor advised him to take a complete rest, the *Trinidad Sentinel* had no choice. It gave Mr Biswas three months notice and continued, up to the time of his death, to supply him every morning with a free copy of the paper.[4]

In that 'had no choice' and the mention of the free copy of the newspaper, bitterness is barely suppressed. But it is governed, nevertheless. Irony has become a means of bringing 'interest and anger' under imaginative control, a means of shaping and distancing distress. It is true that there are also occasions when the irony is directed not at his enemies but at Mr Biswas himself – when he first sees his house in the prologue he notes the affection between the solicitor's clerk and his mother, and 'this touched Mr Biswas whose own mother, neglected by himself, had died five years before in great poverty'. But this is entirely consistent. The novel is much more than a piece of special pleading. The sympathy extended to Mr Biswas is all the more convincing because it follows judgement and is not an alternative to pointing out his failures. It accepts the disorder of his environment. The cruel detachment of the ending of *The Suffrage of Elvira* and the self-indulgence of the worst parts of *Miguel Street* are now fused to a protective irony which balances personal inadequacies against the contradictions of existence itself.

The point can be illustrated another way, by examining Naipaul's use of his sources. We have noted already the acknowledgement that the novel is written by a grown-up Anand, and the point can be confirmed by the external evidence. The details of Naipaul's early years fit Anand's almost exactly, even to the dates supplied in the text. We have already seen something of Mr Biswas in the writings of Seepersad Naipaul, and from the brief biography in Chapter 2 it should be clear that the broad outlines of Mr Biswas's career are taken from life. The family did live in places corresponding to those mentioned in the novel – Chaguanas becomes Arwakas, Tunapuna becomes Pagotes, Verdant Vale becomes Green Vale, Chase Village becomes The Chase, Petit Valley in Diego Martin becomes Shorthills. Some of the characters are given even thinner disguises. Naipaul's elder and younger sisters are indeed named Savi and Kamla, but in the reverse order. Anand's rival at Queens Royal College is his cousin Vidiadhar. Vidiadhar is, of course, Naipaul's own name; Anand is borrowed from his cousin, R. N. Permanand. The various houses in the book are fictionalised only in their addresses. The Lion House, Chaguanas, where Naipaul was born, becomes Hanuman House – the lions on the balustrade being changed to images of Hanuman, the

Monkey God. Otherwise, the description is accurate in every detail – even the visitor's disappointment at finding the shop itself so small compared to the building's outside bulk is featured in Naipaul's account. Obviously, changes have taken place over the years. The original wooden house in the backyard has been replaced by a smaller building and the bridge connecting the two has disappeared – there are marks on the wall where the first floor entrance has been bricked up. But when I visited the Lion House in 1968, the paintings of Hanuman over the back door were fresh and vivid, and it was still possible to distinguish from the fading colours which had been the blue room and which the rose room. Similarly, the house in Sikkim Street – the 'huge and squat sentry box' – is an exact replica of Seepersad Naipaul's final address, and is still owned by the family. More surprisingly, perhaps, there exists in Esmerelda Road, Cunupia, the wooden house Seepersad Naipaul occupied when he worked as an overseer on one of the family estates – Naipaul's first version of the storm scene (in the story 'The Enemy') was set not in Green Vale but Cunupia. The house was not built by Seepersad Naipaul (it was in a similar house, built by himself a short distance away in Montrose, that he was taken ill in 1934), and the barracks which he initially occupied have long since disappeared.

There is a good deal of innocent satisfaction to be got out of visiting the scenes Naipaul describes, fitting the book to the place and trying to trace the originals of his characters. Naipaul comments in *An Area of Darkness* that landscapes are not truly real until they have been given the quality of myth, and for those for whom parts of the Trinidad landscape have come to exist primarily as the setting of Naipaul's novels, it is very pleasing to be able to follow Anand down Victoria Avenue, across Tragarete Road and past the walls of the Lapeyrouse Cemetry on his way to drink milk at the Dairies. It is amusing to study back numbers of the *Trinidad Guardian* and to find that the Neediest Cases for 15 December 1942 (the day after the Exhibition results appeared) are indeed written up without any of the usual harrowing details, or to see that the films *Jesse James* and *The Return of Frank James* were showing in Port of Spain shortly before the examination (though Naipaul has trusted his memory too far: Brian Donleavy, whom Anand abuses along with Henry Fonda, actually starred in *When the Daltons Rode* which Anand champions). Moreover, this over-simplifying emphasis on autobiography does illuminate one, perhaps unconscious feature of how the material is presented. Anand is not born until a third of the way through the book, and it is not until his waking thoughts one Christmas morning where he momentarily fears there is no present for him, that he becomes a character with a mind of his own. But one feature of the opening Anand-less pages is the number of times we are referred to the future – 'Mr Biswas never ate another banana', we are told after the incident at Jairam's which 'marked the beginning of his stomache trouble': two pages later we learn of his arrival home and of the poem he wrote about Bipti's welcome 'thirty years later when he was a member of a literary group in Port of Spain'. Then, when Anand begins to play a real part of his own in the book, his most important experiences turn on his growing awareness of his father. Sometimes Mr. Biswas talks directly of his past, as for instance when he soothes Anand's humiliation at having soiled himself at school by caricaturing his own similar disaster at Jairam's. Sometimes Anand makes discoveries for himself, as when he ransacks his mother's drawer and finds Savi's altered birth certificate and Shama's letters from England. Sometimes Mr Biswas's conversation presupposes a knowledge of the past – Alec's trick of peeing blue is recalled when Mr Biswas wonders why his new editor needs a separate urinal. The book is not written from Anand's point of view – among the most poignant moments are those when Mr Biswas is assessing Anand – but the deepening relationship between father and son does give the novel, as it were, a focal point. We are told how Anand knows because – as we have seen – Anand grows up into V.S. Naipaul. Anand's discovery of his father is Naipaul's own rediscovery of Seepersad Naipaul. The effect is very moving. The impression is conveyed that all these tiny details are doubly important. Mr Biswas's life becomes a journey towards the time when everything he has been will be sympathetically reviewed, a journey towards the time when the meaning of his name will be fulfilled – for 'Mohun', as the Pundit explains to Bipti, 'means the beloved'.

But this sort of activity, however enjoyable, is no substitute for studying the novel itself. It is not the materials that matter but what has been made of them. Naipaul has expressed surprise at the extent to which the book has been praised as vivid documentary and protests that a good deal was written out of his imagination:

> For instance, I never lived in the country in Trinidad; I never spoke anything but English, though in very early childhood I heard some Hindi spoken around me; I have never worked in a newspaper office, in Trinidad or anywhere else. What I would do was to write according to my imagination, and then consult people on little items of inconsequential information to lend vividness and verisimilitude to the story: I wrote to my relatives to ask them for suitable names for characters, what time of year the sugar harvest was, and little things like that. For the shop sequence I asked a solicitor here in England what could happen in a shop in a situation like this which would give the sort of result I wanted, and so on. I'm afraid I was quite unscrupulous about this: in the scene with the flying ants, I wasn't at all sure that there were such things (actually I've found out since that there are), but I needed them for the scene, so flying ants I put in. In a way it's like a sleight of hand; you mention a chair and it's shadowy; you say it's stained with wedding saffron, and suddenly that chair is there, palpable.[5]

What needs to be emphasised even more than the bits the author can claim to have invented is the shaping imagination which has seen beyond the particular and given it the quality of myth. Seepersad Naipaul did work as sign-painter, shopkeeper, overseer, journalist and welfare officer; but not in that order. Within a few months of his marriage in 1929, he was established in Port of Spain working for the *Trinidad Guardian* under Gault McGowan. He returns to Chaguanas only in 1932, and he returns as the paper's local correspondent. During the next two years, so far from being shut up in lonely obscurity in Chase Village, he is famous throughout the island for the business of the goat sacrifice (see Chapter 2). His abilities are sufficiently recognised for him to be assigned to the lead stories of 1933 – the hurricane of July, the Port of Spain floods of August. So far from being humiliated by Seth's family tribunals, we find him reporting court cases in which Seth's original is charged with violence during the 1933 elections. It was not until McGowan's dismissal in 1934 and his resignation from the *Guardian*, under whose new editor Major Lionel Hannington Seepersad Naipaul found it impossible to work, that he became shopkeeper in Chase Village and overseer in Cunupia. His illness, and his quarrel with the Capildeos over his support for the Aryan missionaries from India, belong to this period. After the death of Hannington in October 1937, he returned to the *Guardian* to write his features on the Belmont Orphanage and the Chacachacare Leper Settlement and to investigate his Neediest Cases. From this point onwards (from 'The New Regime', Part II, Chapter 2), the novel records events in roughly the order in which they actually occurred and the most significant changes are ones of omission – Mr Biswas does not spend six months in Jamaica training for the post of welfare officer; nor does he publish his stories.

What Naipaul has done, in other words, has been to abstract from his father's life not a sequence of events but a quality of experience which he has shaped in such a way as to project his own vision of its significance. The novel is based on fact, but only in the sense that from the facts has been distilled a philosophy which the rearranged facts are then used to express. For the basis of this rearrangement, we must return again to the rich paragraph I quoted at the beginning of this chapter:

> Soon it seemed to the children that they had never lived anywhere but in the tall square house in Sikkim Street. From now their lives would be ordered, their memories coherent.

For the children the house brings security, distancing all that has been painful in their past. The house brings order, giving coherence to their memories. It is movingly appropriate that its final significance to a grown-up Anand should be that the house becomes the pivot of the novel in which he explores his father's life, a central image giving coherence and significance to the multitude of details and ideas. The unity of *A House for Mr Biswas* is not the result of a central thesis (as in *The Mystic Masseur*) or of a tightly-knit story (as in *The Suffrage of Elvira*) but of this single integrating metaphor. In real life Seepersad Naipaul spent the five years following his marriage in a series of houses in the vicinities of Port of Spain and Chaguanas, and then after his illness and the period as shopkeeper and overseer, returned to Port of Spain. It is the author who has ordered this to a pattern as Mr Biswas moves from humiliation at Hanuman House to independence at The Chase, from frustration at The Chase to fresh independence in his own house at Green Vale, from collapse and submission at Green Vale to a sobered Mr Biswas, sitting in the bus taking him for the first time to Port of Spain, his eyes glued 'on a house as small and neat as a doll's house, in the distant hills of the Northern Range'. The house stands at the centre, and everything that Mr Biswas's experience signifies is contained in the various meanings the metaphor accumulates in the course of the novel. To analyse them is to emphasise the quality of the novel, to bring out just what Naipaul has done to his past as he turns autobiography into art.

But to analyse them is at the same time to realise the new quality of Naipaul's irony. We first see the house in the prologue, long before it has acquired metaphorical significance. At first, it is no more than a building in a suburb, fulfilling an ordinary middle-class dream. Ten weeks before his death Mr Biswas has won 'his own house, on his own half-lot of land'. But even as we appreciate his achievement, doubts are raised about it. We learn that Mr Biswas has lost his job, that he has not the slightest prospect of ever paying for the house, that the house itself is uncomfortable and badly built, that it cost him far more than it is worth, and that it is proving expensive to maintain. We find the house came into his hands not through his own initative but because the solicitor's clerk was looking for someone to swindle. We learn, in other words, that the truth is not simply that Mr Biswas has achieved his ambition, but that his ambition opened the way for him to be cheated. But then, having made us see how dubious this 'stupendous' triumph really is, Naipaul goes on to list Mr Biswas's possessions, and concludes:

But bigger than them all was the house, his house.

How terrible it would have been, at this time, to be without it: to have died among the Tulsis, amid the squalor of that large, disintegrating and indifferent family; to have left Shama and the children among them, in one room; worse, to have lived without even attempting to lay claim to one's portion of the earth; to have lived and died as one had been born, unnecessary and unaccommodated.[6]

Already, the statement rings true. Mr Biswas is cheated, but it would have been terrible not to have been cheated, terrible to have died among the Tulsis with all that such a death would have implied. Achievement and failure are aspects of a single experience. The truth lies in the paradox, and the house is the image of that paradox. But, as we have just seen, the house as metaphor is the core of the novel. The novel presents a world which is shot through with contradictions. It is written around the assumption that every judgement automatically implies its opposite – that the loss of India is also gain, that rebellion is both futile and creative, that writing is an escape as well as a means of coming to terms, that relationships are an imposition as well as a necessary extension of oneself, that the little anti-hero is indeed heroic. I spoke earlier of the irony of A House for Mr Biswas as a protective irony, combining sympathy and judgement, balancing personal inadequacies against the contradictions of life itself. It should now be clear how deep this irony goes, how much more it is now than just a tone of voice, a deliberate restraint on sentiment, a trick of style distancing through mockery. Irony at this level is satire's antithesis, a mode of acceptance. It has ceased to be a stance and has become a philosophy.

2

When after six frustrating years Mr Biswas finally leaves The Chase, he cycles to Arwakas ostensibly to see his newly-born third child. He arrives after dark and has to wheel his bicycle past the evening assembly of old men in the arcade of Hanuman House. Caring nothing for Trinidad, a place where they had 'stayed longer than they had intended', and knowing no English, they gathered every evening to smoke and to talk of India. Upstairs is the new baby who will know no Hindi, who will sit for a scholarship, who will look for escape not to India but to Europe. Wheeling his bicycle between the generations is Mr Biswas, to whom the old men already look 'foreign' and 'romantic' but who has as yet no home in Trinidad to offer his new child. He spends his whole life crossing from East to West, and the first significance of the house is that it stands for a successful transition.

There is never any possibility of Mr Biswas's remaining in the Indian world. The first words spoken in Chapter 1 are 'Fate. There is nothing we can do about it', and from the start Mr Biswas's horoscope is against him. He is born, significantly, away from his father's house. He is born at midnight, the wrong way and with six fingers, and the Pundit predicts he will be a lecher and a spendthrift and that he will have an unlucky sneeze, but that much harm will be averted if he is kept away from trees and water — not an easy proposition in the tropics! The predictions are fulfilled; his enchantment with the stream does lead to Raghu's death. Had he not been cursed, he might have been better off in what survives of the Indian world — his brother Pratab owns a concrete house long before he does. But the villagers cannot afford his presence and they drive him away by destroying Bipti's garden. At the age of six Mr Biswas is expelled from the 'only home to which he had some right', and his family is dispersed. Only once does he seriously attempt to re-enter the world of his childhood. After almost six years at school in Pagotes, and just when he is beginning to be equipped for Trinidad, he is apprenticed to Jairam as a trainee-pundit. Already, he has begun to leave the Indian world behind — he performs the *puja* 'mechanically' — but the attempt is futile anyway. It is only a matter of time before he defiles Jairam's oleander tree and Jairam, who has met the Pundit who cast Mr Biswas's horoscope, sees it once again confirmed. Mr Biswas clearly belongs elsewhere.

His history is far from being a special case. Not every Indian is cursed with such a horoscope, but the Indian world is shrinking. When Mr Biswas returns as a reporter to his birth place, there is nothing left. The neighbours who expelled him have been forced to follow. 'Indianness' soon becomes a cult of the privileged. Tara, for instance, who sends Mr Biswas to Jairam's, is a defender of the old ways: 'I am oldfashioned', she says with pride, adding significantly, 'It is expensive to be oldfashioned.' While she talks about the old values, she is busy establishing herslf in an elaborate house where traditions can be cherished in comfort, where she can hang the photo of Raghu's funeral among prints of the English countryside. Mr Biswas, unable to afford such luxuries of nostalgia, regards his Hinduism first as a distasteful game and then as an actual obstacle. When he realises he has been trapped into marrying a Tulsi daughter simply because of his caste, his rebellion against Hanuman House grows into a rebellion against all things traditional. He joins the Aryans, the reformed Hindus, in protest against idol worship and cat-in-bag marriages. He makes a point of speaking English even when addressed in Hindi. He regrets the Hindu squeamishness which prevents him stocking lard in his shop at The Chase. When profits fall he blames his failure on Hari's blessing, the joke becoming serious when he begins to lose faith in his house at Green Vale – 'Hari blessed it', he keeps muttering, the words standing in his disordered mind for the curse of orthodoxy on his efforts to establish himself in the new world.

Yet his position is ambiguous. While abusing the Tulsis for idol worship, he also attacks them for their catholicism and for their refusal to give him a dowry, and the placards he paints and the prayers he chants at Green Vale make it clear that his atheism is partly a pose. By contrast with Anand, in fact, Mr Biswas seems positively orthodox. His *puja* at Jairam's is conducted without understanding, but Anand's performance of the same ceremony at Shorthills is a mockery – he diverts himself by sticking flower stems under the god's chin, produces a note like furniture being dragged across floorboards from the conch shell, and then makes his tour of the house to offer the milk and tulsi leaves 'which, unbelievably, he had consecrated'. As always, Naipaul is attending to the smallest details; the loss of India occurs not at once but by stages.

Underlying such surface betrayals of Mr Biswas's origins,

however, is something more significant. It is expressed most poignantly in Mr Biswas's reaction to Bipti's death and his feelings at her funeral:

> Mr Biswas went past Dehuti to look at the body. Then he did not wish to see it again. But always, as he wandered about the yard among the mourners, he was aware of the body. He was oppressed by a sense of loss: not of present loss, but of something missed in the past. He would have liked to be alone, to commune with this feeling. But time was short, and always there was the sight of Shama and the children, alien growths, alien affections, which fed on him and called him away from that part of him which yet remained purely himself, that part which had for long been submerged and was now to disappear.[7]

What survives from the past in the form of rituals or taboos or sticks of broken furniture in no way does justice to the India that has gone. Mr Biswas recognises that something important has disappeared, something which was a part of himself yet which lies beyond his present experience and eludes definition. Later, whenever Mr Biswas thinks of Bipti, he remembers a moment not from childhood but from the fortnight she spends at Shorthills, a moment when as she works in the garden at sunset the 'intervening years fell away'. What stirs him – and he later writes about the experience – is the vision of his mother shrouded in evening light.

The image takes us back to the darkness which in Chapter 1 dominates each of the three crucial scenes of Mr Biswas's childhood. He is born at midnight and his grandmother has to set out at once for cactus to keep out evil spirits. Later, after he has lost the calf, he returns home at dusk – the scene is beautifully evoked – and hides while his parents and brothers quarrel over their evening duties. They disappear to search for him and he is left 'alone in the dark room, and frightened'. Raghu dives as the colour fades from the sky and he dies in the darkness at the bottom of the pond. After the funeral, Mr Biswas screams himself to sleep in the wavering light of the oil-lamp 'which left the corners in darkness', and the night scene follows with the hostile villagers destroying Bipti's garden. All these incidents from Mr Biswas's first six years blend to a picture of a hut in the swamplands surrounded by darkness and precariously lit by fire and oil-lamp, and variants of this image are always associated with Mr Biswas's impressions of the past. Raghu used to make walking sticks of poui wood, and it is the cutting down of the poui trees at Shorthills that reminds Mr Biswas of his vow to invite Bipti to stay with him when he had a house of his own – a sequence of events which is explained by an earlier image at The Chase where the roasting of the poui sticks for stick-fighting brings sensations of the past, of 'an evening meal being cooked over a fire that shone on a mud wall', sensations 'sadly evanescent, refusing to be seized or to be translated into concrete memory'. When Naipaul discusses his own sense of the past in *An Area of Darkness*, he uses the same key image:

> To me as a child the India that had produced so many of the persons and things around me was featureless, and I thought of the time when the transference was made as a period of darkness, darkness which also extended to the land, as darkness surrounds a hut at evening, though for a little way around the hut there is still light. The light was the area of my experience in time and place. And even now, though time has widened, though space has contracted and I have travelled lucidly over that area which to me was the area of darkness, something of darkness remains, in those attitudes, those ways of thinking and seeing, which are no longer mine.[8]

But when Mr Biswas is expelled from his birthplace, he does not leave the darkness behind. In the new world, too, darkness surrounds him – in the 'low sooty thatch' of the hut at Pagotes, the 'perpetually dark' room at Bhandat's, the windowless gloom of Hanuman House, the sooty kitchen at The Chase, the 'wall of flawless black' trees at Green Vale – and it is soon clear that these are more than just realistic details. The darkness which in Chapter I veils the Indian past follows Mr Biswas into the new world. Here another aspect of his transition from East to West becomes relevant, for the metaphor is precise: the darkness of the new world is its ugliness and disorder. F.Z. Ghany's office at Pagotes is a lopsided wooden building, its paintwork 'turned to dust', and F.Z.

Ghany himself sits in a broken kitchen chair, surrounded by dusty books and picking his teeth. The birth certificate, so promisingly suggestive of organisation, is just a scrap of paper, dignifying Bipti's guess at the date but of no further significance. Mr Biswas's first possession is the broken rubber from the date stamp. The first Indians he meets – Lal the Presbyterian who despises Hindus and F.Z. Ghany the Muslim who distrusts them – are divided against themselves. Nothing Mr Biswas brings with him from his Indian past is of the slightest relevance – his first lesson is that 'ought oughts are ought'; his status as a Brahmin is only a game played irregularly; his horoscope which, after all, offered some sort of pattern in terms of which his career could be assessed, becomes just another subject for irony – 'Spendthrift,' he tells Bipti, 'on two dollars a month'. To be fated was at least to be acknowledged. The new world, lacking any patterns, does no more than note the fact of his existence, and forget him. He longs for an ordered society in which, if only he could *look* like a shopkeeper, a lawyer, a doctor, a labourer, there would be a place and a style ready and waiting for him. When he first arrives in Port of Spain, he gets the impression from the sweepers and the bread van and the street lights all going on together that here at last is a place against which he can begin to define himself. But soon, not even the excitement of his job can conceal from him the fact that the city is only a repetition of the dingy cafe in which, fleeing the crowded Tulsi house, he spends his evenings – 'the chipped counter, the flies thick on the electric flex, the cracked glass case'.

His fundamental problem, in other words, is that he lacks the morally and aesthetically coherent environment in terms of which he can begin to discover who he really is. He reads Samuel Smiles and tries to see himself as young and poor and struggling. But the romantic sagas of self-help make sense only in countries where ambitions are credible, where heroes can propel themselves up ladders already in existence. He takes up sign-painting, the one talent he discovered at school. His first victory ever was achieved when he won the support of the class for the stylish lettering of his blackboard inscription, 'I am an ass'. But this ironic substitution of style for meaning is only an expedient – it is sign-painting that takes him to Hanuman House where, with a light heart, he outlines 'Bargains! Bargains!' as he waits to be bullied into marrying Shama. He becomes an artist. Whenever he moves, to The Chase or to Green Vale or to Port of Spain, his brushes are the first things to be packed. But his paintings feature 'cool ordered forest scenes' with graceful trees and companionable serpents, not 'the rotting mosquito-infested jungle he could find within an hour's walk'. He learns to write short stories, but the only two he ever completes are the prose-poem celebrating an unreal past with his mother as the central figure, and the many-versioned 'Escape'. When Mr Biswas does eventually get a job that suits him, it is because his sardonic awareness of the discrepancy between style and content appeals to the *Sentinel* editor, who recognises qualities the paper is looking for. Mr Burnett has fobbed off requests for a job by making him paint signs in the yard:

> 'I could eat the Gill Sans R,' the editor said. 'You know, I don't really see why you should want to give up your job.'
> 'Not enough money.'
> 'Not much in this either.'
> Mr Biswas pointed to a sign. 'No wonder you are doing your best to keep people out.'
> 'Oh, No Hands Wanted.'
> 'A nice little sign,' Mr Biswas said.
> The editor smiled and then was convulsed with laughter.[9]

But Mr Biswas's joy at finding that his fantasy and invective do after all have their place is short-lived. His stories only distance through caricature, and the excitement of the *Sentinel* office is partly the excitement of escape – he feels in contact with 'abroad'. When Mr Burnett gets the sack, he is left with the task of forming words into the pretence that all is for the best in Trinidad, that even the blind and the insane have their place in a coherent and compassionate society. He becomes an expert on destitutes and joins the Welfare Department, only to discover a further irrelevance in the categories of sociologists. And so on, each attempt at coherence exposing further disorder and leaving him still more confused about his own nature and identity.

Appropriately, then, wherever Mr Biswas goes in this new
world which condemns him to nonentity because it offers him no
foothold, he is surrounded as before by darkness. At The Chase,
where his first attempt to paddle his own canoe has left him stranded, the image of the glowing hut at dusk returns in an extended
form. Mr Biswas remembers an evening when he was conducting
one of Ajodha's buses:

> It was late afternoon and they were racing back along the ill-
> made country road. Their lights were weak and they were
> racing the sun. The sun fell; and in the short dusk they passed a
> lonely hut set in a clearing far back from the road. Smoke came
> from under the ragged thatched eaves: the evening meal was
> being prepared. And, in the gloom, a boy was leaning against
> the hut, his hands behind him, staring at the road. He wore a vest
> and nothing more. The vest glowed white. In an instant the bus
> went by, noisy in the dark, through bush and level sugar-cane
> fields. Mr Biswas could not remember where the hut stood, but
> the picture remained: a boy leaning against an earth house that
> had no reason for being there, under the dark falling sky, a boy
> who didn't know where the road, and that bus, went.[10]

The image occurs this time in the context of Mr Biswas's fears for
the future. It evokes powerfully the featureless disorder of the
world in which he is trying to find his place, the menacing void
into which, penniless and hopeless, he feels himself falling. During
the Green Vale episode, it is developed further. On a brief visit to
Hanuman House where he is trying to claim his children, he sees
Anand standing under the pillars, 'staring like that other boy Mr
Biswas had seen outside a hut at dusk'. This time, he is brought to a
resolution, to rescue himself and the children from the void by
building his own house. The house is a failure, for reasons we shall
see in a moment. What matters in the present context is that Mr
Biswas's collapse is described in terms of his surrender to the darkness. The image occurs on virtually every page of his breakdown,
until the climax:

> Then there was a roar that overrode them all. When it struck the

house the window burst open, the lamp went instantly out, the rain lashed in, the lightning lit up the room and the world outside, and when the lightning went out the room was part of the black void.

Anand began to scream.

He waited for his father to say something, to close the window, light the lamp.

But Mr Biswas only muttered on the bed, and the rain and wind swept through the room with unnecessary strength and forced open the door to the drawingroom, wall-less, floorless, of the house Mr Biswas had built.[11]

Surrender and return to Hanuman House bring temporary peace – 'the darkness, the silence, the absence of the world enveloped and comforted him'. But surrender is no solution, if only because he is still alive. He travels to Port of Spain, promisingly, at dawn. But the menace is renewed in starker terms. He lives on the brink of the slums with their 'dark concrete caverns' and their 'gaping black windows'. The years stretch 'ahead, dark'. Night after night he sinks 'into the void'. When at last he succumbs to his final illness, the 'darkness seemed to come from within'.

Mr Biswas's journey from the old world to the new, from the generation of the old Indians in the arcade of Hanuman House to that of the new baby upstairs, thus becomes a journey from darkness to darkness, from a world where he is a creature of fate to a world in which he becomes a victim of circumstances, from an order which seems irrelevant to a disorder in which he is a nonentity. He is rescued by the vision and ultimately the fact of his house. He first vows to get a house of his own after being beaten up by Bhandat – 'I am going to get a job of my own', he tells Bipti, 'and I am going to get my own house too.' This crucial declaration seems at first to reflect little more than dissatisfaction with the hut in the trace to which he is ashamed to take his school friends – and perhaps, too, with his dependence on Tara who has already tried to thrust him back into the Indian world to be trained as a Pundit. But within three pages it is given a new significance by the meeting with Ramchand, Tara's former yardboy and Dehunti's new husband. By marrying Dehuti, Ramchand has offended Tara and broken caste – and he has got away with it. He cultivates his Brahmin brother-in-law and is still sensitive to rebuff. But when Mr Biswas sits in the neat house 'which indicated lowness in no way' and compares it with the hut in the trace, caste seems an absurdity. Naipaul's equation is deliberate; in the new world, the Brahmins are those who possess houses. When Mr Biswas many years later stands irresolutely at the crossroads between his brothers and Bipti in the south and Port of Spain in the north, it is Ramchand he remembers, Ramchand who with a job and a house has freed himself from the humiliations imposed on him by his low-caste birth and has proved the old world's impotence by simply stepping outside it.

In the new world, the Brahmins are those with houses. If Port of Spain seems chaotic there are at least elementary divisions to be made, between rich and poor, between the employed and the jobless, between those with houses and those without. By achieving a house of his own, Mr Biswas rises to a position where the disorder can be kept at bay, its immediate threats distanced. We have studied already the claim that it is the house which brings order into the children's lives, a centre round which their memories can be organised. Mr Biswas's experience is this, and more. At Green Vale, half the excitement of building his own house lay in the physical details – the gleaming nails, the fresh sawdust, the neat wooden frame on the newly cutlassed site. Later, in the Tulsi house in Port of Spain, he is delighted to live 'where everything worked as it was meant to', and he expresses his appreciation by adding a pond and a rose garden. When at last he achieves his own house, all his impulses towards aesthetic order find fulfilment in the rose bushes, the orchids on the coconut stumps, the anthurium lilies, the sweet-smelling laburnum tree. Returning from hospital after his first illness, he steps into a 'ready made world' of his own creation, with a tidied garden and newly-distempered walls, the Prefect waiting in the garage and all his possessions ranged around him, justifying his claim to this portion of the earth. The house is the equivalent of the stories he never finishes, the paintings he never makes relevant, his own island of status, coherence and beauty in the ramshackle world he first entered at Pagotes.

The point is clinched by the imagery. The climax of Mr Biswas's success is the visit to Sikkim Street of W.C. Tuttle and his wife. Naipaul ends the book in Dickensian fashion with Mr Biswas triumphing over all his rivals, silencing all but the reader's doubts. The rivalry with W.C. Tuttle is a late development, beginning at Shorthills where Mr Biswas dismissed W.C. Tuttle's westerns (by the author of that name) as 'trash', thus inaugurating a battle of possessions which the Tuttles usually seem to be winning. Victory seems final when, before Mr Biswas moves, they buy an old wooden house. Their surprise visit to Sikkim Street is for purposes of assessment, and Shama (from whose point of view the scene is presented) prepares carefully. But the Tuttles arrive after dark. The house about which Shama has so many anxieties is 'shining' and 'softly-lit', the weak bulb shedding a cosy exclusiveness, and they are deceived into jealousy. Mr Biswas's journey is from darkness to darkness, but his house, like all the huts and houses of the novel, is a centre of light. Even before his marriage, in the hut in the trace at Pagotes, Mr Biswas working late into the night finds romance and purpose by the 'light of a gas lamp'. Cycling home to Green Vale he passes other people's houses 'lightless and dead or bright and private'. In the rented house at Sans Souci the family gather round the oil-lamp, their security against the 'unknown surrounding darkness'. There are many other instances, summed up most vividly in the recurring image of the hut at dusk, containing an oil-lamp or a cooking fire whose welcoming light throws a wavering circle a little beyond the eaves. All that was implied by darkness — the loss of identity with the loss of the past, the featureless present, the menacing void of the future — finds its reassuring answer in the vision of the brightly-lit house. Mr Biswas's rival, another Tulsi son-in-law, envies him his cosy area of order and security, his house enclosed and glowing in the night.

Yet the light is deceptive. The Tuttles do not see the rickety staircase, the ill-fitting doors and windows, the cracks in the masonry which would be so obvious in daylight. Naipaul's paradoxes are maintained, and reflect back on all that the house represents. If Mr Biswas has triumphed we are left in no doubt about how little has been won, how uncertainly it is preferable to what has been lost. If the house is a centre of beauty and order and light, it is also very nearly falling apart. If his status as a Brahmin was 'a game', his new status as householder remains tenuous, for he is still heavily in debt. Fittingly, therefore, there is a final twist. For the debt is to Tara, the champion of the old ways. Mr Biswas's house becomes in the end the place from which he urged Anand to believe in God, the home from which he can be carried for cremation as an orthodox Hindu.

3

The first word used of Hanuman House in Chapter 3 is 'fortress'. Nothing that is said afterwards about tyranny and decay quite invalidates this first metaphor. Compared to the other tumbledown buildings in the High Street, it is solid and impregnable, alien and self-sufficient. It commands respect, not only in Arwakas where it is the home of the leading Hindu family, but throughout rural Trinidad where the Tulsis are Ajodha's only serious rivals for wealth and power. It is a place of order, a communal organisation with degrees of precedence all the way down from Mrs Tulsi and Padma to Mrs Biswas's own children, well down the scale but valued and protected as future assets. It seems, in other words, to provide a good deal of what Mr Biswas meant by his vow to get a house of his own. Cycling home after his first conversations about marriage, he feels he has 'achieved status'. Even six years later, after his efforts to break free, he realises how much he needs such a 'sanctuary' as Hanuman House, a community to which he can withdraw from the chaos around him, an island of India with a backyard called 'Ceylon', a house within whose gates he exchanges nonentity for the privileged position of clown. Later still in Port of Spain, he can tell Anand 'We could all go back to Hanuman House', and the words are not just a threat. Retreat to the fortress 'bright with lights' remains a last, comforting possibility.

In so far as Mr Biswas's vision of a house means no more than his desire for security, a place of his own in an ordered community, a centre of light in the darkness of past and future, then he gains all this very early with marriage to Shama. His rejection of the Tulsis reveals how much more comes to be involved in the house metaphor than what has been discussed so far. Equally relevant to questions of order and security are the terms on which they are gained. If Hanuman House is a fortress, it is also a gaol. Mr Biswas's wedding day, the climax of all his dreams of romance, is spent 'imprisoned', thinking of 'escape', and all that is implied by these words is more than confirmed by the terms he subsequently finds himself offered. He can gain his place in a secure world, but only by becoming a Tulsi. Instead of taking Shama home to serve and respect Bipti, he must himself become the *doolahin*, occupying the subservient position of the Hindu daughter-in-law. This does not simply mean putting his talents, such as they are, at the disposal of the house and accepting its discipline. It means the total surrender of his identity. Years later, when Mr Biswas is investigating destitutes, he is visited by the five widows from Shorthills. They want to be 'destitutes', and when Mr Biswas objects that they will be known to belong to one of the richest families in Trinidad, they have their answer ready. They can be anonymous: they can use their husbands' names. The prison image seems inadequate. The Tulsi sons-in-law are not so much inmates as slaves — or domestic animals: Mr Biswas calls the fortress 'a blasted zoo'.

The paradox is underlined by the contrast between Seth and Mrs Tulsi. Seth is the nominal head, managing the estates and exacting obedience in the interests of efficiency. His competence over the *insuranburn* or over Mr Biswas's 'baby' court-case makes it clear he knows his way around the picaroon society better than anyone else in the novel. Moreover, he is a likeable figure, and Mr Biswas is wrong to regard him as the real enemy. Seth genuinely cannot understand why Mr Biswas refuses to co-operate — 'This is a helluva man. When a man is married he shouldn't expect other people to feed him.' — but he bears no grudges, joking roughly with Mr Biswas about his first child, and scorning the idea of charging him rent for the site at Green Vale. He enjoys people's dependence on him, and cannot see why they should object to his handling their affairs for them. It is significant that he is absent from the scenes of Mr Biswas's worst humiliations, when he is beaten up by Govind or when the doll's house is demolished. Seth presumably acquiesces, but he never lays his own hand on the trouble-maker.

What makes the trial scenes so squalid is the intervention of Mrs Tulsi:

> The younger god frowned even more. 'Is not because my father dead that people who eating my mother food should feel that they could call she a hen. I want Biswas to apologise to Ma.'
>
> 'Apologise-ologise,' Mrs Tulsi said. 'It wouldn't make any difference. I don't see how anyone can be sorry for something he *feels*.'[12]

The statement parallels her earlier question, 'How can anyone be sorry for something he *thinks*?' and clarifies the contrast between Seth and herself. What she demands is total submission of thought and will, absolute devotion to herself. She works through blackmail, inviting victims to share her maudlin nostalgia, then springing her demands at a moment when it will seem insulting to refuse. Her ultimate weapon is her faint, an elaborate performance uniting the household in resentment against the offending son-in-law for whom equally elaborate penance is prescribed. That hers is the real controlling hand is revealed when she spends most of her week with Owad in Port of Spain. In her absence, Seth's rule declines; he commands obedience, but he cannot impose the harmony that comes from submission to a moral tyrant. As usual, Naipaul underlines the irony, for Mr Biswas, by rebelling, follows her to Port of Spain. Had he remained in Hanuman House, he might have achieved a desirable combination of security and freedom. By escaping to the city, he merely remains under her control. At times, she seems almost to be specialising in him, so perfectly matched are her self-delusions to his vulnerability. 'She expected much of Mr Biswas and always had', knowing that he is ambitious, 'which was why she had been so ready to agree when he came that afternoon to ask for Shama's hand', knowing that he is romantic. When she wants Mr Biswas to join the move to Shorthills, she excels herself. 'There would be no Seth', she promises as if it were

Seth who had made Hanuman House unbearable; and there would be 'many good sites for houses', as if it were not such blackmail, such studied manipulation of his deepest self that he was trying to escape.

Mr Biswas is not immediately aware of all this in the days following his marriage, but he learns enough. He packs his brushes and leaves. But his marriage is known. Back at Pagotes he is feted by Bipti and consoled by Tara. His marriage is final, inescapable. So he returns to Hanuman House to parade in his floursack pants and open his campaign of caricature – and the pattern of his rebellion is established. He becomes an Aryan, preaching the irrelevance of caste in a world where 'my sister better than anybody here, and better off too'; he accuses the Tulsis of being Catholics, of denying his rights as a bridegroom, of dabbling in Western customs for simple profit. It is true, but too late. The time to complain about being picked for his caste but denied a dowry was before the wedding took place. All his subsequent rebellion follows the same course of resistance to what has already happened. His chief weapon is caricature. He attacks the inconsistencies of his persecutors, shifting ground with so little regard for his own consistency that he lays himself wide open to reply, were any of them as intellectually alive as he is. His performance is brilliant. His wit, depending as it does on a real sensitivity to language, is the most creative thing in the book. One should not emphasise the differences between *A House for Mr Biswas* and the earlier novels to the point of forgetting that this too is a very funny novel. The wit of *The Mystic Masseur* is put into the mouth of Mr Biswas himself, with Naipaul standing back pointing the sad irony that it is all a response to events which cannot be altered. The most effective phrase for it comes after Bipti's death. Mr Biswas learns at the funeral that the doctor who signed her death certificate did so with impatience and disrespect. He had never loved his mother but her loss, as we have seen, means much to him and he feels the need to honour her. His rebuke to the doctor takes the form of an eight page letter, a 'long philosophical essay on the nature of man'. By the time the letter is despatched, his shame has turned to exhilaration and he is proposing to Anand a series of similar letters to be published as a booklet. But despite the comedy,

the wound was still there, too deep for anger or thoughts of retribution. What had happened was locked away in time. But it was an error, not a part of truth. He wished this stated; and he wanted to do something that would be a defiance of what had happened.[13]

This is one of the few occasions when his protest actually brings results — the doctor acknowledges the error by returning the letter. Much of his rebellion involves no statement of his position and is limited to caricature and abuse. But it is all equally an attempt 'to do something that would be a defiance of what had happened'.

This does not mean it is irrelevant. Twice when Mrs Tulsi tries to reassert her emotional dominance, when Hari is blessing the shop at The Chase and when he sees his first child at Hanuman House, Mr Biswas effectively counters her mood with facetiousness — 'Nobody has a house these days. They just want a coal barrel'. Irony cannot alter facts, but it saves him from servility. He replies, moreover, in English to Mrs Tulsi's Hindi. Hindi is, of course, the language of Chapter 1, of the world into which Mr Biswas is born. But when Tara addresses the photographer at Raghu's funeral ('Draw your photo now') she has to speak English, and in the new world, in F.Z. Ghany's office at Pagotes, Tara's and Bipti's Hindi becomes 'a secret language'. In the stories of Seepersad Naipaul, Hindi was represented by standard English as opposed to dialect. V.S. Naipaul borrows the device but extends it to underline the distinction between the two societies. For the shrinking Indian community, Hindi is not only a private language, but the language of privacy — of family loyalties, of friendship, of rebuke and apology, of love between man and wife or parent and child. English, by contrast, is the language of the picaroon world outside, a language of mockery and abrasion. Mr Biswas, discussing his marriage with Tara, avoids Hindi as 'too intimate and tender', and though Tara replies in Hindi she uses the English for 'love-letter', making it sound something vicious. Mr Biswas and Shama begin their marriage in English 'for there was as yet little friendship between them'. In Hanuman House both languages are used, one for its intense emotional claustrophobia, the other for quarrels or for dealings with the outside world. The long quartet at the end of Chapter 4, when Mr Biswas returns from The Chase for the last time, illustrates the point neatly. The scene has been arranged beforehand by Mrs Tulsi, Seth and Shama to persuade Mr Biswas to accept the job as driver at Green Vale. Inevitably, Mrs Tulsi casts herself as invalid. She addresses Mr Biswas from her bed in the Rose Room where she lies suffering, complaining, forgiving the inattentions of her family – and all in Hindi which Mr Biswas unwillingly finds himself using. But when Seth enters on cue, the arrangements for the *insuranburn* are conducted in English, and even Mrs Tulsi manages an English joke. In the context of this distinction, Mr Biswas's determination to use English 'even when the other person spoke Hindi' becomes, for his purposes in Hanuman House, a rejection of his Indianness, a deliberate choice of the language of abrasion, a refusal to be cowed by Mrs Tulsi's claims on his mind and spirit.

He refuses, in other words, to model himself on any of the other brothers-in-law, with two of whom Naipaul continuously contrasts him. The first is Hari, the constipated Pundit, the only other member of the household regarded as intelligent enough to be excused labouring jobs. Hari has won for himself a definite place in the hierarchy and Mr Biswas more than once envies him his position – 'Would Hanuman House care to have two sick scholars?' After his death at Shorthills he is discovered to have been indispensable. Yet he is a completely negative character, avoiding even those disputations appropriate to his role. The myth of his goodness seems to be founded on the complete absence of any qualities which would have made him a dangerously individual member of the household. Earning his place has left him as colourless as his complexion.

The other comparison is with Govind, whose wife Chinta is Shama's closest sister. One particularly insensitive review of *A House for Mr Biswas* described Mr Biswas as 'small and unsightly . . . cowardly and ugly, definitely not the stuff that heroes are made of' and therefore 'simply not worth all the detail' the author spins around him.[14] If heroes have to be 'tall, slender, smiling,' brave enough to fight and strong enough to rescue, then Govind certainly fits the bill. From the moment when Mr Biswas sits in the hall with Seth and Mrs Tulsi discussing his love-letter and Govind enters to report to Seth 'with many sighs, laughs and swallows', there is a continuous contrast between them. Mr Biswas sees Govind as one who has succumbed and he tries to spur him to rebellion. But his seditions are reported, for Govind and Chinta are the court favourites. It is Govind who thrashes Mr Biswas for insulting Owad just as it is Chinta who leads the 'puss-puss' over the doll's house. It is Govind who carries Mr Biswas home in the storm from Green Vale, Chinta supplementing his claim to authority by fussing over Anand. But such triumphs are only those of the slave serving his master. Time and time again when Mr Biswas reflects on his situation, his mind turns to Govind – unable to find a place, he defines himself against other people – and he congratulates himself on the comparison, not for anything he has achieved but for what he has avoided. His campaign of caricature may at times seem little more than the verbal equivalent of his spitting into the rum at Bhandat's, but it does at least save him from becoming as drab as Hari or from collaborating in his own degredation like Govind.

Yet after the collapse of Hanuman House, Govind who found it a fortress and Mr Biswas who found it a prison both live in the same Tulsi house in Port of Spain. Their rivalry is continued through Anand and Vidiadhar, who sit for the exhibition together, but Anand's victory over 'the little thug' (the insult is revealing) cannot disguise the fact that their fathers' situations are exactly similar. Mr Biswas's rebellion has taken him no further than Govind's servility. If Govind is lost without Hanuman House, lapsing into a maniacal surliness and eventually taking to wife-beating, Mr Biswas is no less misplaced and just as bad-tempered. Irony alone cannot feed his family or put a roof over their heads. What was marvellously subversive when directed against a tyranny becomes mere eccentricity when flung at Port of Spain. Mr Biswas can demolish Mrs Tulsi's nostalgia with remarks about coal barrels, but he cannot answer the questions which follow –

'But perhaps he could change . . . But go where? And do what?' He can win Anand's loyalty through wit and caricature, but it takes more than clowning to save Anand's life at Docksite – when Shekhar pulls Anand to the shore, Mr Biswas's flippancy is cruelly misplaced. So long as his rebellion lacks any more positive aspect, Mr Biswas remains in a real sense as emotionally dependent on Hanuman House as is Govind. But Mr Biswas is sustained by his vision of a house of his own, to which his experience of the Tulsis now adds a whole new dimension. The house stands not only for status and security, order and beauty, a centre of light in the menacing void of past and future. It now becomes the creative side of his rebellion, the concrete proof that he is not anonymous, a positive achievement founded on and justifying his refusal to capitulate.

Shama recognises this immediately she is confronted with the beginnings of the house at Green Vale. She knows it is a declaration of independence, and she attacks him for 'setting up in competition with people who have a lot more'. It is significant that he begins the house not only as an attack on the darkness, an attempt to 'arrest his descent into the void', but as a reaction to the labourers whom he is supposed to be overseeing and whose open mockery he is powerless to discipline. A clown at Hanuman House was a rebel; a clown at Green Vale is an incompetent, a nonentity. The house becomes his statement that he is more than a rebellious buffoon, that he really is a person capable of leaving on the world the marks of his existence. The house becomes, temporarily, his identity. This is why he begins it with such exuberance. This is why he resents the materials he is forced to buy cheap from Hanuman House. This is why the breakdown occurs while he is anxious about getting it finished. 'What is the matter, Mohun?' Seth asks, 'You are the colour of this', placing his hand on one of the grey pillars but not realising that it is precisely such identification with the house that is the problem. This is why the house is never completed, for independence is impossible for Mr Biswas at this stage. Finally, this is why his own mental collapse is paralleled by the partial destruction of the house in the storm, and why even after his surrender he cannot find peace at Hanuman House until

Seth brings the welcome news that the remains of the house, the incomplete symbol of himself, have been burned down by the labourers.

Green Vale represents a false start, a premature claim. But it is far from futile, and it adds yet another layer of meaning to the central metaphor of the novel. The house is built, Mr Biswas keeps insisting, for 'the children sake', and its merit is that for the first time he claims them as his own. He has already involved them in his campaign against the Tulsis, providing Savi with effective replies to make during his absence on the estate, and removing Anand's shame after the incident at school which Chinta finds so amusing by joking about his own disaster at Jairam's. Now, he involves them in the vision of his house. His gift to Savi of the doll's house provokes the bitterest of all his quarrels with the Tulsis. The scene is superbly described, with Mrs Tulsi rebuking him for showing favouritism to his own child and the sisters affronted at this display of individualism. When Shama breaks up the house, its wreckage is described in human terms with 'delicate joints' and 'torn skin', and Mr Biswas running back from the yard to confront her rips his own skin on the wall of Hanuman House: the doll's house is temporarily identified with his very existence as a father. He reacts in the only way possible. He claims Savi and carries her off into the darkness of his life at Green Vale. But his cycle, significantly, has no lights and they are stopped by a policeman. Eventually and inevitably, Seth comes to the rescue, quashing the case with a bribe. The pattern is repeated with Anand. The decision to build the Green Vale house follows immediately upon his vision of Anand, like that other boy, standing at dusk outside Hanuman House. Anand responds with enthusiasm. It is he who objects to using the rusted corrugated iron, a comment which is the turning point in Mr Biswas's own attitude to the house, and he reports confidentially to his father about how carelessly the stuff was loaded. It is Anand who in another scene of high intensity resolves to stay with his father not because of the crayons but because 'they were going to leave you alone'. The decision is followed by many happy moments at Green Vale where Mr Biswas establishes a real relationship with his son. But when the storm hits the house, the windows are blown open and the oil-lamp dies. Anand screams in terror, waiting for his father to 'say something, close the window, light the lamp'. But Mr Biswas is helpless. Anand, like Savi, has to be rescued by Hanuman House.

The claim is premature, but at least it has been made, and Mr Biswas never loses hold of his children again. The very next time he sees them, reurning to Hanuman House as the Scarlet Pimpernel, they run to claim him as their now famous father, and within three pages they have joined him in Port of Spain. Once they are established together as a family, what was begun at Green Vale grows into a mutual love, between Mr Biswas and Anand especially, that adds a whole new dimension to the novel. Five years after the Green Vale episode, Mr Biswas builds a similar house at Shorthills. This time it has concrete pillars, good timber, new corrugated iron for the roof and proper glass for the windows. It occupies such a site 'as he had always wanted', and it is completed – actually completed with no help from the Tulsis and no blessing from Hari – in less than a month. He seems to have achieved his ambition, and he invites Bipti to share his triumph. But the meaning of his original vow to Bipti has long since been superseded. The children are dissatisfied. Their choice of Mr Biswas was partly a choice of Port of Spain, and the new house 'imprisoned them in silence and bush'. Mr Biswas's independence must involve his children, and a house which denies his responsibilities as a father is no longer relevant, no matter how many of his earlier needs it fulfils.

Nor is it only the children who dislike the Shorthills house. Shama has over a mile to walk to the shops, and she regards the move as provocative – if the children want a house in town, their mother wants to stay with the Tulsis. From the earliest days of their marriage, the problem has been that Mr Biswas has nowhere better to offer Shama. 'What you got?' she asks not unreasonably when he refuses to be summoned by Seth, and his reply ('I ain't got nothing. But I not going to see Uncle.') makes no sense to her in her own home. She enjoys his wit; it is after he has drawn her into the game of name-calling that he first takes her as his wife. But she fears it also because it threatens to make her life unbearable. Unable to offer her anything, Mr Biswas seems bent on undermining the only security she knows, for however much she disowns him she remains the wife of the rebel, the mother of the rebel's children. It is significant that Mrs Tulsi's anger over the doll's house includes Shama from whom she demands 'notice' before 'you move into your mansion'. Shama is terrified. For the first time in her life she is completely alone, and despite the horror of her action it is impossible not to sympathise with her. Away from Hanuman House, the need to disown Mr Biswas disappears. At The Chase, she treats him with morose affection which contrasts sharply with her behaviour among the Tulsis. Visiting him at Green Vale, she even apologises for destroying the doll's house, blaming Chinta for jealousy. But she still goes back to Hanuman House. Ultimately, she understands as little as Seth the necessity for Mr Biswas's rebellion. Ambition for her is 'a series of negatives: not to be unmarried, not to be childless, not to be an undutiful daughter, sister, wife, mother, widow.' She has no memory for quarrels, for the injustices which spur Mr Biswas on. What she wants for herself and the children is to be achieved through the established rituals of Hanuman House. If this leads her into secret negotiations, as over the job at Green Vale or when she discloses only after the move to Shorthills that Mrs Tulsi had planned to raise the rent of their rooms, she has no sense that she is being disloyal.

Mr Biswas reacts to her mistrust by seizing Savi and Anand. But the attempt to separate them from their mother is an attempt to be father without being husband. Even when he is telling Anand to 'remember Galilyo' and stick up for himself, Shama at Hanuman House is expecting their fourth child. Is he to continue claiming more and more children without claiming her? The baby is born a few hours after Mr Biswas learns his house has been burned down. At the very moment of release, the reasons for his efforts are being redefined in a manner which must include Shama. He leaves for Port of Spain without bothering to see her or the child, but his first *Sentinel* stories feature four children roasted in a hut blaze while their mother watches helplessly, and four kiddies and a wife anxiously awaiting the return of explorer Edman from Brazil. Shama actually joins him in Port of Spain before Savi and Anand do, and she sets about creating her own Hanuman House. But her existence remains a lonely one:

> She was often alone in Port of Spain. The children were not anxious to go with her to Hanuman House, and as dissension there increased she went less often herself, regretting the old warmth, fearing to be involved in new quarrels. She had hardly moved outside her own family and did not know how to get on with strangers. She was shy of people of another race, religion or way of life. Her shyness had got her a reputation for hardness among the tenants, and she had done little to get to know the woman who lived in Owad's old room.[15]

When the Tulsis move to Shorthills, she nags Mr Biswas into joining the adventure, preferring still the security of her family to his precarious independence. In this context, with the children pulling one way and Shama the other, the house in the bush is clearly a mistake. There can be no solution now until Mr Biswas can persuade Shama that a move has become inevitable. His ambition must involve Shama too, and a house which denies his responsibilities as a husband is once again irrelevant.

Mr Biswas discovers, in other words, that his identity lies in his relationships. Increasingly, his most important experiences are family experiences. When, after six years in Port of Spain, after losing forever all satisfaction in his work, when one night he realises he has come to accept his situation as unalterable and that he has 'lost his vision of the house', the vision is rekindled by the brief, enchanting holiday at Toco. He, Shama and the children discover the 'new, shy pleasure of being a family together'.

4

Hanuman House thus adds a whole new range of meaning to Mr Biswas's dream of a house of his own. His search for security and status, for an order which is aesthetically pleasing and morally co- light in the menacing dark void, expands into a struggle nny, an urgent need to leave the mark of his existence d, and into the slow recognition that his identity lies in hips he has created, in the wife and children for whom a home must be provided. But the process by which he gets his house has still to be described. Naipaul does this in a complex and quite brilliant chapter in which all the novel's themes are rehearsed as Mr Biswas, in a manner absolutely in character, achieves his ambition.

From Shorthills, Mr Biswas returns to the Tulsi house in Port of Spain. But the Tulsi organisation has broken up. Without Seth, all that remains is a terrible destructiveness, no longer confined to the doll's house or Mr Biswas's rose garden, but wildly indiscriminate. Without an organisation to channel their energies, those who depended on Hanuman House disintegrate. Seth, who never struck Mr Biswas, is charged 'with wounding and with insulting behaviour'. Govind, the loyal slave, becomes 'the terror of the household'. Mrs Tulsi herself is perpetually ill and 'as her body decayed so her command of invective and obscenity developed'. Meanwhile, the Port of Spain house becomes a hostel for the readers and learners. From now on, it is everyone for himself with education the only protection. This sounds, perhaps, like progress of a sort. But the education which supersedes Hanuman House is as remote from Trinidad as Hanuman House, ever was. At least Hanuman House was an island of India in an island partly Indian. Anand's exhibition lessons are pure, sustained fantasy. Like Lal's oases and igloos twenty-five years earlier, like the horoscope Mr Biswas is told about at Pagotes, Anand's 'hampers – laden hampers' are so utterly irrelevant as to seem meaningfully ironical. Education, like Hanuman House, offers only the security of escape. But then Owad returns from England, equipped with a degree in medicine, and Hanuman House is recreated. Naipaul draws his themes together with a detailed contrast between Book 2, Chapter 6, the chapter of Owad's return, and Book 1, Chapter 3, in which Mr Biswas first became entangled with the Tulsis. Nowhere is Naipaul's controlling imagination more in evidence than here. Mr Biswas makes his final commitment in a manner that unites all that the house has come to signify with all that was originally at stake.

For a brief, happy period, the sisters are able to pretend they are back in Arwakas. Mrs Tulsi is revivified; old hierarchies are re-established – it is 'just like an old Hanuman House festival', just as if 'they were still sisters in the hall of Hanuman House', just like 'the old days which seemed to have returned with Owad'. Yet, as Mr Biswas never tired of pointing out, the old days contained their contradictions; the orthodox Tulsis made their own compromises with the West, marrying their daughters without dowries and sending their sons to the Catholic college. No sooner has Owad set foot in Trinidad than the decision to send him abroad has its inevitable consequence. Seth is among those waiting on the wharf. In Hindi which 'thrilled them all', he claims Owad as 'Son, son'. This is the last Hindi we hear in the novel, and the last we see of Seth whom Owad rejects – in English. In that moment, the past is finally destroyed, with all its warmth and sweetness, with all the protection Seth provided. No matter how Owad flatters the sisters that they are the last custodians of Hindu culture, there can be no real return to Hanuman House.

The old days are gone. Yet the Tulsis remain a threat. Even before Owad arrives, Mr Biswas is relegated to the tenement slum and then to one room at the back of the house. Driving to the wharf on the great day, he has to carry people he doesn't know, his family having 'split up and gone in other cars'. He recognises the pattern, and when he witnesses Seth's humiliation he again rebels – partly out of sympathy for Seth whose worth he has come to appreciate, but principally because he sees in the returned Owad a grown-up version of the younger god. Back in Hanuman House it was Owad who was the pampered favourite, Owad who spoke up at the trials demanding total submission, Owad whose *puja* Mr Biswas rejected, Owad who got food tipped on his head and who urged Govind to 'Kill him!' Now that Owad is back, he turns out to be an infinitely more harmful version of Indarsingh. Nowhere is the returned scholarship boy more devastatingly exposed. An education in Trinidad which taught him nothing about himself, supplemented by the delights of Europe, has produced only a spoilt and opinionated hypocrite. But his victims welcome him. Building on the family illusion that old loyalties are still binding, he sets up a new and more irresponsible form of tyranny. The scene which greets Mr Biswas when he returns from welfare work on the evening of Owad's return is richly ironical. Once, after Mr Biswas's second trial, Seth rebuked them all with 'This house is a republic already'. Now Mr Biswas finds even the Pundit reading *The Soviet Weekly.* Once, he was hated as a subversive. Now he hears Owad describing with relish 'what they did to the Czar'. The former atheist, the former 'spy', continuing his rebellion into the new era, finds himself 'a capitalist lackey'.

Another trial scene follows. But the victim this time is Anand. He has loyally championed Owad's opinions at school, basking in the glory of knowing a man who 'knows' T.S. Eliot. But he is identified with his father whose humour, though eventually tolerated and even enjoyed in Hanuman House under Seth, has no place in the family Owad has recreated in his own image. Again, unlike Seth, Owad actually strikes his victim. Hanuman House was a fortress for the weak; under Owad's rule the weak are insulted to feed his vanity. But the real point of the scene is that Anand is undergoing the same humiliations as his father. The past is being recreated, the cycle repeated. In Book 1, Chapter 3, Shama gaily disowned her husband. This time she cannot evade her responsibilities. She persuades Anand to apologise, but she cannot avoid seeing that her children, sitting quietly with Anand while the rest of the house prepares for enjoyment, are united in resentment. The rebellion now involves the whole family, and however much she runs up and down stairs between her children and the sisters, she has to accept facts. Mr Biswas knows nothing of these events. But Anand's appeal to him — 'We must move. I can't bear to live here another day' — is more direct than ever before. Just as the children force Shama to take sides, so the children press Mr Biswas into his final commitment. That same night, Mr Biswas demands that the light should be put off. A quarrel develops in which he insults Mrs Tulsi and Owad. Last time this happened, he was beaten up by Govind. Govind's wife Chinta is as delighted as anyone by the recreation of Hanuman House; she becomes the sisters' spokesman throughout the chapter. Govind's son Vidiadhar is the 'free, unoffending' partner in the card game when Anand is slapped. But Govind has changed. He is the only son-in-law to be absent from the party on the wharf. Now, as in Book 1, Chapter 3, he races into Mr Biswas's room:

> A wonderful sentence formed in Mr Biswas's mind, and he said, 'Communism, like charity, should begin at home.'
>
> Mr Biswas's door was pushed open, fresh light and shadows confused the patterns on the walls, and Govind came into the room, his trousers unbelted, his shirt unbuttoned.
>
> 'Mohun!'
>
> His voice was kind. Mr Biswas was overwhelmed to tears. 'Communism, like charity,' he said to Govind, 'should begin at home.'
>
> 'We know, we know,' Govind said.
>
> Sushila was comforting Mrs Tulsi. Her wail broke up into sobs.
>
> 'I am giving you notice,' Mr Biswas shouted. 'I curse the day I step into your house.'[16]

At last he has committed himself, and Govind is the first to approve. But immediately, as so often before, the family is left 'appalled' in 'the darkness'.

It will be appreciated how much of what has gone before is resolved by these events. Hanuman House is recreated in its most repressive form, and Mr Biswas rejects it. He rejects its swamping of his identity, its denial of his right to speak and act for himself. He rejects the Indianness it claims to uphold. He rejects its philistinism, its power to destroy the beauty he cherishes – the conversations over the card game are about books and art. He rejects the specious security it offers to those who conform. He rejects the light it still provides in the world, preferring the darkness which is not to be dispelled until the light goes on in the house in Sikkim Street. He rejects all this not only for himself, but for the children who are at the centre of the chapter. Mr Biswas sees the humiliations of the past repeated in a new generation. Shama sees the responsibilities she has evaded in the past thrown back in her lap. The result is that Mr Biswas's claims on his children and his wife are finally consummated. They arrive in Sikkim Street a united family. It is all the more satisfying because in the process Hanuman House is finally overthrown. Seth has long been rejected; Govind has joined the rebels; now Owad, the new ruler, leaves the house in a temper and

Mrs Tulsi is unable to coax him back. He marries the Presbyterian violinist and joins a new caste of doctors and lawyers. 'This', said Seth once, expelling Mr Biswas to The Chase, 'was a nice united family before you come.' The prophecy is fulfilled. The tyranny is over, and it is Mr Biswas who gives the final push.

But if this makes him seem too heroic, the sequel is wholly in character. Having made his commitment, he lapses yet again into loquacious inactivity. He can only get his house by being cheated into it. Yet, as we saw earlier, the cheating hardly matters. The house is still a stupendous triumph. A lifetime of defiance has at last brought him to the point where he can be fittingly and desirably swindled. For Naipaul insists that the house is the culmination of former efforts. What makes its purchase possible is the four hundred dollars Mr Biswas is offered the same evening for the materials of the Shorthills house. The house in the bush which fulfilled all he had hoped for as an individual but which denied his responsibilities as husband and father, now makes possible the house which is needed to save his family from Woodford Square. Once the move has been made and despite all its drawbacks, the house becomes for the children a centre of security, a home such as their father never enjoyed, a jumping-off ground for studies abroad. It becomes for Shama a place where she learns new family loyalties, to her husband and her children, a possession of which she can boast to the Tuttles 'this is just right for me'. It becomes for Mr Biswas a 'ready-made world' of his own, not just the setting for final victories over the Tuttles and over the solicitor's clerk's plans to cheat him of part of his land, but the climax to a lifetime's vision, the 'place which had been hollowed out by time, by all that he had lived through,' the place where right at the end – despite the debt and Anand's absence – he can rejoice in Shama's attentions, in Savi's cleverness, in the butterfly-orchid and the sweet-scented shade tree.

For a grown-up Anand it becomes, as we have seen, the pivot of the novel in which he records the quality of his father's experience of Trinidad, a means of organising in a fresh and deeper perspective his vision of that colonial society. Being written around a central metaphor, a symbol of ever-broadening significance, and containing in the character of Anand an acknowledgement of the urgency of these problems for an author who is himself deeply implicated in them, *A House for Mr Biswas* becomes the first of Naipaul's novels to reach confidently beyond Trinidad. No longer concerned with defining or exposing a single society, it is a novel dealing with human problems of universal application, drawing on a mass of local detail to make itself credible, but open to all whose identity is at odds with their society, who understand homelessness and the threat of disorder, who feel condemned permanently to provincialism, who are ready to sympathise with struggle and failure and triumph. For the first time, Trinidad exists as an area which the educated imagination has to acknowledge. Naipaul has ceased to be a purely regional writer.

At the same time, it is in another sense the last of the Trinidad novels. It is not, of course, the last to be set on a Caribbean island, but it is the last in which the author accepts, with little modification, his characters' view of the outside world, the last to stay inside Hat's or Ganesh's or Mr Biswas's feelings of colonial inferiority. From now on, Naipaul spends his time exploring that larger world. By 1961, when *A House for Mr Biswas* was published, he had spent eleven years in England. Apart from a three-month visit to Trinidad at the time of the 1956 elections, his material was drawn from his memories of his first eighteen years. But before his next novel *Mr Stone and the Knights Companion* is published in 1963, he spends seven months touring the West Indies and a whole year in India. With such new experiences to be absorbed, his writing now enters a completely new phase.

CHAPTER FIVE

'. . . an experience of nothingness . . .'

I

A House for Mr Biswas obviously marks the climax of one line of development. 'It was like a career', Naipaul said afterwards, 'I've been feeling unemployed ever since.' But in fact, the years following its publication in 1961 were exceptionally busy. In addition to the travel books *The Middle Passage* (1962) and *An Area of Darkness* (1964), Naipaul wrote three of his finest stories, 'A Christmas Story', 'The Night Watchman's Occurrence Book', and 'The Baker's Story', a short novel, *Mr Stone and the Knights Companion* (1963), and a story only about 7000 words shorter than the novel, 'A Flag on the Island', written in 1965 and published two years later in the volume of that name. *Mr Stone and the Knights Companion* is set in England and deals entirely with English characters; 'A Flag on the Island' has an American hero and is set in an unnamed but newly independent island in the Caribbean. Both look like new beginnings, attempts to capitalise on the experience of travelling in England, the West Indies as a whole and India, and in fact, quite apart from the obvious relevance of Naipaul's years in England, both books do lean heavily on the material of the travelogues. Naipaul is in a sense serving a second apprenticeship, and *Mr Stone and the Knights Companion* and 'A Flag on the Island' bear something of the same relation to *The Mimic Men*, his second masterpiece, as did the early Trinidad novels to *A House for Mr Biswas*, his first. But there is also a sense in which they are both footnotes, looking backwards rather than ahead. *A House for Mr Biswas* is a deeply ironical book, modifying every statement to paradox, but one assumption which is scarcely challenged up to the closing pages is Mr Biswas's belief that real life is going on elsewhere, that disorder is something peculiar to societies like Trinidad and that

127

England by contrast is a coherent place where everyone is born to a position and an identity. In addition, although it is not overtly political, the very fact that it deals in a colonial context with an individual's struggle against tyranny inevitably gives the novel political overtones. The characters may lack the political awareness of those in *The Mimic Men*, but it is impossible not to read Mr Biswas's struggle with the Tulsis as to some extent a nationalist parable, arguing in 1961 the case for that self-governing democracy which came to Trinidad in 1962. For Mr Biswas, the solution lies in the establishing of his right to speak up for himself from his own corner of the earth. Now, in *Mr Stone and the Knights Companion* and in 'A Flag on the Island', Naipaul qualifies these assumptions and shows us two further kinds of placelessness – the placelessness of a man who, owning a house in London, finds the physical world irrelevant to his humanity; the placelessness of a people who, in the acquiring of a political identity, have become uprooted within their own land.

Mr Stone and the Knights Companion was written in Srinagar, Kashmir, during his stay in 'A Doll's House on the Dal Lake' described so excellently in Part II of *An Area of Darkness*. The distancing which he finds necessary (his first four books were written in England about life in Trinidad), and the change of landscape which he seems to find stimulating (Mr Stone's inspiration comes to him on holiday in Cornwall) are all the more necessary now that Naipaul is dealing with entirely new problems. The difficulty in writing about Trinidad, as we saw in Chapter 2, was that for all his intimate knowledge of his subject he had no examples to guide him. In applying to one society a genre imported from another, he had to start from scratch, with his father's stories his substitute for a tradition. But to write about the English raises for him precisely the opposite problems. How can he, as a foreigner, ever know enough to get beyond the most obvious clichés? How can he, as a colonial, bring anything like a fresh approach to people mythologised from his childhood in the pages of 'Eng. Lit.'? It is a sign of how seriously he tackles the problem that after eight years' residence, he admits in his article 'London' how little he has learned. He complains about the privacy of English life with so much going on behind locked doors, about the lack of obvious 'characters' exposing themselves in a moment, about the modes and conventions of English speech, the habitual irony and understatement so difficult to interpret and reproduce:

> I feel I know so little about England. I have met many people but I know them only in official attitudes – the drink, the interview, the meal. I have a few friends. But this gives me only a superficial knowledge of the country, and in order to write fiction it is necessary to know so much.[1]

These remarks were made at a time when well-wishers were urging him to 'cease being a regional writer', at a time when the impatience with Trinidad of the closing pages of *The Suffrage of Elvira* seems to have set him wishing he could turn his hand to larger subjects. They were made, in fact, a year after he wrote the two English-based stories now collected in *A Flag on the Island*.

'Greenie and Yellow' and 'The Perfect Tenants', written in 1957, describe events in an English boarding house, packed with tenants, and presided over by Mrs Cooksey the landlady. From his flat somewhere in the middle regions, the narrator observes in the first story Mrs Cooksey's passion for budgerigars and the events which lead her husband accidentally to poison them, and in the second her behaviour towards the Dakins, welcomed initially as ideal tenants but expelled after a long war of nerves. The stories begin in cliché – the Englishman and his pets, the battle of tenant and landlady in that boarding house where all West Indian writers seem to have stayed (though Mrs Cooksey, mercifully, is not sexually demanding, nor her husband racially bigoted). They are successful because Naipaul accepts readily that he is dealing only with externals and because of the rightness of the role he assigns himself as storyteller. When Mr Dakin is taken suddenly ill and the whole household is convulsed, the narrator says, 'I went and stood on the landing as a sympathetic gesture', and later, 'I went back to my room. After some thought I left my door wide open: another gesture of sympathy'. This is a far cry from the sophisticated boy of the last stories of *Miguel Street* or of *The Mystic Masseur*, inviting the characters to reveal themselves by co-operating gaily in their eccentricities. The narrator here is a tentative observer, trying to make his contribution but uncertain what note to strike. When Mrs Cooksey weeps over the budgie's death he records the tears but he clearly wasn't expecting them and 'it was hard to know what to say'. When Mrs Dakin weeps over her husband's illness he ventures to remark to another tenant 'he was such a nice man', but he is only repeating what Mrs Cooksey told him four lines earlier. With this reassurance that there is more to the lives of these people than he is yet able to cope with, we accept the amusing externals at the level at which they are offered:

> The Knitmistress took the cocktail and sipped without enthusiasm.
> 'And you?' Mr Cooksey asked.
> 'Guinness,' I said.
> 'Guinness!' Mr Dakin exclaimed, looking at me for the first time with interest and kindliness. 'Where did you learn to drink Guinness?'
> We drew closer and talked about Guinness.[2]

Such an approach, however, can hardly be adequate for a full-length novel, from which one expects some insight into the characters or at least into the workings of their society. As Naipaul eschews what he calls the gimmicks of sex and exploitation which might have supplied him with a simple framework many years earlier, it is not until 1962 that he writes *Mr Stone and the Knights Companion*. Even then, after twelve years' residence in England, a certain hesitation remains about going beyond appearances, not marring the novel in any way but helping to dictate the terms in which it is written. He begins, naturally enough, with what he knows best. 'I know them only in official attitudes,' he wrote in 1958, 'the drink, the interview, the meal.' There are no less than six meals described in this short novel – the two dinner parties at the Tomlinsons', the splendidly embarrassing evening at Mr Stone's, the chilling teashop in Cornwall, the Knights Companion celebration dinner and Whymper's wonderful Hampstead meal of 'chipped grass' and olive oil washed down with retsina.

He is excellent on clothes. Every character has a costume: one thinks of Mr Stone's black city overcoat from Simpson's, of Margaret's dark red silk dress, her bony hands subsiding into its spread lap after each brittle remark, of Whymper's ill-fitting jacket which makes him look round-shouldered. The observation is clinically exact – the overcoats, lower buttons alone undone, of Fred's keepers in the teashop, and Fred himself, his steel-rimmed glasses and hearing-aid flex making him look dangerously attenuated. He is, as one would expect, especially sensitive to the atmosphere of different houses. The bright reassuring permanence of the Tomlinsons' Christmas display contrasts sharply with the 'time-created shabbiness' of Mr Stone's house, which contrasts in turn with the genteel decay of Margaret's rooms in Earls Court, or with the permanently 'unfinished look' of Olive's houses as she moves to avoid burglars. He is good on conventional phrases, on that accretion of cliché around a character that is like a second costume, and he captures the tone of those letters to *The Times* with a punch and a relish that takes us back to the vivacity of *The Mystic Masseur*.

Yet even as Naipaul's eye registers styles and conventions, he insists that they *are* only externals. When Mr Stone attends the first of the Tomlinsons' dinner parties, he looks forward to seeing Tony 'in action', cultivating his annual contact. But he finds the centre of attention is Mrs Springer, whose voice and delivery recall those of 'celebrated actress'. Grace appears 'to be acting as cheer leader', and she rebukes Mr Stone for attempting a joke (a pun which draws 'pretended groans') by whispering that Mrs Springer is 'in profound mourning'. The conversation turns to films, and Tony exercises his prerogative as the party's intellectual by mentioning *Rififi* – though his enthusiasm about its lack of dialogue threatens to kill conversation altogether until Mrs Springer comes to the rescue with her witticisms about sub-titles. Mr Stone spends the evening hunting for a role, until he successfully caricatures himself to Mrs Springer and is accepted as her understudy. The emphasis here on acting is obvious. Words like gesture, part, performance, mask, manner, are used regularly throughout the novel. Margaret, after her marriage, discards her 'party manner' and concentrates instead on her 'functions as a woman and a wife'; later, she develops further from the 'wife who waited for her husband at home' into the 'wife who encouraged and inspired her husband in his work'. Grace changes from a self-effacing hostess into a globe-trotting merry widow, with appropriate alterations in her clothes and hair-style. Whymper, whose every action is rehearsed and whose job as a P.R.O. is concerned with appearances, is having an affair with an actress. So quickly does Naipaul establish the point that when, midway through Chapter 2, Richard and Margaret throw their expected dinner party (another evening of modulating poses), he shows us Gwen insulting Margaret by copying her public voice in a dramatic recitation.

But Naipaul's purpose is far from being Gwen's. The theatrical metaphors are the equivalent of the hesitant narrator of 'Greenie and Yellow' and 'The Perfect Tenants', a means of indicating that there is more to the lives of these people than the gestures they present to the world. Moreover, there is a good deal of that same hesitant narrator in Mr Stone himself. At moments of crisis – when he is appalled by Fred in the café or by the prisoner of Muswell Hill – he is reduced to silence and inactivity, a trapped spectator of events which nevertheless affect him deeply. I do not mean that Mr Stone, like Anand or the boy of *Miguel Street*, is another version of Naipaul – the brief scene in Earls Court where Mr Stone, the elderly Englishman, notes with anxiety and distaste those 'foreigners of every colour' is a triumph of sympathetic detachment. But his constant uncertainty about the levels at which other people are operating surely echoes Naipaul's own position in England. 'What strange things must happen behind the blank front doors of so many houses', Mr Stone reflects at one point, and the phrase is lifted from Naipaul's 1958 article on the problems of writing about the English. His hesitations culminate in the problem of assessing Whymper. Whymper is the most competent performer in the novel, greeting every situation with a rehearsed gesture, a practised phrase. For a time, Mr Stone is almost convinced of his commitment to the cause. Yet Whymper's misconceptions run deep. Even as he works on a scheme to solve the problems of old age, he longs to be old himself, 'having tea on a fresh clean tablecloth on a green lawn'. When Mr Stone is treated to his confessions and visits his flat for a meal, he discovers in Whymper an uncertainty and a rootlessness which complements his own. But a rootlessness which matches his own is equally what Naipaul has discovered in Mr Stone. By projecting on to Mr Stone his own problems of assessment, he has laid bare another kind of displacement. Mr Stone's problem is that he can no longer make sense of the rituals with which he is surrounded. He is a man for whom the gap between the solid world and the inner life has suddenly become too great. The order of a lifetime has come to strike him as mere theatre. The point is suggested by Naipaul himself in a discussion of English fiction in *An Area of Darkness*:

> To this dependence on the established and reassuring might be traced the singular omissions of English writing in the last hundred years. No monumental writer succeeded Dickens. In the English conditions the very magnitude of his vision, its absorption into myth, precluded as grand an attempt. London remains Dickens's city – how few writers since appear to have *looked* at the city! There have been novels about Chelsea and Bloomsbury and Earls Court; but on the modern mechanised city, its pressures and frustrations, English writers have remained silent. It is precisely this, on the other hand, which is one of the recurring themes of American writers. It is the theme, in the words of the novelist Peter de Vries, of city people who live and die without roots, suspended 'like the fabled mistletoe, between the twin oaks of home and office'. It is an important theme, and not specifically of America; but in England, where narcissism applies to country, class and self, it has been reduced to the image of the bank clerk, always precise, always punctual, who farcically erupts into misdemeanour.[3]

This paragraph, though only loosely related to the argument about imperial consciousness which is its immediate context, tells us a good deal about the novel written in India one year earlier. Naipaul's theme is the fraudulence of the big city, the irrelevance of its apparent order. Even as recently as *A House for Mr Biswas*, escape to London was seen as a solution. But Mr Stone begins where Mr Biswas leaves off, entering on page one the house Mr Biswas achieves only in the final chapter. All that seemed desirable in *A House for Mr Biswas* – a secure position in an ordered society with a set of dependable modes and conventions – is now profoundly questioned. All that Mr Biswas's house represented is now dismissed as costume and scenery. For a house, even in London, is no substitute for companionship, and no shield against death.

'Stone' is the perfect name – something settled, solid, grey – and Mr Stone approximates to the house he has lived in for twenty-four years. He and it have aged together, he priding himself on the accumulating years, the 'protracted calm' of his adult existence, the house carrying in its personable shabbiness the marks of his habitation. The cat, by contrast, is a creature 'of the jungle' whose daily attacks on his property require daily reparations – the image of Mr Stone in his black overcoat raising a twenty-two year old briefcase to shield his head from the cat captures the essential antithesis exactly. It is significant that although he likes to think in numbers – the thirty years with Excal, the forty-four years of friendship with Tony – he measures time not from his childhood but from the death of his mother when he was seventeen. The fact is mentioned only briefly in this most economical of novels, but it is clear that the whole of Mr Stone's adult life has been spent in the shadow of this grief, and in moments of solitude he still indulges himself in pity for 'a boy of seventeen walking back alone from school on a winter's day, past the shops of the High Street . . . going home, unaware of what awaited him there.' This is the context in which his house, his rituals, his colourless docketed experience must be viewed. They are another version of what Mr Biswas spends his life pursuing, a means of bringing what has been unbearable under control.

But the novel begins with Mr Stone at sixty-two just three years from retirement. Within three years the order of a lifetime will be overthrown. He senses for the first time that the passing days are not so much adding to his experience as hastening him towards death. His conservatism, which formerly worked itself out in harmless resentment against his neighbours, becomes perverse as he cherishes images of cruelty and death. Then, at the start of the

Christmas holiday when all comforting routine is dislocated, he meets Mrs Springer, the name again appropriate with its suggestion of renewal. He meets her at a time when she too is engaged with the problem of translating grief into behaviour which will make it manageable, and Mr Stone is impressed with her success. Between them, they take the story of Mr Stone and the cat and turn it into something amusing and endearing, something far removed from the fear and loneliness out of which it arose.

Their marriage, however, despite its origins, is not a piece of play-acting. It is a deliberate choice of human companionship, a deliberate substitution of love and concern for property and convention. Marriage does involve them in new roles, Margaret as the helpless, dependent woman, Mr Stone as the Master or the Brave Bull, but what matters is clearly their choice of each other. When Margaret, at their dinner party, is mocked by Gwen for her public actressy manner, Mr Stone is fiercely sympathetic and he has a sudden coherent vision of the meaning of the choice he has made, a realisation

> too upsetting to be more than momentarily examined, that all that was solid and immutable and enduring about the world, all to which man linked himself (the Monster watering her spring flowers, the Male expanding his nest), flattered only to deceive. For all that was not flesh was irrelevant to man, and all that was important was man's own flesh, his weakness and corruptibility.[4]

The vision is sharpened, and then modified, by his experiences in Cornwall where he and Margaret go for a belated honeymoon. There the landscape is not simply indifferent but actively hostile, and the ancient Celtic houses, where an extinct race sheltered 'from more than the elements', are squalid and depressing little hovels. Yet, as at Christmas, the suspension of normal routine together with one terrifying moment of halucination, a moment which remains with him as 'an experience of nothingness, an experience of death', re-emphasises his dependence on order and the physical world. The solid and immutable, the Monster and the Male, cannot be written off so easily. On the last day of his honeymoon, he meets a workman pensioned off after forty years, a man reduced to caricature by his loss of a position in the world, utterly in the control of the women in his life whose functions are redoubled now that he is useless. The experience leads Mr Stone into the one creative act of his life.

He devises the scheme whereby retired Excal staff can keep themselves active by keeping in touch with each other. The hours of writing are the most satisfying he has ever known (all Naipaul's heroes relish the trappings of authorship), and when his idea is officially approved he knows all the joy of success. He feels at one with the tree outside his bathroom window, not now because its cycles are adding years to his experience but because its reawakening with spring is an image of himself. But before his private vision can become official policy, it needs to be 'licked into shape'. The phrase is Whymper's, and what happens to Mr Stone's idea in Whymper's hands is that it is gradually detached from the 'concern and fear' out of which it was born and licked into a venture in public relations. The metaphors for this process are significant. Mr Stone feels that the ideas which catch on are those which seem 'theatrical and cheap'. The old men are called Knights Companions (the name suggesting youth), and are presented with badges and archaically worded scrolls of appointment. The department magazine is called *Oyez! Oyez!* And although Whymper's idea of borrowing costumes from the Old Vic is turned down, the celebration dinner is dominated by ritual from the gothic invitations to the presentation of *Excal*ibur to the Knights Companion of the year.

Mr Stone's inspiration, in other words, is diverted back into the social play-acting whose irrelevance has troubled him since Chapter 1. Yet he enjoys the role thrust upon him. He savours Margaret's sudden release of energy, her enthusiasm about new carpets and wallpaper, the resurrection of her party manner. He relishes Whymper's metaphors — words like unit, operation, intelligence, confer grandeur and give him the illusion of paramilitary power. For the first time in his life, people actually listen to what he is saying. The 'climax of his life' comes when he and Margaret are the guests of honour at what turns out to be the last of the

Tomlinsons' dinner parties. They are the 'stars' of the evening. He studies his gestures, playing up to his attentive audience – and now it is *his* words that Tony echoes with that annually pained expression. Yet, by its very theatrical nature, the brilliance recedes, leaving him with a sense of unease which is part anger that other people should be riding to success on his back and part shame that success should have buried his original feelings so completely. Over the next few weeks, no less than five events conspire to remind him of his earlier vision that 'all that was not flesh was irrelevant to man'. Tony's sudden death removes his oldest friend, destroying finally that evening of brittle triumph, and the strenuous efforts of Grace to forget him – so strenuous that Mr Stone wonders if they have not been successful – and takes him back to his initial meeting with Margaret when she too was recently widowed. Miss Millington becomes senile and has to be retired, but not before Mr Stone has been shamed by her assertion of dignity over the phone to a friend. The neighbours move away and their cat, with which Mr Stone has begun to establish an old man's communion, is destroyed, leaving him horror-struck that his impulses of pity were not strong enough to make him rescue it. Added to these is his own sense of increasing irrelevance at the office where the jokes about his retirement have a double bitterness. Finally, one Sunday afternoon in early spring, he hesitatingly suggests man's oneness with the reawakening world. It is only a year since the plane tree had seemed an image of his own renewal, but now the possibility that 'we too will have our spring' is dismissed by Margaret as 'a lotta rubbish'. There is no evading death, no point in deluding oneself that the physical world has any pity or reassurance to offer. Mr Stone had realised this before, but now he goes further:

> Nothing that was pure ought to be exposed. And now he saw that in that project of the Knights Companion which had contributed so much to his restlessness, the only pure moments, the only true moments were those he had spent in the study, writing out of a feeling whose depth he realised only as he wrote. What he had written was a faint and artificial rendering

of that emotion, and the scheme as the Unit had practised it was but a shadow of that shadow. All passion had disappeared. It had taken incidents like the Prisoner of Muswell Hill to remind him, concerned only with administration and success, of the emotion that had gone before. All that he had done, and even the anguish he was feeling now, was a betrayal of that good emotion. All action, all creation, was a betrayal of feeling and truth. And in the process of this betrayal his world had come tumbling about him. There remained to him nothing to which he could anchor himself.[5]

One is tempted to insist that these conclusions are, of course, Mr Stone's and not the author's. For one thing, the novel is not yet finished. The speech with which Mr Stone greets the news of Gwen's pregnancy and her elopement with Whymper is superbly abusive, uniting scattered moments of irritation with other people's pretensions – Olive's 'living for her child', Gwen's borrowed phrases, Whymper's deceptions, Margaret's 'impresario-like manner' – in one splendid ironic outburst. But the speech is destructive, a symptom of hatred, and must therefore be as great a betrayal of his earlier vision of man's vulnerability as the Unit can possibly have become. He still has to learn that he can only acknowledge the validity of his original pure emotion by an act of love – hence the final scene in which Mr Stone the destroyer surrenders to pity and love for the kitten which, as in Chapter 1, greets him on the stairs. Furthermore, there is a strong element of unreasonabless about the conclusions he is drawing. Creation and action, writing and administration, are lumped together as aspects of one betrayal. Yet he acknowledges that it was only as he wrote that he realised the depth of those feelings which subsequent actions have betrayed. There is a further inconsistency. Mr Stone's idea was to provide the old men with a role, to rescue them from retirement by giving them something to do. It is not a vision which *can* be preserved in the purity of silence. To be puritanically ashamed of the success it has brought to to himself is to ignore the benefits it has conferred on the people he wanted to help. For the scheme works, even to the extent of uncovering cases of cruelty and neglect. It grows into a crusade. At the very least, it possesses the merit of Ganesh's cure of the boy with the black cloud, a dramatic performance which serves a human need. It offers the old men what Mr Biswas sought – a continuing role in an ordered society. What Mr Stone objects to (apart from his own loss of credit for the scheme) is the conversion of something inspired into something 'theatrical and cheap'. But the issue here is not between creation and silence. It is a question of taste, a matter in which, silence being impossible, one has to compare forms of expression.

Yet it is not so easy to dismiss this powerful paragraph in the same fashion as the partly irrational outburst of one of Naipaul's case studies. Those reviewers who assumed that Mr Stone by this stage is very close to Naipaul himself and·that the thoughts are more or less the author's can find a good deal of support in the novel. Not only does Naipaul now openly question all that seemed desirable in *A House for Mr Biswas*, he seems to take absolutely seriously the attack on writing itself. He has, in fact, reached a point of self-questioning which can only be understood in terms of his experience of India, where *Mr Stone and the Knights Companion* was written. Before this problem can be examined, however, another work needs to be discussed. For in the long story 'A Flag on the Island', a complementary analysis is brought to strikingly similar conclusions.

2

'A Flag on the Island' was written for a film company, and is set on a newly independent Caribbean island. It contains (the film company's requirement) 'much sex and much dialogue', to which Naipaul has added much drinking. It has (another requirement) an American hero. It has several crowd scenes, and it ends with an impromptu carnival. It lacks a single East Indian character. All this is new to his fiction and suggests that, however sardonically, he is at last writing of the Caribbean everyone knows, the calypso islands, the crazy tourist resorts. Yet there is a disturbing staleness about the story. Too much of the material has been used before in *The Middle Passage*. It was on his return to Trinidad that Naipaul was told of the Grenadian whose girl friend, the mother of his four children, wanted to 'rush' him into marriage; this now becomes Henry (who, like Harbans, holds up his trousers with a tie). It was in Surinam that Naipaul met the nationalist writer who wanted to translate the world's masterpieces into patois; this now becomes Mr Blackwhite. The ritual dancing in Henry's yard, the complaints about the allocation of black sand and white beaches, the Abyssinian myths, the preoccupation with culture as a night-club turn, even actual phrases ('What do the Surinamers do when they are doing nothing') – we have read it all before in *The Middle Passage* (though the singing of 'Flow Gently Sweet Afton' comes from *An Area of Darkness*: in *The Middle Passage* it was 'Loch Lomond'). Perhaps only the Naipaul enthusiast will feel a little cheated by this. Perhaps only one who has lived in Trinidad will feel that the new material (the explanation of 'fishing', the joke about Mr Lambert as the legal head of a Scottish clan) sounds like the work of a writer who has paid a brief visit to collect local colour. The story was written in Trinidad, but one wonders how much after fifteen years of learning about England Naipaul really knows about the new Caribbean. He writes about independence. His thesis is striking, a genuine development. But the details used to place it in this island with a flag lack the spontaneity of the earlier novels.

The story is written around an American hero. Once, discussing his own future as a writer in 'London', Naipaul condemned the device as 'good business but bad art'. Now, however, in the character of Frank who revisits the island he once knew as a serviceman, he finds opportunities. Americans are mentioned in the earlier novels – as tourists flocking to Ganesh's temple, as the source of the materials for Mr Biswas's house – but they have not so far been dramatised. Yet the American bases are an important part of recent history, on which the film company's requirement of an American hero now permits Naipaul to pass ironic comment. He uses Frank firstly as a means of illustrating the part played by Americans in releasing the island from its 'Englishness', and secondly as a way of bringing together two kinds of rootlessness – that of the metropolitan who, like Mr Stone, cannot connect with city life, and that of the small islanders, waving from the edge of the world. But the problem remains of creating a credible American, and there is no hint in the story that Naipaul has approached this problem with anything like his usual care. We know from *The Middle Passage* that he can manage the externals. Mr Winter who accompanies him up the Kamarang river in British Guiana is summed up, adequately for a travelling companion, by his straw hat and camera, his gum-chewing, his drawling speech with its built-in anticlimaxes, his elaborate precautions against infection. But we never see Frank like this from the outside. Naipaul's meticulous eye, his greatest asset in reproducing the unfamiliar, is useless because he has chosen to see the island through Frank's spectacles. We know from *An Area of Darkness* that he has strong views on the 'new type of American', scrounging his way around the world 'exacting a personal repayment for a national generosity'. But although Mr Blackwhite tells Frank he too is just a beach-comber looking for sympathy, this is hardly enough to make him a convincing American.

What we are left with is a few conventional Americanisms (Frank sells encyclopaedias, worries about radiation, speaks a hearty dismissive slang) and the irresistible impression that the narrator is Naipaul himself in an ill-fitting disguise. Frank has the same preoccupations as the author, makes the same statements about landscapes existing in the imagination, about poverty as something to be concealed, about identity and labels. He falls into the same cadences ('the time was tremendously announced'), has the same fondness for words like disturb, exhaustion, accommodate. Arriving by sea like Naipaul in *The Middle Passage*, he shows the same jumpy irritation – it would be tedious to elaborate the point. The problem is once again that we have read so much of it before and never before with the pretence that this was not Naipaul himself speaking. The story is, of course, a film script with much of Naipaul's usual business being handed over to the director, and it is possible that this central weakness might be overcome by aggressive acting. It is fair to add that Frank's relationship with the other characters and particularly their reflection of his Americanness in their own lives is convincingly done. But reading 'A Flag on the Island' as we possess it, as a long story, it is impossible to avoid the impression that Frank is Naipaul himself, spuriously Americanised as a prop for ideas about American influences, but in reality revisiting the island he knew as a boy and recording what he describes in *The Middle Passage* as 'the fantasy' of being American 'which Trinidadians live out every day of their lives'.

Fantasy is, of course, a key word in this story which Naipaul describes on the title-page as 'a fantasy for small screen'. Yet the story is written in three parts, and the middle section describes a world which is still vividly real. The alcoholic blur of Part I, the deliberate burlesque of Part III, contrast sharply with the presentation of Frank's wartime 'occupation' on the street in Part II. Frank as a serviceman lived alongside an unemployed street philosopher, an eccentric preacher, a black writer without a style, a Chinese shopkeeper, an amiable policeman, a poet who enjoys an early morning glass of rum — we are back, of course, in Miguel Street. Henry is Hat, Priest is Man-man, Mr Lambert is Popo, Mr Blackwhite is B. Wordsworth with something of Titus Hoyt. Once, Naipaul began his career with a salute to this world of his childhood. Now, a mature novelist, he looks again. He still finds the old eccentric humour, the delight in picaroon trickery, the admiration for style. 'You got to learn tolerance', Henry tells Frank, and it might be Hat speaking. But Naipaul's assessment has changed. 'This place I tell you is nowhere. It doesn't exist', says Mr Blackwhite, assuming like the narrator of *Miguel Street* in his adult moments that the problem is simply lack of opportunities, that living at the edge of the world there is nothing to do but go mad, that even Churchill would have ended up working in a bank or the civil service. But Frank, the beach-combing American, creates opportunities. The effect of his interference is to undermine the original thesis, to destroy a way of life which in retrospect turns out to have been real after all. Frank and his fellow Americans turn the island of *Miguel Street* into this fantasy island with its mimic flag.

There is one story in *Miguel Street* which hesitates around the point. Morgan the pyrotechnist dreams of making fireworks for the King of England and the King of America. Failing that, he will settle for being a memorable eccentric — the fact that these *are* the alternatives is one key argument of the book. But Morgan is laughed at by the whole street when his massive wife, catching him in adultery, holds up his naked body, and the firework display is spectacular when he burns down his house. Hat's comment, 'When he get it he don't like it', is not quite opposite. What breaks Morgan is not so much achievement as fate's unkind parodying of his ambitions. But the words look forward to a comment of Henry's:

'Frankie, I think you trying too hard with Mano. You should watch it. You see what happen to Mrs Lambert. You know, I don't think people want to do what they say they want to do. I think we always make a lot of trouble for people by helping them to get what they say they want to get.[6]

This time the words do apply. Mano and the Lamberts are people whom Frank has tried to raise from Miguel Street 'down-couragement'. He steals a truck from the base and gives it to the Lamberts, who hire it back to the Americans at twenty dollars a day. He devotes a lot of time to training Mano, helping him overcome the urge to run which has disqualified him in previous walking races. The effects are disastrous. Mrs Lambert, the poor Corsican who was once glad enough to marry a man with a regular job, suddenly has a position to maintain. She rejects the street, rebuilds her house, and disowns her black husband who is reduced to drunkenly boasting of his Scottish ancestry. Mano wins his walking race, and kills himself. He had always really wanted to be a runner.

Frank looks at the street and offers to help. He helps Mano fulfil an ambition which turns out to have been misinterpreted. He releases in Mrs Lambert a destructive desire for respectability. So, after the double funeral, he vows not to interfere again. But when he returns, some twenty years later, he finds American help has run its course. All those private fantasies which were the product of displacement have been recklessly and expensively indulged. The result is a public fantasy. Independence with its rejection of British standards and assumptions (that the island is small and distant) has left a vacuum which can only be filled by the tourist's vision. The islander's dream of escape to a larger world has been answered by the American dream of a tropical paradise with friendly, amoral people and colourful customs. The island exists now. It is the people who are 'not real', says Frank in Henry's revamped nightclub, 'I could put my hand through them'; and he has a nightmare image of Leonard, the pied piper with a million pounds to give away, walking down the street 'followed by processions of steelbandsmen, singers and women calling for his money'.

If, as has been said, a landscape does not exist until it has been recorded by artists and a society has no meaning until it has been written about, so we felt we existed only when we were known by others. We were truly dependent. To know ourselves, to get a necessary self-esteem, we did not need writers. We required tourists: the psychology of the colonial and the small-islander came together. Writers occurred; but they became real and acquired value only after they had been acknowledged abroad and often after they had gone abroad. They sublimated the tourist complex, the desire to be known, to *exist* in the way that other countries existed; they provided the camouflage of phrases like 'the search for identity' . . . Politics had a similar sublimating effect: the intellectuals and the proletariat were at last bound by a cause.

Self-discovery went hand in hand with that other discovery, from the north, of the West Indies as that crazy resort place. We became exotic even to ourselves. The exotic was not the middleclass colonial culture of club, sport and food . . . the exotic was the local *patois*, the calypso, the steel band – lower class creations in which meaning had suddenly to be discovered. So, in independent Trinidad, English deteriorates in the law courts, in university debates; a labour movement, newly aware of its power, becomes perverse. 'Massa day done,' sums up the mood. Yet the larger dependence always remains. Is there a West Indian culture? Yes; and the tourist sees the truth.

The article in which these comments appear was written during the same visit to Trinidad in 1965 as 'A Flag on the Island'. It sums up neatly what Naipaul dramatises through the change that overtakes each of his main characters. Henry was the philosopher and

spokesman, the man who successfully managed the picaroon society. But more and more Americans come to his establishment; he
develops from a person into a character; what his nightclub offered
is relabelled 'culture'; he is put into a suit and given an M.B.E.; the
woman from Grenada catches up with him. When Frank returns,
he finds Henry miserable and impotent, surrounded by plastic
flowers, longing for the impermanence of the old days before the
Americans championed his existence. Priest was the preacher, who
abused the island in stylish English and used magic to protect the
street from Frank's influence. He was also an insurance agent. His
transformation, when a new American company offered him a
higher salary, came a little too quickly for the rest of society and
left him vulnerable to an elementary bit of picaroon trickery at
Ma-Ho's hands. But he cherished the American image of himself.
When the rest of the island was equally transformed, he was there
in the van, championing it in stylish American as Gary Priestland,
the TV personality, perfectly attuned to unreality. And Frank, on
his return, finds Selma, who once had nightmares about walking
down Regent Street dressed like an English princess – except for
her bare feet. Selma resisted a permanent home as a threat to her
independence. Now she lives in Manhattan Park, surrounded by
shrubs and a swimming pool, conforming exactly to the idea of
the tropics the Americans brought with them. She welcomes
Frank on an eiderdown, like Norma Shearer in *Escape*.

The most interesting transformation, however, is that of Mr
Blackwhite into H.J.B. White. Mr Blackwhite is far from being
an absurd character. His English accent, his stories about lords
and ladies, may seem comically irrelevant. But the pose, as he
himself explains, is an attempt to exist, to identify with the only
reality available. He is as vulnerable as Priest to recognition, and
when Frank suggests that he writes about the street Mr Blackwhite responds. He begins to talk of the island's culture, he
champions patois ('damn Jane Austen'), he organises ballets
which feature a symbolic slavery. It looks like self-discovery, a
liberation from mimicry. In fact, his new pose is a double self-
deception. Once he accepted his displacement as a starting point;
now by denying it he is doubly displaced. Once he rejected

unreality; now he champions that same unreality as his culture. The vision is not even his own – it is the Americans, looking for the exotic, who tape-record the steelbands, who dance with the happy-go-lucky natives; it is they who pretend the island exists, overriding Mr Blackwhite's earlier insistence that Frank is only beach-combing. So Mr Blackwhite becomes H.J.B. White, writing stories called *I Hate You* with the help of money from American foundations, producing versions not of the life he lives but of the myths the Americans require. When he tries to escape from their vision of his life, by offering to write about a black man loving a black woman and perhaps even ill-treating her, he is abandoned.

Escape: the word is part of all Naipaul's conclusions – escape from Miguel Street, escape from Elvira, escape from Mr Biswas's Port of Spain. But there can be no escape from this island with a flag, for the flag was a proclamation that escape was no longer necessary. To that fantasy, only the hurricane can offer a solution. With the prospect that the island will soon be destroyed, people are released from the pretence that this is their landscape. They can be real again because a denial of the island, an acceptance of its smallness and unimportance, has always been a condition of their reality. Now Henry smashes up his night-club. Priestland reverts to Priest. Selma is once again the *wabeen*. Mr Blackwhite is released from 'the strain of seeing himself' and becomes 'a private man at last'. The streets of the city fill with revellers dancing without an audience, dancing as they once danced in Henry's yard. But deliverance fails; the hurricane changes course. They are left once more with the weary problem of making the island their home, the task of possessing consciously an imported view of themselves. And there is a last cruel joke, a mocking prophecy. Leonard's million pounds never existed. For the first time in the story, Sinclair speaks – 'We have had our fun. It is time to go home.' The lavish Americans have enjoyed their beach-combing. Now the game is over and it is time to withdraw.

3

It should now be clear that the two stories spring from complementary visions. Mr Stone discovers the fraudulence of the big city, whose concrete order and theatrical modes are irrelevant to his humanity. The islanders discover the fraudulence of their attempt to link themselves to a landscape they have always denied. If Mr Biswas could read the history of Mr Stone, he would recognise as illusions his dreams of escape to a larger society; if he read 'A Flag on the Island', he might insist rather less on the virtues of independence. But there is another shadow which falls across their pages, the shadow of Naipaul's experience of India. Naipaul has acknowledged that on his return, he tried but failed to write a novel about India – the experience was 'too particular' for anything other than a first person travelogue.[8] But *Mr Stone and the Knights Companion* was written in Kashmir (in a Srinagar shop window, Naipaul sees a photograph of an English cavalry officer, his boot on a dead tiger: this becomes Margaret's former husband). 'A Flag on the Island' was written on his next trip abroad, the year after *An Area of Darkness* appeared. Both these works are attempts to take imaginative account of his visit to India. Both carry the impact of 'that journey that ought not to have been made' and which 'had torn my life in two'.

The difficulty is that even for a writer as attuned to paradox as Naipaul, India offers no point of rest, no moment of final resolution – no equivalent to Mr Biswas's house. He ridicules Indian mimicry of the fairy-tale land of the Raj, yet he hears the absurdity of his own voice every time he opens his mouth. He condemns the Indian withdrawal in the face of starvation, the 'refusal to see' squalor and hunger, yet he recognises in himself a similar detachment, an ability to separate the pleasant from the unpleasant, to sit at his desk in London congratulating himself on the honesty of his lack of commitment. Beneath his resolution to 'remain what I was', he discovers a longing to be able to accept India, to rid himself of anger and compassion and come to terrms with the 'total Indian negation'. Returning to Europe, he is overwhelmed by the 'insubstantiality and wrongness' of the Boeings and Caravelles and of the booted air-hostess at Rome airport; he is unable 'to summon up a positive response' to London, that concrete city of separate warm cells where he has lived and worked. This is clearly the mood in which, while still in India, he records Mr Stone's sudden vision:

> And just as sometimes when travelling on a train he had mentally stripped himself of train, seats and passengers and seen himself moving four or five feet above the ground in a sitting posture at forty miles an hour, so now he was assailed by a vision of the city stripped of stone and concrete and timber and metal, stripped of all buildings, with people suspended next to and above and below one another, going through all the motions of human existence.[9]

Yet Naipaul remains the outsider, the colonial. In a brilliant chapter about Gandhi, whose early years were spent in South Africa, he discusses the advantages of seeing an Indian community removed from the setting of India, so that 'contrast made for clarity, criticism and discrimination for self-analysis'. The effect of channelling his criticisms of India through Gandhi's own words is, of course, to give them enormous impact. But the statement applies equally well to himself. It is with 'the straight simple vision of the west' that he recognises, among other anomalies, the immense break with history that nationalism demanded:

> It is perhaps only now that we can see what a clean break with the past the Raj was. The British refused to be absorbed into India; they did not proclaim, like the Mogul, that if there was a paradise on earth, it was this, and it was this, and it was this. While dominating India they expressed their contempt for it, and projected England; and Indians were forced into a nationalism which in the beginning was like a mimicry of the British. To look at themselves, to measure themselves against the new, positive standards of the conqueror, Indians had to step out of themselves. It was an immense self-violation; and in the beginning, in fact, a flattering self-assessment could only be achieved with the help of Europeans like Max Muller and those

others who are quoted so profusely in nationalist writings.[10]

'It resulted in the conscious possession of spirituality', he continues; 'it resulted in the conscious possession of an ancient culture'; and later, in a phrase which sums up his whole argument, 'in the acquiring of an identity in their own land they became displaced.' This assessment is not entirely Naipaul's own. A good deal of the analysis in the 'Fantasy and Ruins' chapter is lifted (with some actual phrases) from the long, concluding essay of Nirad Chaudhuri's magnificent *Autobiography of an Unknown Indian*, which, with a curious ungraciousness, Naipaul mentions not as a source but as an example of Anglo-Indian bewilderment. But the similarities between this version of Indian nationalism and the situation of Priest and Mr Blackwhite, equally displaced by the acquiring of an identity, are obvious. For India, read the Caribbean, for the British, read Americans, and you arrive at something very close to the thesis of 'A Flag on the Island'.

A Western view of all that is most sadly ridiculous about independent India: an Indian view of all that is most fraudulent about the West. The antithesis does little justice to the complex honesty of *An Area of Darkness*. But it pinpoints the common experience behind these two fictions. The London of Mr Stone is reduced to theatre, with its actors, costumes, scenery and conventions of speech. The island has become a 'fantasy for a small screen'. Linking them both is a newly-awakened sense of the world as illusion. For there is no other way out; the contradictions are unresolved. Only in negation can there be release, and the stories end. Thus Mr Stone walks through London 'as the destroyer, as the man who carried the possibility of the earth's destruction within him'. The islanders dance in the streets of the capital, grateful for the 'benediction' of the hurricane which has restored them to themselves.

We have come a long way from *The Mystic Masseur* with its jokes about Ganesh's autobiography or with its reduction of Hinduism to prejudice and taboo. But we have moved on in other ways. This 'total Indian negation' extends to the act of writing, and both these stories, written in the shadow of India, incorporate serious doubts about the purpose of fiction. In *Mr Stone and the*

Knights Companion, there is scarcely an incident which is not used to reinforce the impression that language is an elaborate system of distortion. Mr Stone's story about the cat and the cheese, as told to Margaret at the start of their relationship, is amusing and endearing. But it takes no account of the fear and loneliness out of which it arose. His newspaper, so far from dealing with real issues, is – like the tabulated accounts of his career – an 'insulation against the world'. Conversations are conducted in a kind of code, the real meaning of statements intelligible only to the initiated. By the time Mr Stone's idea begins to be 'licked into shape', the processes of distortion reach their climax – the name suggests 'youth', the concern for old people's welfare becomes a publicity drive. It is tempting to link this with that comment of Naipaul's on his father's stories – 'They taught me to look at things that had never been written about before, and seemed dull in life, yet when transformed to paper became very surprising.'[11] The ambiguity here, between whether writing clarifies and defines, or whether it distorts and glamourises, is all the more significant in that the comment appears in an interview immediately prior to the novel's publication. Certainly, it is no accident that *Mr Stone and the Knights Companion* is the shortest of Naipaul's novels. He has claimed that he felt the need to react against *A House for Mr Biswas* and write 'a compressionist novel' in which every sentence of every paragraph would contain something important.[12] Given his current suspicions of language together with the difficulties of writing about England and the English, it is perhaps surprising he got anything down on paper at all.

In this context, we can understand why Mr Stone's diatribe against 'all action, all creation' should incorporate an attack on writing. Once again, reference to *An Area of Darkness* is helpful. Naipaul's comic portrait of himself, in the Kashmir section, as the effete Westerner with an impressive but impotent typewriter – his invitations to tea disregarded, his testimonials giggled over in the kitchen – surely throws light on this aspect of the novel. Towards the end of his stay ('My work was almost done'), he reflects on his relationship with Aziz, his illiterate servant:

Would he have gone far if he had learned to read and write?
Wasn't it his illiteracy which sharpened his perception? . . . To
us illiteracy is like a missing sense. But to the intelligent illiterate
in a simpler world mightn't literacy be an irrelevance, a dissipation of sensibility, the mercenary skill of the scribe?[13]

I do not think it fanciful to suggest that it is such doubts as this that
are written into Mr Stone's outburst, and that are responsible for
the inconsistencies we saw there. For Mr Stone's speech doesn't
quite convince. It is one thing to be suspicious of 'all action, all
creation'. It is another to sweep them away in the context of a story
in which they have been demonstrated to be humanly necessary.
What animates Mr Stone is the sense that his inspiration has been
inadequately expressed, and the knowledge that he has won success out of other people's misery makes him feel he has betrayed his
original good emotion. Naipaul perhaps shares something of this
feeling – he has, after all, won acclaim for turning his father's life
into a masterpiece. But he also projects on to Mr Stone a type of
Hinduism which, while it is supported by incidental details, is not
sustained by the plot as a whole.

It is also, as we have seen, modified by the ending. Mr Stone's
former readiness to assert himself through destruction now sub-
sides to pity and love for the kitten which greets him on the stairs.
The novel closes, in other words, not in negation but with an
appropriately muted reminder of that 'concern for the condition of
men' which Naipaul, in *An Area of Darkness*, describes as the essential, westernising ingredient of the novel. But in 'A Flag on the
Island' there are no such concessions. The doubts about language
are again part of the analysis – 'We turn experience continually
into stories to lend drama to dullness'. Frank recognises this truth
about himself when he is trying to persuade Mr Blackwhite to stop
writing about lords and ladies and to look instead at the street. But
he fails to see that Mr Blackwhite will end up doing the same,
using language not to explore and define but to dramatise his life,
building his self-respect on borrowed phrases. When Frank
returns, almost his first exclamation is, 'I need a new language', for
the slogans of independence, slogans now supported by literature

and art, are obvious fantasy. But this time there are no comforting modifications. Naipaul offers no hint that a fresh start with different words, a new expression of concern, might provide solutions. For the only other available words are 'smallness', 'unimportance', words which assume a rejection of the island and which make the hurricane welcome and necessary.

But there is an even more disturbingly negative aspect of this story, and that is Naipaul's deliberate undermining of our trust in the narrator. There is a good deal of Mr Stone in Frank. He has the same sense that his 'time is short'; he lacks the energy and courage to cope with city life; yet, like Mr Stone in Cornwall, he realises with increasing panic his dependence on the 'safe, solid earth'. The trouble is that, unlike Mr Stone, Frank is the narrator, and the effects of displacement on him are a fatigue, a dissipation of energy — a sense that 'the world is being washed away'. These are not ideal qualifications for an observer. Has the island become a fantasy or could it be, as Frank wonders, that 'the blurring of fantasy with reality which gives me the feeling of helplessness exists only in my mind'? The possibilities cancel each other out. 'I was drunk', says Frank in Part I, but he adds, infuriatingly, 'on more and on less than alcohol.' Instead of a steady advance through paradox to a house for Mr Biswas, or even to a muted gesture of concern from Mr Stone, we reach narrative stalemate. The islanders welcome destruction, the narrator embraces the 'total, empty response'. Naipaul's sense of negation has become absolute, undermining both subject and form. It is not a position from which he can advance as a novelist without a drastic reappraisal.

CHAPTER SIX

So writing, for all its initial distortion, clarifies, and even becomes a process of life.'

I

The house: in *Miguel Street*, simply a spot from which the street can be viewed, an excuse for being there; in *The Mystic Masseur*, in Ganesh's new house in Fuente Grove, the image of a compromise; in *A House for Mr Biswas*, a central unifying symbol; in *Mr Stone and the Knights Companion*, suddenly fraudulent, irrelevant to flesh and blood. Now, in *The Mimic Men*, there is a series of houses — Kripalsingh's childhood house whose collapse he anticipates daily; Browne's house, a racial prison; the boarding house in Kensington High Street, packed with immigrants and owned by an exiled Jew; the Roman house, the Beach house, the Scandinavian house in the hills, expressions of expatriate taste. None of them are homes, islands of order, centres of light and beauty and achievement. They are the temporary residences of shipwrecked people; their meanings culminate in that London hotel where the fatigued narrator seeks truth, the 'final emptiness'.

I suggested at the beginning of the previous chapter that *A House for Mr Biswas* marks the climax of one line of development. When Mr Biswas eventually moves into his heavily mortgaged house in Sikkim Street, Naipaul's early work comes to a point of resolution. Even when all the ironies have had their say, it is still better to accept the West, still desirable to declare independence for oneself and one's family, still possible to escape to more meaningful societies, still useful to explore experience through writing. But no sooner was the novel published in 1961 than its basic assumptions began to be undermined by the deep disturbance of Naipaul's travels in the West Indies, India, and in 1966, East

Africa. The two works of fiction which first express that disturbance are, as we have seen, not entirely satisfactory. In *Mr Stone and the Knights Companion*, rather too large a conclusion is forced upon rather too small a plot. In 'A Flag on the Island', the vision is blurred by the author's deep scepticism about the form he is using. But the stories do dramatise the necessity for reappraisal. Naipaul has called *A House for Mr Biswas* 'very much a south London book', and while this is partly provocation, it does pinpoint the extent to which his early achievement is geared to a single assumption. [1] If the order of London is genuine and if escape to London is easy, there is no need to take colonial problems too seriously; taking them seriously becomes, in a sense, an act of generosity – for which the author even deserves credit. But if London is an illusion and the possibility of escape just another colonial myth, what and where then?

The starting point of *The Mimic Men* is a passage which resolves precisely this difficulty:

In that period of my life which was to follow, the period between my preparation for life and my withdrawal from it, that period in parenthesis, when I was most active and might have given the observer the impression of a man fulfilling his destiny, in that period intensity of emotion was the thing I never achieved. I felt I had known a double failure, and I continued to live between their twin threats. It was during this time, as I have said, that I thought of writing. It was my hope to give expression to the restlessness, the deep disorder, which the great explorations, the overthrow in three continents of established social organisations, the unnatural bringing together of peoples who could achieve fulfilment only within the security of their own societies and the landscapes hymned by their ancestors, it was my hope to give partial expression to the restlessness which this great upheaval has brought about. The empires of our time were short-lived, but they have altered the world for ever; their passing away is their least significant feature. It was my hope to sketch a subject which, fifty years hence, a great historian might pursue. For there is no such thing as history nowadays; there are only manifestoes and antiquarian research; and on the subject of empire there is only the pamphleteering of churls. But this work will not now be written by me; I am too much a victim of that restlessness which was to have been my subject.[2]

The importance of this passage in the making of the novel as a whole can scarcely be over-emphasised. Instead of London as the centre of order, we have the world before Columbus. Whether the past was ever really like this — whether Shylock, for instance, Kripalsingh's first landlord in London, would recognise this contrast between medieval stability and post-renaissance homelessness — is hardly relevant. This version of history is a vision of security, a golden age indefinitely placed, in terms of which Naipaul can overthrow the purely colonial framework within which he worked until *A House for Mr Biswas*, and from which in succeeding books he has escaped only into negation.

When, after completing *A House for Mr Biswas*, Naipaul returned to Trinidad at the start of the seven months' tour of the West Indies which he describes in *The Middle Passage*, one of his fellow passengers was an Indian from British Guiana, summoned home after years of 'studying' in England. Naipaul calls him Kripal Singh. It is appropriate that he should use this same name for the hero of *The Mimic Men*, for in that novel he re-examines all his major themes in the light of his discoveries since 1961. Within the framework of this new antithesis, between the security of the past and the widespread disorder caused by the voyages of discovery, he reappraises the whole cycle of events in which he has been involved. Deliberately, he begins again at the beginning, focusing on that alternative to escape which has been in the reader's mind ever since *The Mystic Masseur*. He returns, to put the point another way, to that figure he once ridiculed — the figure of Indarsingh, the rootless graduate, who finds his place campaigning for independence.

He returns at the same time to one of the oldest novel forms, the fictional autobiography. Significantly, it is the form of the first novel about the Caribbean, Defoe's *Robinson Crusoe*. The shipwrecked adventurer who has to make the best of what is at hand but who can never lose the sense of being abandoned on a distant island and whose principal satisfaction is the written account of his shipwreck; this Crusoe archetype appears in *The Castaway* by Derek Walcott, published in 1965 while Naipaul was working on *The Mimic Men*:

> So from this house
> that faces nothing but the sea, his journals
>   assume a household use,
> We learn to shape from them, where nothing was,
>   the language of a race,
> and since the intellect demands its mask
>   that sun-cracked, bearded face
> provides us with the wish to dramatise
>   ourselves at nature's cost[3]

It may seem a long way from the goat-skinned Crusoe to the impeccably suited property-magnate Ralph Kripalsingh. But the underlying metaphor is the same, and – like Defoe – Naipaul lets his narrator tell his own story of shipwreck without distancing and without postulating alternatives.

Kripalsingh is a fallen politician. Like Crusoe, he has had to flee the island he once ruled. It is not difficult to see why the idea of writing Kripalsingh's memoirs should have appealed to Naipaul. The device enables him, as I have suggested, to return to the figure of Indarsingh, and to inquire whether, in the light of all he has learned since *The Mystic Masseur*, some form of commitment might not have been healthier – whether, in short, his devotion to the pose of honest pilgrim pursuing disturbing truths in romantic isolation and eschewing the 'corruption of causes' might not have been the greatest corruption of all. It enables him to bring together ideas from *Mr Stone and the Knights Companion* and from 'A Flag on the Island' as aspects of a single experience, to question both escape to London and escape into independence as solutions to colonial disorder. It allows him, under the cover of his politician narrator, to indulge his growing taste for direct exegesis – if *An Area of Darkness* is a commentary written with the insight of a novelist, *The Mimic Men* is something of a novel by a commentator, its plot anecdotal, peppered with generalising intrusions. It enables him to examine yet again the meaning and purpose of writing. Kripalsingh, whose first book this is, discovers as he proceeds that words are not necessarily dishonest, and that events which have seemed random and chaotic can be reduced to a deeply satisfying order. Lastly, the device provides Naipaul with a final solution to the problem which has pursued him ever since *Miguel Street*, that problem, in novels about displacement, of placing the narrator. In Kripalsingh we have no longer a boy confident he will soon grow up and escape, no longer an Anand referred to only obliquely as the author's younger self, but a narrator who at last acknowledges openly that he too is 'a victim of that restlessness which was to have been my subject'.

This leads us directly into the problem raised by all reviewers of the novel, namely, the relation between the author and his narrator, the extent to which Kripalsingh is a spokesman for Naipaul. Naipaul, of course, has never been a politician. He is five years younger than the book's chronology suggests Kripalsingh must be, and he knows far too much about writing to have ever assumed that the memoirs could be the work of three or four weeks. But when we move beyond such obvious fictions, clear distinctions are impossible. Naipaul's irony is both subtle and resonant, hard to reduce to simple antitheses. But it is impossible to find in this book any sustained effort to see the narrator ironically, any attempt to detach the author from Kripalsingh in a manner which suggests judgements essentially different from those Kripalsingh is making. There are occasions when one wishes one could do so. The court-ship of Browne's sister and her policeman fiancé is mocked at one point as 'ugliness coming to ugliness' – as though Kripalsingh has come to accept his cousin Sally's absurd claim about nostrils shaped like peas. But there are no grounds for concluding that Naipaul intends to mock Kripalsingh (Wendy Deschampsneufs, also coloured, is also described as ugly), or that the cruel phrase is not ultimately his own. Kripalsingh's intended inadequacies are all underlined by the narrator himself. He views his past actions with irony, but there is no hint that he is still deceiving himself – not even the acknowledgement which blurred the ending of 'A Flag on the Island' that the narrator's judgements might be invalidated by his personal crisis of displacement.

Moreover, for those who have followed Naipaul's work from the beginning, the task of distinguishing the author from his creation in all but matters of obvious fact is virtually hopeless. Even more closely than Frank in 'A Flag on the Island', Kripalsingh resembles the patrician, fastidious, hyper-sensitive spectator of the travel books, a blend of intensity and inaction, caught up in events he perfectly comprehends but lacks the energy born of conviction to control. It is not just that he expresses similar opinions – about slavery visible in the Caribbean landscape, about East Indians as intruders between master and slave, about industrialisation in ex-colonial territories, about the inevitable substitution of symbolic for real action. He has the same tastes – Lorraine, the American girl to whom Naipaul is attracted during his pilgrimage to the Cave of Amarnath, clearly foreshadows Sandra, with a similar leanness disguising pendant breasts and that quality of graining in her skin. He has the same obsessions – 'wife', he says, 'is a terrible word', and for the whole of *An Area of Darkness*, although Naipaul was accompanied around India by his wife, he never refers to her except once as 'my companion'. He analyses his disillusionment with London in exactly parallel sentences:

> I came to London. It had become the centre of my world and I had worked hard to come to it. And I was lost. London was not the centre of my world. I had been misled; but there was nowhere else to go. It was a good place for getting lost in, a city no one ever knew, a city explored from the neutral heart outwards until, after years, it defined itself into a jumble of clearings separated by stretches of the unknown, through which the narrowest of paths had been cut. Here I became no more than an inhabitant of a big city, robbed of loyalties, time passing, taking me away from what I was, thrown more and more into myself, fighting to keep my balance and to keep alive the thought of the clear world beyond the brick and asphalt and the chaos of railway lines. All mythical lands faded, and in the big city I was confined to a smaller world than I had ever known.[4]

Is this Naipaul speaking or Kripalsingh? In fact, the paragraph is from *An Area of Darkness*, but it would take a thorough knowledge of both books to be sure. We can meet Kripalsingh, too, outside the travel books, in articles written before and during the novel's composition. 'What's Wrong with Being a Snob?', asks Naipaul in the *Saturday Evening Post*,[5] anticipating not only Kripalsingh's bewilderment at the apparent triumph of working class values in Britain, but his very accents – those long, stylish sentences, with several meanings held in tension, paradoxes contained between balancing semi-colons, the whole welded together by the assurance of its rhythm: and as early as 1961, Naipaul confesses in *The Times*[6] to a passion for Roman history.

Given such evidence of a close identification between Naipaul and his narrator, negative in the sense that none of the book's ironies are directed at Kripalsingh the writer, positive in the sense that many of his characteristics are visibly the author's, it is scarcely surprising that in Part Two of *The Mimic Men* Naipaul draws once again on memories of his childhood. Kripalsingh attends Isabella Imperial, but there are occasions when one feels one is back with Anand in Queens Royal College in Port of Spain. The emphasis is different – on the growth of political consciousness rather than on the absurdities of individual lessons – but the intensity and warmth of the writing, markedly different from that in Parts One and Three, reminds one vividly of *A House for Mr. Biswas*. If it is hard to imagine Mr Biswas as Gurudeva, leading the strikers and the unemployed into voluntary exile, it is perhaps not entirely irrelevant that Naipaul's father did draw attention to himself, when Naipaul was in Form 3B, by publishing *Gurudeva and Other Indian Tales*. Several of Naipaul's former classmates have told me that they can identify Kripalsingh's teachers without much strain, and certainly from the obituary which appears in the Q.R.C. *Chronicle* for 1949 it is not difficult to guess that Captain Achilles Daunt, who joined the school in 1920 and who taught Naipaul Latin and English from 1945 to 1947, must be the original of Major Grant (the obituary records, endearingly, that during Captain Daunt's final illness, the prefects wrote to him in England, 'Keep on fighting, Sir. We need you.'). Naipaul's own name is recorded in the Q.R.C. register as

'Naipaul, Vidiadhar Suraj Persad' – he too, like R.R.K. Singh, having revived an ancient fracture to give himself a more impressive set of initials. Time and time again, in fact, with this section of *The Mimic Men* as with *A House for Mr Biswas*, the details tally with what other records are available. The Q.R.C. *Chronicle* for 1944 confirms the introduction of a house system into the school. The cinema pages of the *Trinidad Guardian* for August 1943 advertise Tyrone Power and Maureen O'Hara in *The Black Swan* – its vision of the pirate island contrasting absolutely with the themes of Seepersad Naipaul's stories, published the same month. One year later the same paper carries a report on the heroic but fatal attempt of Rennie Legendre, aged twenty-two, to save his sisters, Gloria aged eighteen and Joan aged twelve, from drowning – 'Rennie, sitting on the beach when he saw the girls in danger, died a hero's death in a vain but courageous attempt to wrest his sisters from the angry billows . . . Mrs Govia exhorted some men nearby to do something to rescue her sisters.[7] The tragedy occurred at Mayaro on the south-west coast where, as Kripalsingh says, the beach stretches for more than twenty miles.

The crucial point about this merging of identity between Naipaul and Kripalsingh is that it is obviously intentional. Naipaul is perfectly capable of detaching himself from a narrator when necessary. In the case of Frank in 'A Flag on the Island', his failure to do so convincingly was, I suggested, the result of a certain confusion of purpose. The film company commissioning the story required much sex, much dialogue, and an American as the leading character. Naipaul seized the opportunity to dramatise the triumph, throughout the independent Caribbean, of those American fantasies about friendly, amoral, happy-go-musical islanders which presumably lay behind the commissioning of such a script. But at the same time, he was revisiting and reassessing the people he once described in *Miguel Street*, and he projects on to Frank so many of his own attitudes and tricks of style that it becomes impossible for us to believe in the American's separate identity. But to suggest that Naipaul's irony has failed to cope with Kripalsingh is patently absurd. From *The Mystic Masseur* onwards, with its snatches of Ganesh's autobiography, Naipaul has always enjoyed demolishing his characters' claims about themselves.

One short story, 'A Christmas Story' from *A Flag on the Island*, is especially instructive in this connection. It describes the career of Randolph, formerly Choonilal, a Presbyterian convert who, having at eighteen chosen Christianity for its promise of a higher standard of living ('to me the superficial has always symbolised the profound'), finds himself left far behind by his Hindu businessmen relatives. He consoles himself by taking pride in his threadbare jacket and his plain wooden house, symbols of the 'sacrifice' he has made for his faith. Then, after a lifetime as teacher and headmaster in Presbyterian schools, he is given the responsibility of supervising the construction of a new school. It is the climax of his career, the final concrete expression of the decision he made at eighteen. But the building is a disgrace, a cheap gim-crack construction, the result of a corrupted vision undermined (it is implied) by his own embezzlement of the funds:

> I felt myself caught in a curious inefficiency that seemed entirely beyond my control, something malignant, powered by forces hostile to myself. Until at length it seemed that failure was staring me in the face, and that my entire career would be forgotten in this crowning failure. The building went up, it is true. It had a respectable appearance. It looked like a building. But it was far from what I had visualised. I had miscalculated badly, and it was too late to remedy the errors.[8]

He is rescued when his wife (chosen for qualities that 'wear well') and his son (free from any symptom of Hindu 'backwardness') set fire to the school three days before it is due to be inspected by the ministry. Randolph is, in a sense, a Presbyterian Ganesh, an opportunist who has the knack of convincing himself that every act, however dishonest, every triumph and set-back, confirms his special piety. In a sense, too, he provides a fascinatingly sinister contrast to Mr Biswas who also ends his life with a building which is the image of his panicky career – like *Mr Stone and the Knights Companion*, also begun in reaction to *A House for Mr Biswas*, the story was written in 1962.

The particular comparison I wish to make, however, is with *The

Mimic Men, for 'A Christmas Story' is another first person narrative, an attempt at exorcism through frankness. In something of Kripalsingh's style, though with strong evangelical overtones, Randolph describes how he seems to have been caught in a web of ironies. Yet there is never any doubt about Naipaul's detachment, never the slightest difficulty in seeing through Randolph's account to what is really happening:

> How agreeable, for instance, to rise early on a Sunday morning, to bathe and breakfast and then, in the most spotless of garments, to walk along the still quiet and cool roads to our place of worship, and there to see the most respectable and respected, all dressed with a similar purity, addressing themselves to the devotions in which I myself could participate, after for long being an outsider, someone to whom the words *Christ* and *Father* meant no more than *winter* or *autumn* or *daffodil* . . . On these Sundays of which I speak the men wore trousers and jackets of white drill, quite unlike the leg-revealing dhoti which it still pleases those others to wear, a garment which I have always felt makes the wearer ridiculous. I even sported a white solar topee. The girls and ladies wore the short frocks which the others held in abhorrence; they wore hats; in every respect, I am pleased to say, they resembled their sisters who had come all the way from Canada and other countries to work among our people.[9]

The irrelevance of the new religion (*Christ* and *Father* belong with *winter* and *daffodil*), the sheer absurdity of such mimicry (the new religion conceals men's legs but reveals women's), is beautifully established here.

As the story proceeds, the irony bites deeper. At a relative's wedding, Randolph is contemptuous of the groom's Hindu regalia, concealing 'the truck driver that he was', and of the bride's beauty, which is only 'skin deep' – though missionary dress seemed to him earlier to symbolise the profound. He complains bitterly of the 'outward shows of respectability and efficiency and piety' by which his rivals try to cheat him of promotion to headmaster; yet in the next paragraph he speaks of his on 'renewed dedication', the prayer meetings and Sunday school classes which led to 'my later elevation'. As headmaster, he administers ritual floggings for 'the backward' on Friday afternoons – the sadism involved in his contempt for his background is a convincing touch. Finally, after he has married the daughter of a schools' inspector and has gained through the connection the managership of three schools, the maximum number permitted, he relinquishes responsibility for the most derelict to dispel rumours that he is pocketing funds intended for renovation. The action, taken on his father-in-law's advice, proves 'to have its own reward'. For he is given charge of the construction of a new school – the one which eventually has to be burned to conceal evidence of his dishonesty. Sympathy for Randolph is not entirely forfeited. He is a man whose life has been corrupted by fantasy, and there are moments when, like Ganesh, he is almost tragic – when he all but envies Kedar for his marriage to a genuinely beautiful girl, or when after his retirement he takes pleasure in still being addressed as 'headmaster' by villagers whose backwardness he momentarily forgets. But there is never the slightest doubt about Naipaul's intentions. At every stage of the story, evidence is provided which undermines Randolph's version of events. As the gap widens between his pious phrases and the actions they gloss over, the irony becomes as sharp as anywhere in Naipaul's work.

Naipaul, then, is perfectly capable of demolishing his narrator's pretensions should that suit his purpose. But this kind of distancing follows judgement, and the question which arises with Kripalsingh is what such distancing would necessarily imply. *A House for Mr Biswas* concludes with Anand in Britain and with Mr Biswas in his own house. It was in the possibility of such solutions that the ironies of the whole novel finally made sense. Despite all that was said about colonial disorder, it remained possible to lay claim to one's portion of the earth or to escape to a place where things were different. The ironies pointed, in other words, to the availability of alternatives.

But by reference to what alternatives could Naipaul detach himself from Kripalsingh? If Mr Biswas is shipwrecked on a single island, Kripalsingh carries shipwreck within him. If *A House for Mr Biswas* is 'very much a south London book' in the sense that it looks back from the security of escape, *The Mimic Men* places right at the centre of Kripalsingh's experience the knowledge that London has failed him and that visions of order can only be visions of the past. The very form of the novel emphasises this point. 'I tried to write *The Mimic Men* three times', Naipaul told Francis Wyndham at the time he received the W.H. Smith award for the novel; 'Then I realised it needed a physical centre – and this would be the place where the man was writing his memoirs.'[10] The words echo Kripalsingh's:

> And this became my aim: from the central fact of this setting, my presence in this city which I have known as student, politician and now as refugee-immigrant, to impose order on my own history, to abolish that disturbance which is what a narrative in sequence might have led me to.[11]

It is the colonial myth that London is the centre of the world that first defines his sense of shipwreck on the island. It is the shrinking of London to a two-dimensional city of separate cells that drives him back to the island to attempt a new possession. It is the fraudulence of the emotions behind that attempt which makes exile inevitable. Instead of a London which offers an escape from colonial disorder, we have a London which underlines that disorder more acutely than ever before. What can Naipaul do but identify with a narrator who makes such discoveries? In. *The Mimic Men*, he has constructed a fiction which presents more fully than his own story could have done the finality of his displacement. All his former conclusions are reappraised on a canvas of imperial dimensions. But like Defoe, Naipaul lets his narrator tell his own story of shipwreck, without distancing and without postulating alternatives. There can be none, for the only satisfaction that remains is that of compiling the record.

2

Naipaul has, of course, little choice but to invent his own island. These are political memoirs, and quite apart from the possibility of libel (even in *The Suffrage of Elvira* he invents both the constituency and the county to which it belongs), there is the question of verisimilitude. Trinidad's politics are no longer anonymous, and to insert the figure of Kripalsingh into a familiar situation would be intolerably clumsy. Having invented Isabella, however, he is not content simply to tamper with Trinidad – to resurrect Queens Royal College as Isabella Imperial, to turn the Northern range into the Eastern hills, to shift the Carnegie library from San Fernando to Isabella's unnamed capital. He goes to a great deal of trouble amalgamating fact and fiction to supply Isabella with a convincing past and present. The references to Churchill, the anecdote about Stendhal, the mention of Governor Clifford, former Governor of Trinidad and Conrad's correspondent, all support the illusion that Isabella is a real place. J.A. Froude, the historian, is brought in because it was he who recommended, in his account of a tour of the West Indies, the importation of more Indians to work on the sugar estates. From his book *The English in the West Indies*, Naipaul borrows the sub-title *The Bow of Ulysses* and supplies a visit to Isabella by combining two separate incidents – one occurring in Dominica where Froude was annoyed by an uncomfortable climb to an extinct volcano, the other in Trinidad at the Blue Basin waterfall where he rudely demanded the departure of a villager who was bathing there before him.[12] Naipaul also appropriates some paragraphs from *John Morton of Trinidad* by Sarah E. Morton, the official biography of the pioneer missionary to Trinidad East Indians. The paragraphs, which he adapts to provide a background for Kripalsingh's father, are sufficiently extra-ordinary to be worth quoting in full:

> Benjamin Balaram was one of two high-caste Brahmins taught and baptised by Mr Morton in Iere Village days. He was located as a teacher in Couva and further trained there under Mr Christie. We have never forgotten a saying of Rev. George Christie in reference to Balaram, who was accustomed to wear the native dress, his turban having streamers and all in spotless white. Mr Christie caught sight of him in the distance, riding on an ass to his Sabbath work. The ass was hidden by the tall sugar canes lining either side of the narrow road; he saw only the rider with his shining drapery lighted up by the morning sun. 'To

me,' said Mr Christie, 'it was a striking reminder of the 6th verse in the 14th chapter of *Revelations*, 'I saw an angel flying in the midst of heaven, having the everlasting Gospel to preach unto them that dwell on the earth.'

Chancing to read in a copy of the *Presbyterian Record* that Rev. Mr Douglas had been sent as a missionary to Indore, his native place, where his young wife was living as a widow in his father's house, Balaram's heart yearned for home. He was Mr Christie's right hand man, but Mr Douglas had promised to employ him as a catechist and Balaram felt an over-powering desire to work for Christ in his native city of Indore. When he arrived at Indore after ten years' absence, a professing Christian, Balaram's relatives refused to receive him unless he would meet them in their idol's temple. This he refused to do and demanded his wife. She was not yet treated as a widow because twelve years had not elapsed since he left her. After two months he succeeded in getting her away from her father's house but not till she had been dispossessed of her jewels and clothing.

For eight years Balaram preached the Gospel faithfully at Indore and was then entrusted with the opening up of Neemuch as a new station. Writing in 'Harvests in Many Lands', Rev. W.A. Wilson D.D., of Indore, Central India, says, 'Balaram was most in his element in village or bazaar preaching . . . How often when the inexperienced missionary was struggling with a wily disputant and making poor work of it, Balaram would say, 'Let me speak', and, like an old warhorse rejoicing in the battle, would press to the front and silence the antagonist, when he would seize the opportunity, in a rush of burning words, to proclaim the terrors of the law, or to plead with his hearers to receive the Gospel of grace . . . Benjamin Balaram is one of God's gifts to the Indian church in Malwa.[13]

On occasions, Naipaul wanders even further afield. Unlike Trinidad, Isabella has apparently no American bases – there is no substitute for Frank in this novel, no linking of independence with Americanisation. Like Guyana, however, Isabella does have bauxite deposits, which an American company is mining. Perhaps, too,

Naipaul has imported from Guyana the Indian-Negro coalition which collapses in racial disorder – Cheddi Jagan's autobiography *The West on Trial* was published in 1966. On the other hand, the fancy-dress party after which several Europeans are deported for dressing up as African chiefs, is based on an incident which occurred in Kampala, Uganda, on 11 December 1963, when on the night of Kenya's independence celebrations a group of ex-patriates held such a party with similar consequences to celebrate the lifting of 'the white man's burden'.[14] These apparently trivial details are worth attention because they point to a more positive reason for the novel's fictional setting. Naipaul has made little attempt to link Isabella to Caribbean politics generally. Independence for Jamaica and Trinidad was a face-saving consequence of the break-up of the West Indian Federation in 1961, but there is no mention of Federation in *The Mimic Men*. Instead, it is suggested frequently that Isabella is a representative country, not just Trinidad disguised as a legal safeguard or a fictional necessity, but a typical ex-colony whose history is, in a larger sense than Ganesh's, the 'history of our times'. In his account of independence, Kripalsingh generalises continuously about 'territories like ours' where the pattern of dependence to disorder has been repeated with no significant variation:

> It has happened in twenty places, twenty countries, islands, colonies, territories – these words with which we play, thinking they are interchangeable and that the use of a particular one alters the truth. I cannot see our predicament as unique. The newspapers even today spell out situations which, changing faces and landscapes, I can think myself into.[15]

During his final exile in London he keeps coming across the similarly exiled leaders of other colonial revolutions.

In other words, just as Naipaul finds in the fictional autobiography a new solution to the old problem of placing the narrator, so in this fictional setting he finds a new escape from the limitations of being just a regional writer. It is not, however, in the narrow political sense that Isabella is a typical ex-colony. We learn, in fact, very little about the practical issues with which

Browne's government has to deal. We are never told how big a majority he has won, whether a two-party system is set up with an established opposition, whether it ever becomes necessary to imprison political opponents. The renegotiated bauxite contract is presented as Kripalsingh's most solid achievement, but we learn none of the details and we are not shown how it was managed – Kripalsingh merely says that, on advice from Jamaica, the barbecue lunches ceased and were replaced by press photographs of stern delegates in the conference room. When the sugar crisis finally erupts, he does not give us facts and figures to explain why nationalisation is impossible or why, at least, the government cannot take a controlling interest in the companies concerned – why, in short, press photographs in the conference room could not do the trick on this issue as well. Several reviewers of *The Mimic Men* grumbled about this, arguing that Naipaul's imprecision about the substance of power makes it impossible for us to see Kripalsingh as anything other than a special case. Karl Miller, for instance, diagnoses as the novel's central flaw the fact that 'the political material is scanted in favour of excellent studies of childhood and adolescence, and of a tender attention to the narrator's complaining, hyper-sensitive persona.'[16] But such criticisms assume that Isabella has a coherent political life of its own, something distinct from the personal neuroses of its inhabitants, an establishment which survives temporary clashes of personality. Naipaul's whole point is that this kind of comment is meaningless in such territories where there is no ordered middle class independent of the ruling party, and where politics becomes a reckless do-or-die charge. True, Kripalsingh begins by promising that in his memoirs 'the politician, chapman in causes, will be suppressed as far as possible', and he sees the real politician as distinct from himself, a professional taking seriously what to him was 'little more than a game'. But by the beginning of Part Three, when he has completed his study of childhood and adolescence, his conception has altered:

For I find I have indeed been describing the youth and early manhood of a leader of some sort, a politician, or at least a disturber. I have established his isolation, his complex hurt and particular frenzy.[17]

Turning to what was achieved by independence, he dismisses 'politics' as a sustained delusion, a set of imported slogans by means of which the new leaders conceal from themselves the disorder they have created:

> What did we talk about? We were, of course, of the left. We were socialist. We stood for the dignity of the working man. We stood for the dignity of distress. We stood for the dignity of our island, the dignity of our indignity. Borrowed phrases! Left-wing, right-wing: did it matter? Did we believe in the abolition of private property? Was it relevant to the violation which was our subject? We spoke as honest men. But we used borrowed phrases which were part of the escape from thought, from that reality we wanted people to see but could ourselves now scarcely face.[18]

Thus, for Kripalsingh writing in London and determined at last to confront that reality, the facts and figures about sugar hardly matter. To present them would be to continue in that former escape from thought. What matters, he now insists, is that 'we were in the midst of a racial disturbance, but we spoke of it as nationlisation'.

This argument can obviously be carried much too far. Kripalsingh writes at times as though, given the underlying disorder, it makes no difference what policies are adopted. He even speaks of a longing to undo independence, understandable as an expression of insecurity, but blurring the novel's wider relevance when he describes the old Isabella as a 'benevolently administered independency' or when he reduces anti-colonial agitation to 'that bitterness which every untalented clerk secretes'. Colonial tyrannies have existed, and do exist, and their overthrow is not automatically absurd. Naipaul convinced us in *A House for Mr Biswas* that however rickety, however mortgaged Mr Biswas's house is, to have died among the Tulsis would have been terrible. He does not convince us now that the terrors of independence in any way invalidate the revolution. Moreover, it cannot be irrelevant in the long run whether Isabella goes the way of Jamaica or of Cuba, whether money is spent on peasant farming or on industrial projects, whether Browne presides over a dictatorship or an elected government. Despite Kripalsingh's despair, it remains possible for the new leaders to govern well or govern badly. Race riots, for instance, on an island the size of Isabella, are the ultimate catastrophe, and if – as Kripalsingh acknowledges – he bears a heavy responsibility for them, it is reasonable to assume that better leadership might have avoided them altogether.

Nevertheless, given the obvious dangers of over-simplification, Naipaul is surely justified in isolating as the most important – and most representative – factor in Isabella's politics that widespread sense of displacement, that universal feeling of personal shipwreck, which saps energy and corrupts loyalties, producing in the end only an irresponsible desire for melodrama. For despite Naipaul's tender attention to the narrator's hypersensitive persona, Kripalsingh is not the only character to feel abandoned, to yearn for foreign cities and mythical landscapes. There is Cecil, for instance, the apparently enviable heir to the Bella Bella fortune, stamping his name in enormous letters on the sand of a deserted beach. Like Bogart of *Miguel Street*, Cecil lives in the world of the bad movie, his island the setting for feats of self-consuming recklessness. There is Hok, the attractive coloured boy of vaguely Chinese ancestry. When Kripalsingh is reading those tomes about Aryan migrations, he surprises Hok in the Carnegie library going through the Chinese section. But Hok weeps when his classmates see his black mother in the city streets – such a mother is a betrayal of 'that private hemisphere of fantasy where lay his true life'. There is Eden, the blackest boy in the whole school, daily reminded in brutal jokes of his peasant background and slave ancestry. Eden's deepest wish is 'for the Negro race to be abolished'; his 'intermediary wish' to rule as solitary Negro in a remote land – preferably the landscape of *Lord Jim*. There is Browne, the comedian, the singer of coon songs, who grows up to discover why society has accepted him in this role. It is Browne who teaches Kripalsingh that the island's beauties are man-made and degrading – fruit trees in the

city mark a former slave provision ground. He finds a grim satisfaction in the exploration of the past, but can make no pattern from
the facts beyond a statement of distress. Ultimately, he choses the
company of other races, among whom his distress is at least distinc-
tive.

More important of all, there is Gurudeva, Kripalsingh's father,
whose name has passed into island myth. It is this name that
Browne persuades Kripalsingh to acknowledge as the opening
shot of their campaign. To proclaim oneself Gurudeva's successor
is to become the new champion of the poor. It is to rewrite the
island's history, overthrowing Imperial ideas about backwardness
and paternal care, and defining a new pattern of exploitation and
heroic protest. It is to imply that revolts like Gurudeva's – and the
lives of all who identify with him – only make sense in the light of
the present, broader struggle for complete independence. The
movement is established immediately as a portent, beyond criticism and beyond rivalry.

Yet, looking back from exile, Kripalsingh sees a different pattern. His last memory of his father, before the exodus to the forest,
is of that cycle ride in the rain when, balancing on the crossbar, he
shared every skid and wobble of the precarious and illegal journey.
This merging of their identities as they negotiate a slippery surface
is prophetic. Gurudeva's followers are the hungry strikers and the
unemployed. Yet he can achieve nothing for them; he offers them
no food, no jobs. His appeal is positive only in that he brings
drama to an island 'starved of large events'. Country villages and
city slums are glamourised by press pictures of armed policemen
and reports of fires. But to Kripalsingh writing in London,
Gurudeva's revolt is in the end no more than 'a statement of
despair, without a philosophy or a cause'. He sees this clearly because his own movement is similarly built on drama, on name-
giving and symbolic action, attracting the support of the bitter
and the distressed, but unable to alter the island's size or its inevitable dependence. Gurudeva is rescued by two things: by the im-
possibility of his ever seizing power, so that his essential
negativeness is never exposed, and by the war which, turning attention elsewhere, allows his revolt to become historically

defined, the crystallisation of a mood at a particular time. But for Kripalsingh and Browne, there can be no such rescue. No one calls their bluff. Their creation, with its hectic mimicry, has to be followed through to its climax of chaos.

Equally important, however, is the way Naipaul uses this parallel between the 1930s and the 1960s to underline his point about the origin of political feeling in a place like Isabella. Gurudeva's movement not only begins as a purely individual protest; it continues, even at its strongest, to be dominated by his personal feeling of shipwreck. This key word, which Kripalsingh uses repeatedly of himself, is earliest applied to his father. After reading the account of his father in *The Missionary Martyr of Isabella*, Kripalsingh 'used to get the feeling that my father had in some storybook way been shipwrecked on the island'. Whatever talents were stirred by his mission education have long since fallen into disuse. Compared to that romance which the missionary lady saw in him, his subsequent life has been a slow humiliation. What underlies his rebellion is precisely this inability to connect his past with his present. His first political lesson comes when he breaks up four cases of coca cola bottles. The incident is a paradigm of what his rebellion is to be – an act of drama, purely destructive and fulfilling an entirely personal need, yet winning him widespread support because he has succeeded in making the rich look ridiculous. Its immediate cause is the quarrel over the cricket bat, which he interprets as his son's rejection of him for his wife's – the coca-cola bottler's – family. The issues involved here are clarified by the events which precede the rebellion. Gurudeva, as he is about to become, reinstates Sunday lunch as a family occasion. Like Mr Biswas, he is trying to create an island of loyalties in his own house. More important, he is trying to resurrect from his Christian past what he was taught about the family as 'the unit which is at the basis of all civilisation and culture'. But the children giggle. He takes his family on an excursion into the hills, and talks of those voyages from distant continents which make up Isabella's history. Still, the children resist his mood and he deliberately crashes the car. Two pages later, the rebellion begins. Finding himself among the striking dockworkers, he makes an impromptu speech and wins their support. But not with a party programme:

> He broke and told his own story. He told of his early life, of the
> missionary and his lady and the aboriginal young man in a clear-
> ing in the forest. He told of the years of darkness that followed
> his abandonment. He told of his marriage and his service with
> the government. He had never spoken of these things before; he
> held his audience. He told these men as despairing as himself of
> his decision, perhaps made even as he was speaking, to turn his
> back on this darkness.[19]

Having assumed leadership, he remains completely private. He
adopts not his Christian teachings, not a nationalist ideology, but
the robes of a Hindu mendicant. The climax of his rebellion is an
utterly personal statement, the ancient Aryan sacrifice of *Asva-
medha* — and in all the island, where it is assumed that the killing is
an attack on the *Cercle Sportif*, only Kripalsingh understands the
truth.

Naipaul, then, places at the centre of this political novel something which even Kripalsingh understands fully only as his
memoirs take shape — namely, that the basic fact of political life in
colonies like Isabella is that widespread sense of personal irrelevance, that longing to escape to more important places, which
defines itself in childhood and which experience never completely
eradicates. New leaders may play on it bitterly to achieve power
themselves, but it remains their most fundamental problem, undermining energy, sapping the will to build and to defend, ultimately
demanding fresh satisfaction in further upheavals. In the whole
novel, in fact, there is only one family which feels it has a stake in
Isabella. Shortly before he leaves for the School in London, Kripalsingh visits the Deschampsneufs family. He is offered a vision of
the island which contrasts absolutely with everything he has met
before:

> 'You know, you are born in a place and you grow up there. You
> get to know the trees and the plants. You will never know any
> other trees and plants like that. You grow up watching a guava
> tree, say. You know that browny-green bark peeling like old

paint. You try to climb that tree. You know that after you climb it a few times the bark gets smooth-smooth and so slippery you can't get a grip on it. You get that ticklish feeling in your foot. Nobody has to teach you what the guava is. You go away. You ask, 'What is that tree?' Somebody will tell you, 'An elm'. You see another tree. Somebody will tell you, 'That is an oak'. Good; you know them. But it isn't the same. Here you wait for the poui to flower one week in the year, and you don't even know you are waiting. All right, you go away. But you will come back. Where you born, man, you born. And this island is a paradise, you will discover.[20]

The appeal is powerful, its poetry genuine. By this stage of the novel, the island's beauty has been convincingly established – in the wonderful descriptions of the cocoa valleys with their endless varieties of purple and gold, the flooded grottoes, the cool estate house; or in the account of that long day at the beach, the scene of the drownings, evoked with an abundance of photographic details, but capturing too the feel of the place, the effects of light and temperature at different times during the day, leading up to the moment when Kripalsingh is 'alone on the beach, smooth and shining in the dying light'. Deschampsneufs reinforces the appeal of this vision with the story of Stendhal and his ancestor, a story which reduces the outside world to ordinariness, and mocks the idea that real life goes on elsewhere in places essentially different to Isabella. Against his will, Kripalsingh is impressed. Yet when he gets up to leave, old Deschampsneufs refuses to shake hands with him, unwilling to share such a simple courtesy with an Indian. Even the Deschampsneufs family, apparently rooted, apparently content, is part of the total pattern. They are the makers of the man-made slave island. Paradise for them is still shipwreck for others; paradise is a battlefield.

3

After the failure of Kripalsingh's mission to London on the nationalisation issue, his political career is finished. Reluctant to return to Isabella, he breaks his journey with a stopover, to which a complete chapter is devoted. Sixteen hours are passed in an unidentified city, part of them with an unnamed woman:

> Judgement disappeared, I was all painful sensation. Flesh, flesh: but my awareness of it was being weakened. I was turned over on my belly. The probing continued, with the same instruments. The self dropped away, layer by layer; what remained dwindled to a cell of perception, indifferent to pleasure or pain; neutral perception, finer and finer, having validity, existing only because of that probing which, growing fainter, yet had to be apprehended, because it was the only proof of life: fine perception reacting minutely only to time, which was also the universe. It was a moment that was extended and extended and extended. There could be no issue; it was a moment which, when release without fruition came and perception widened again, defined itself as an extended moment of horror. It is a moment that has remained with me. After three years I can call it back at will: that moment of timelessness, horror, solace.[21]

It is an image of total placelessness, man reduced to anonymous flesh, concerned only to keep his body intact, man purchasing physical pleasure as the only proof of his existence at isolated moments in an unknown place. The scene is the climax of those intense moments of desolation which have stood out in earlier chapters of the novel. After watching three young people drown, Kripalsingh walks alone on the empty beach, overwhelmed by a feeling of 'abandonment at the edge of the empty world'. He is saved from despair by the prospect of escape, the conviction that leadership and fulfilment await him elsewhere. He comes to London, the centre of the world as he has known it. He is enchanted by snow; he conjures with the famous street names; he studies with a painter's eye the marvel of light in a temperate zone, the soft shadows revealing colour everywhere, the slow gradations of twilight. Yet he is lost, reduced to caricature, an immigrant living with other immigrants in rooms rented from an exiled Jew. Not even the city's magic can disguise the forlornness of the christening ceremony, the swiftness of a London death, or prevent that surrender of himself to one anonymous woman after another. He is saved from suicide by his trust in Sandra. Relying on her forthrightness, her gift for words and sense of occasion, her seeming ability to control situations, he returns to Isabella. Slowly, he comes to realise that she too is lost, that despite her apparent confidence she has been relying on him to save her from nonentity in England. The house-warming party is a disaster, underlining the fraudulence of their marriage. As Kripalsingh drives off angrily into the night, Naipaul again employs that powerful and evocative image of 'children outside a hut at sunset, the fields growing dark' to picture Kripalsingh's despair at 'the lack of sympathy between man and the earth he walks on'. Yet again, there is an alternative to save him. The Roman house becomes the fitting centre of the campaign for independence.

Now, on the stopover, with every escape route closed and every commitment turned sour on him, he faces his homelessness as never before. He tries to keep moving. He returns to Isabella and unintentionally provokes a racial war. He flies back to England and spends eleven days at different hotels. But the timelessness and horror of that stopover remain with him, supplemented in intensity by one final image of homelessness on a holiday afternoon at a country station:

> A man sitting at the limit of desolation with sixty-six pounds of luggage in two Antler suitcases, concentrating on the moment, which he mustn't relate to anything else.[22]

Mr Biswas in the storm at Green Vale, Mr Stone on the moors in Cornwall, experience similar moments of terror when the physical world is suspended and there seems nothing to halt their descent into the void. For Mr Biswas, the moment becomes a measure of his later recovery, a redefinition of his need for a house. For Mr Stone, it is the spur to creation, an experience 'of nothingness' whose direct consequence is his Knights Companion scheme. From Mr Biswas's search for a house through Mr Stone's idea of the Unit, the line is direct to Kripalsingh's writing his memoirs. For Kripalsingh's discovery of himself as a writer marks his personal salvation. In the act of writing, he finds at long last that order and coherence which have eluded him in every other activity.

Kripalsingh has long intended to write a book. Few pages of *The Mimic Men* are more appealing than his description of the estate house where, the revered elder statesman, he will give expression to 'the deep disorder of our times' in a work illuminated throughout by his personal experience of power. But the dream is of something to occupy his retirement, a substitute for more compelling activity, and the setting evokes a way of life his politics has abolished. Before he can begin his present work, he has to come to terms with a new subject and a new setting. The subject is not Empire, but his own brief career; the setting, a London hotel, the image of his homelessness. But even when these changes have been absorbed, he remains singularly ill-equipped for his task. He sits down at his desk expecting his book to be the work of 'three or four weeks'. He has still to discover that the fluency which once permitted him to write five thousand words in an evening was the product of a deep dishonesty. He begins to learn what Mr Stone and Frank knew, that words distort and deceive and that their glamour must be resisted. This discovery becomes a running theme, an antidote to further self-deception – he remembers how seductive was the thought of Mr Shylock's 'mistress', how he was led astray by the 'magic' of London's street names, how unreliable and destructive was Sandra's 'gift of the phrase', how 'rooted in contempt' were those wildly successful political speeches in which it didn't matter what was said.

But he discovers more than the capacity of language to cheat him. He finds, what he expected even less, that his opinions alter as he writes. He finds that patterns of which he was never even dimly aware begin to assert themselves. We have noticed already how he begins by insisting 'I was never a politician', but comes to realise, by the beginning of Part Three, he has after all been describing the development of 'a leader of sorts'. He begins with the feeling that his character has all along been moulded by the vision of others, that his marriage and his political career were 'accidents' following his acquiescence in roles provided for him. But a later view is that the 'personality hangs together'. He learns to share the blame between himself and his society, and to accept that though his actions have often been dishonest they have never been entirely arbitrary. He begins with a strong sense that his active life is over, and that he has half a lifetime of retirement before him. By the closing pages he has come to see that his present residence in London has been the most fruitful of all. He wonders how he could ever have believed that writers were 'incomplete' people, engaged in an activity which, however enjoyable, was only 'a substitute for what it then pleased me to call life'. He sees now that, paradoxically, his marriage and his political career were the real acts of withdrawal, and that his memoirs have at last released him from the barren attempt to combat his homelessness. He concludes that writing 'for all its initial distortion, clarifies, and even becomes a process of life'.

Kripalsingh discovers, in other words, what Naipaul has called the 'slow magic' of writing, the excitement of working towards unexpected conclusions.[23] Yet all the discoveries of *The Mimic Men* depend on a single page. Kripalsingh sits at his desk after breakfast, expecting to make quick progress. But he is stuck:

I was overwhelmed as much by the formlessness of my experiences, and their irrelevance to the setting in which I proposed to recount them, as by the setting itself, my physical situation, in this city, this room, with this view, that lustreless light. And it was not until late afternoon, excitement gone, the light faded, the curtains about to be drawn, my stomach, head and eyes united in a dead sensation of sickness, that the memory at last came which, forcing itself to the surface all day, had kept the first page of the Century notebook blank except for the date: the memory of my first snow and the memory, incredulously examined, of the city of the magical light.

Fourteen months have passed since, in a room made overdry by the electric fire, I re-created that climb up the dark stairs to Mr Shylock's attic to look through a snowfall at the whitening roofs of Kensington. By this re-creation the event became historical and manageable; it was given its place; it will no longer disturb me. And this became my aim: from the central fact of this setting, my presence in this city which I have known as student, politician and now as refugee-immigrant, to impose order on my own history, to abolish that disturbance which is what a narrative in sequence might have led me to.[24]

This is the crucial moment in the writing of the novel, the discovery of its centre, a union of character and setting to which all the book's meanings can be related. I discussed earlier the significance of London as first the cause and finally the setting of Kripalsingh's shipwreck. But his discovery that London must be the pivot of his memoirs involves more than just a final facing of the facts. It becomes the means of organising those facts, a means of distilling order from what has seemed chaotic. Once the union is realised of 'this man, this room, this city: this story, this language, this form', the experiences fall naturally into place. Kripalsingh is able at last to see coherence in the cycle of events which has left him high and dry in his London hotel.

With coherence comes release. There is one event in Kripalsingh's political career which prepares us for such a use of language. Shortly before his final departure from Isabella, he is visited by some Indian victims of racial violence who, despite his apparent betrayal of them, have no one else to turn to. He offers them the anaesthetising comfort of newspaper phrases – 'Do not tell me how people died. Say instead, "Race riots occurred". Say, "There was loss of life".' In the long run, such distancing phrases are not, he recognises, adequate for their purpose. Mr Biswas needed more than a gift for caricature; he needed a house. Kripalsingh needs more than Sandra's 'gift of the phrase'; he requires what only the larger myth can provide, the satisfaction of coherence. Only when, with the acceptance of London as the pivot of his memoirs, he has discovered the centre round which everything else revolves, only then can he know which are the right phrases, avoiding the cheating and the distorting, rejecting satire with its assumption of alternatives, achieving for himself the comfort he offered elsewhere by seeing his homelessness as a general condition. Gurudeva in his final phase as a *sanyani* also offers the remnant of his followers the comfort of simple phrases, and even Lord Stockwell is impressed. But the phrases were supported by his own adapted vision of the good life as laid down by his Aryan ancestors. They drew their logic from the larger myth. Kripalsingh's memoirs fulfil something of a similar function. In the closing paragraphs it gives him joy to reflect he too has fulfilled Aryan precepts about the 'fourfold division of life . . . I have been student, householder and man of affairs, recluse'.

The climax of *The Mimic Men*, then, marks Naipaul's most confident statement yet about the purpose of writing. In *The Mystic Masseur*, he shared Ganesh's excitement over the 'thrilling, tedious, discouraging, exhilarating process of making a book'. But he placed his narrator in England, and acknowledged that Ganesh's Indian view of things contradicted ludicrously the requirements of a novelist. In *A House for Mr Biswas*, he followed with even greater sympathy Mr Biswas's development from sign-painter to journalist to writer of short stories. Yet Mr Biswas's best journalism never rose above the level of caricature, and the story which obsesses him is always called 'Escape'. By the time of *Mr Stone and the Knights Companion* and of 'A Flag on the Island', Naipaul's suspicions about language and form seem, as we saw, to have reached proportions which threaten his very continuance as a writer. Now, in Kripalsingh's discovery of writing as a means of releasing himself from a barren cycle of events, Naipaul recovers from this negation. The recovery is all the more significant in that while *The Mimic Men* carries as postscript the dates August 1964 – July 1966, 'A Flag on the Island', in which the negation seemed absolute, is dated August 1965. Kripalsingh's discoveries about writing seem, in their actual chronology, to refer directly back to Naipaul's own recovery of confidence in his art.

Derek Walcott, from whose poem 'Crusoe's Journal' I quoted earlier, has argued an opposing point of view. In his review of *The Mimic Men*, he draws attention to the improbability of Kripalsingh's producing at his first attempt such a highly wrought work of art, faultless in shape and consistently elegant in expression. He suggests that Naipaul might have been truer to his subject had he permitted Kripalsingh to write 'a deliberately bad book . . . weakest at its centre'. But his conclusion is that the paradox is intentional, that Naipaul is deliberately mocking an art in which he has lost all confidence. Instead of a Kripalsingh who finds ultimate release in the shaping of his memoirs, Walcott offers us Kripalsingh the mimic man, trapped in the ultimate posturing of art. Hence the novel becomes 'a celebration of inertia in a powerful style, a despair that has syntactical confidence', the contradictions pointing to the enigma of Naipaul:

> that he makes art but now distrusts it, that he loves and suffers with and for his people but that love chokes on abhorrence, that there is despair but it lacks resonance, that the writing of novels seems a futile occupation yet no West Indian writer is so prodigious.[25]

It is a stimulating thesis yet, as my argument indicates, it insists on a negation from which the Naipaul of *The Mimic Men* has already recovered. It is true that the style of the novel is nervously elegant to the point of self-parody. Yet it is hard to believe that Kripalsingh's claims about the satisfaction he has found in writing are meant to be read as proof that he is once again deceiving himself. There is nothing in the novel to indicate that Kripalsingh is under any broader ironic attack than that which he mounts against himself. Naipaul can, in fact, be shown to be working out in fictional terms ideas which he expresses in articles published before and during the composition of *The Mimic Men*. In the most explicit of these, 'The Documentary Heresy', he protests vigorously against that kind of writing which seeks only to record, which concentrates on documenting 'anonymous flesh' in photographic detail, and abandons that 'larger vision' which is the artist's responsibility:

> The violence some of us are resisting is not the violence which is a counter of story-telling. It is the violence which is clinical and documentary in intention and makes no statement beyond that of bodily pain and degradation. It is like the obscene photograph. It deals anonymously with anonymous flesh, quickened only by pleasure or pain; and this anonymity is a denial of art. *The Magic Mountain* is a painfully physical book; yet even when it reduces man to flesh, and the components of flesh, it never

violates. There is concern here, and wonder, absorbing and annihilating violation. This is the effect of art, and is the opposite of violence as an end in itself: violence as therapy, violence as the releasing response either to the extreme placidity of the age or its insecurity . . . The artist who, for political or humanitarian reasons, seeks only to record abandons half his responsibility. He becomes a participant; he becomes anonymous. He does not impose a vision on the world. He accepts; he might even make romantic; but he invariably ends by assessing men at their own valuation. The time comes when he is content to communicate the egoism of the brute.[26]

This attack on violence and obscenity as 'the final dereliction of artistic reponsibility' may seem at first of dubious relevance. Yet the antithesis on which Naipaul bases his outburst, the antithesis between documentary and art, is substantially Kripalsingh's antithesis between a narrative in chronological order which would have recorded everything but solved nothing, and that shaping of his material round a central truth which has made it 'historical and manageable'. It broadens into the contrast between the desolation of the stopover, when he learns about flesh 'through poor, hideous flesh', and the calm of his memoirs as he shapes his 'larger vision' of the displacement of all peoples.

   The significance of this is that Naipaul's recovery of confidence in his art seemed to proceed directly from his repudiation of a concern only with man's physical condition. Writing in India, and feeling all the 'insubstantiality and wrongness' of European cities, Naipaul seemed to share Mr Stone's insistence that 'all that was not flesh was irrelevant to man; and all that was important was man's own flesh, his weakness and corruptibility'. In the end, Mr Stone longs for destruction, prepared to sympathise with other flesh, but waiting for death to relieve him of the effort to come to terms with a world whose creations he cannot believe in. We saw in Chapter 5 how, even at the time, this emphasis caused Naipaul trouble with his conclusion. He seems, I suggested then, to have projected on to Mr Stone a sense of negation which is not properly supported by the working out of the plot. We saw, too, how in 'A Flag on the

Island', a similar preoccupation with lassitude and knowing disillusion led directly to a welcoming of the hurricane and to narrative stalemate. Now, in his attack on violence and obscenity, inevitable products of the writer's preoccupation with the flesh 'unquickened by spirit', Naipaul returns to something of the mood in which he closed *A House for Mr Biswas*:

> So later, and very slowly, in securer times of different stresses, when the memories had lost the power to hurt, with pain or joy, they would fall into place and give back the past.[27]

Kripalsingh on the empty beach, in the snow-dimmed attic, in his car on the abandoned sugar estate, in the prostitute's hotel on the stopover, or waiting cumbered with luggage on a country station platform; these climaxes of negation are distanced, their ghosts are laid, by the discovery of a pattern which acknowledges and transcends them.

With this realisation, we can appreciate how complete is the novel's cycle of meanings. I began this chapter by showing how Naipaul works within the framework of a new antithesis, not now between a chaotic Trinidad and an ordered London, but between a chaotic present and the established social organisations of the past. Kripalsingh's memoirs become, in effect, his substitute for those older myths whose passing he so powerfully regrets, an attempt to recapture privately that state of calm, before the voyages of discovery, when the peoples of the world achieved fulfilment within the landscapes 'hymed by their ancestors'. The act of writing becomes an attempt to undo the effects of imperialism, an attempt to re-establish the rooted coherence of a vanished past. In Chapter 1 of *An Area of Darkness*, Naipaul describes his grandfather leaving his village in Uttar Pradesh on that courageous, startling journey across half the world, but capable of such action and unshaken by its consequences because he carried India within him. The importance of *The Mimic Men* in terms of Naipaul's own development is that it recaptures something of that calm state of mind. It releases him from the cycle begun in *Miguel Street* and continued through *Mr Stone and the Knights Companion*, opening the way, his world now intact within him, for fresh discoveries and for fresh achievement. By the closing pages, he has – in Kripalsingh's words – 'cleared the decks, as it were, and prepared myself for fresh action. It will be the action of a free man'.

CHAPTER SEVEN

'It's their country. But it's your life.'

I

Out of her fidelity to her experience, and her purity as a novelist, Jean Rhys thirty to forty years ago identified many of the themes that engage us today: isolation, an absence of society or community, the sense of things falling apart, dependence, loss. Her achievement is very grand. Her books may serve current causes, but she is above causes. What she has written about she has endured, over a long life; and what a stoic thing she makes the act of writing appear.[1]

The Mimic Men concludes on a note of optimism. Just as *A House for Mr Biswas* ended Naipaul's preoccupation with colonial Trinidad set against the assumed alternative of London, so *The Mimic Men* puts into final and liberating perspective that preoccupation with London which is now seen as both cause and focus of his homelessness. But what has Naipaul done since its publication in 1967? What are the consequences of his having cleared the decks and prepared himself for fresh action? Four books have followed, of which one, *A Flag on the Island* (1967), was written earlier, and another, *The overcrowded Barracoon* (1972), is a selection of articles some of which date back fourteen years. More important are *The Loss of El Dorado* (1969), a history of Trinidad, and *In a Free State* (1971), a 'novel' comprising three linked stories and two journal extracts. Perhaps it would be unfair to see in this signs of a slackening off – one can hardly expect Naipaul to maintain indefinitely his earlier rate of nine books in eleven years. What is striking, however, is the confirmation of a real shift of interest towards non-fiction. Since 1961, in fact, when in response to the invitation of Eric Williams Naipaul toured the West Indies, he has – by bulk at least – published more non-fiction than fiction: two travelogues, a fat history and a collection of articles, set against three brief novels, some short stories, and *The Mimic Men*. If judging by bulk reflects 'a grocer's attitude to literature' (as Naipaul described a threat to refer him under the Trade Descriptions Act for calling *In a Free State* a novel), it does lead us to ask why such a distinguished novelist should dissipate his energies in this way. The two travel books have been discussed in earlier chapters. But what is the status of his recent non-fiction? How do his history and his journalism reflect 'the action of a free man'?

The Loss of El Dorado was begun in September 1966, a matter of weeks after *The Mimic Men* was completed. The book describes, firstly, the struggle between the Spanish Antonio de Berrio and the English Sir Walter Ralegh for possession of Trinidad as a base for El Dorado explorations, and, secondly, the attempt to open up Spanish America to British commercial interests by organising revolution from Trinidad. The stories are separated by two hundred years and they are complicated by the presence of other races with stronger claims. Spanish settlement involved the extermination of the Amerindians; British efforts to promote freedom on the mainland coincided with the trial of Sir Thomas Picton for using torture to maintain discipline in his slave colony. The complications are reflected in Naipaul's presentation of the material. On the one hand, he sees the two episodes as comprising the 'history of Port of Spain', the two moments when the island ceased to be a remote colonial backwater and acquired some political and economic importance. On the other hand, his sympathies are entirely with the Amerindians and the Negro slaves who, nameless, faceless, denied a voice in history, are present throughout the book as the oblique side of every irony.

Apart from its importance as an illuminating and carefully researched history, the book is in a sense a supplement to *The Mimic Men*, reinforcing Kripalsingh's displacement with an academic and fully documented version of the same themes – a discipline to which other novelists might well subject themselves. It could only have followed the novel. 'How can the history of this West Indian futility be written?' Naipaul raged in *The Middle Passage*:

> The history of the islands can never be satisfactorily told. Brutality is not the only difficulty. History is built around achievement and creation; and nothing was created in the West Indies.[2]

Eight years later, in the Epilogue to *The Loss of El Dorado*, describing how history was taught in Port of Spain in the 1940s, Naipaul has his terrors under control:

> Port of Spain was a place where things had happened and nothing showed. Only people remained. History was a fairytale about Columbus and a fairytale about the strange customs of the aboriginal Caribs and Arawaks; it was impossible now to set them in the landscape. History was the Trinidad five-cent stamp: Ralegh discovering the Pitch Lake. History was also a fairytale not so much about slavery as about its abolition, the good defeating the bad. It was the only way the tale could be told. Any other version would have ended in ambiguity and alarm.[3]

'Ambiguity and alarm' are precisely what have been exorcised by *The Mimic Men*. The 'free man' is evident on every page. For the first time since *A House for Mr Biswas*, the writing is free from doubts about itself. The style is bald, unrhetorical, the clauses brief, the diction colourless, the irony the product not of the author speaking at the expense of his subject but of the historical facts themselves colliding with each other in a manner that needs no comment. For the first time, too, since *A House for Mr Biswas*, he is clear about where his sympathies lie. In a pre-publication interview, he describes his 'enormous satisfaction in this non-fiction book I've been doing. It's awfully hard to take sides, you know.'[4] Never have the atrocities of conquest and slavery been more effectively exposed. Naipaul writes as a novelist: he seeks the human being behind the records – the Amerindians, identified by Ralegh, glimpsed fleeing from their cooking pots by Dudley and Wyatt, but vanished completely by the time Charles Kingsley two and a half centuries later next visits the same high woods: and the Negroes, reduced to caricature by names like Paly, Belchy, Pig-

Foot, Ham, Scipio, Sampson, coming to distant life only as the victims of the slave codes, the inhabitants of Vallot's jail, the creators of those fantasies of mimic power that lie behind carnival. It is impossible to revive them as individuals, but their presence is insisted on throughout the book. Naipaul is not prepared to allow their scourging to be, like the killings in *In a Free State*, 'something that never happened'.

At the same time, the colonialists and slave-owners – Spanish, French, British – are presented as real people:

> In 1807 one of the objections from Trinidad to the abolition of the British slave trade was that it was unfair to the Africans, who would now not only be denied civilising contacts but would also be transported in cruel conditions in foreign ships. The argument, with its remote reference to several ideals, is recognisably English. The objection in 1823 to the regulation forbidding the whipping of Negro women is different. The regulation, it was said, was a means of ruining white families, who were already sufficiently hard-pressed. Negro women were notoriously insolent; the regulation would encourage them to provoke their owners; a story was told of a very old and devout French couple who, obscenely provoked at table one day, had reacted with the whip and had found themselves ruined by a fine. The objection comes from people who have accepted the values of the new society, who have accepted the values of the new society, who have ceased to assess themselves by the standards of the metropolis and now measure their eminence only by their distance, economic and racial, from their Negroes.[5]

Underlining the brutality is the revelation of its context – that artificial society, mimicking Europe, knowledgeable only about sugar and tobacco and managing Negroes, turning the imported words on their head to keep reality at bay. It is this awareness of the conflicting drives of different cultures, of the ways people from different backgrounds have different ways of *seeing* – Berrio, 'committed to a holy war and an outdated code of chivalry', Ralegh with his 'lucid, three-dimensional view of the world', Pedro Vargas describing the 'simple' people of Venezuela and missing the European sophistication that 'found romance in the deficiency' – that marks this book off as something special, not just history written with the insight of a novelist but history written from the widest of viewpoints, Naipaul turning his placelessness, his lack of identification with any single culture, to fresh and startling advantage. The discussion of the character of Miranda, the Venezuelan revolutionary, is especially illuminating. Naipaul describes 'the deeper colonial deprivation, the sense of the missing world, that Miranda spent a lifetime making good', and later comments, 'he had developed the exile's compensating sense of temporariness, in which reality is defined by negatives and ever recedes.' Eventually, after many years in Europe and after his disastrous expeditions, Miranda – like Ralegh, like Kripalsingh – accepts confinement as a solution. Insights such as these resound beyond their context and seem not only to echo Naipaul's own experience but to dramatise the new detachment and calm which will permit him to form them.

After completing *The Loss of El Dorado*, Naipaul announced late in 1969 that he had sold his house in London and was leaving England for good. England, he said, was 'closing up. People cease to examine themselves and ask questions.'[6] In fact, after a short absence, he has once again made England his base as a writer. But the notion of fresh travel together with the search for a society where 'the individual adventure' is still possible, dominates *The Overcrowded Barracoon*. About one quarter of the volume consists of pieces done before *The Mimic Men*. The rest is a selection of articles and interviews which have taken Naipaul to a number of new places, not only back to India and the West Indies, but to New York, California, Tokyo and Mauritius. Most of them were commissioned by the *Daily Telegraph* and *Sunday Times* magazines, and by the *New York Review of Books*, and they take us up to July 1972, since when Naipaul has added South America and the *Observer* to his territory. Not since he was a reviewer for the *New Statesman* has Naipaul devoted so much attention to journalism. His current interest amounts almost to a new career. For a writer who could complain in 1971 that the income from his books amounted to only £400 a year ('with occasional goodies in the form of translations'),

something more profitable is clearly necessary.[7] But Naipaul insists
that he takes his journalism 'very seriously', choosing his own
'missions', and relating them closely to his fiction. He has described how the title piece was written in illness brought on by distress at what he had seen in Mauritius – though so 'unimportant'
was the subject that the *Sunday Times* held back the article for ten
months.[8]

The *Overcrowded Barracoon* is the most political of Naipaul's
books. Two major articles, on Ajmer and on Norman Mailer, describe the actual conduct of elections; the pieces on St Kitts,
Anguilla, British Honduras and Mauritius are built around political analysis; and the remaining articles in the volume are chosen
for the further light they throw on the problems of colonial and
ex-colonial territories, Naipaul having included only those of his
reviews which bear directly on his present concerns. One sympa-
thises with his wish to bring home to a mass newspaper audience
the urgency of these problems, to emphasise that these countries
are not just 'Commonwealth Lit.' fodder but situations of acute
distress and danger. He has a powerful case: there are many such
parts of the world, anomalies of imperialism, territories 'dangerous
only to themselves' which cannot be made to function. One recognises, too, the purely literary reasons for writing of them in this
manner. Societies like Mauritius, under-developed, over-
populated, utterly dependent despite independence, are too
simple for sustained fictional treatment, and Naipaul's position as
visitor is far too much of a special case. It is the old problem –
Naipaul has no society; a novelist of exceptional subtlety lacks the
material appropriate to his talents; the points that need to be made
are better handled in journalism.

Yet one fears for the fiction. The dangers that Naipaul once
noted in the foreword to *The Middle Passage* still exist:

> The novelist works towards conclusions of which he is often
> unaware; and it is better that he should. To analyse and decide
> before writing would rob the writer of the excitement which
> supports him during his solitude, and would be the opposite of
> my method as a novelist. I also felt it as a danger that, having

factually analysed the society as far as I was able, I would be unable afterwards to think of it in terms of fiction and that in anything I might write I would be concerned only to prove a point. However, I decided to take the risk.[9]

It is perhaps significant that although Naipaul has been able to turn his English and African experiences into novels, he has since *An Area of Darkness* written nothing about India save additional articles and a few pages of one short story. Moreover, despite the brilliance of many passages of *The Overcrowded Barracoon*, the marvellous sense of scene and occasion, the pithy generalisations, it is hard to find anything in it he has not said before. Just as *The Loss of El Dorado* is in a sense a historical supplement to *The Mimic Men*, tracing the same patterns back over five hundred years of Trinidad's history, so *The Overcrowded Barracoon* becomes an investigation of how widely, in the geographical sense, Kripalsingh's experiences can be made to look relevant. Naipaul visits not only samples of those 'twenty countries' to which Kripalsingh keeps referring but older, larger societies, and he finds an equal rootlessness – not just the West Indies, the 'third world's third world', or Mauritius where 'the escape routes are closed', but also California where he watches 'a culture parodying itself' and New York where he approves Mailer's diagnosis of 'a dying city, alienation its major problem, a complete political reorganisation the only hope'. More recently, he has found it again in Argentina and Uruguay, where the victims this time are European immigrants, Spaniards and Italians, who in a couple of generations have become as lost as any other races:

> Now already, there is decay. The British Empire has withdrawn *ordenadamente*, in good order; and the colonial agricultural economy, attempting haphazardly to industrialise, to become balanced and autonomous, is in ruins. The artificiality of the society shows: that absence of links between men and men, between immigrant and immigrant, aristocrat and artisan, city dweller and *cabecita negra*, the 'blackhead', the man from the interior; that absence of a link between men and the meaningless flat land. And the poor, who are Argentines, the sons and grand-

sons of those recent immigrants, will now have to stay.[10]

> Uruguayans say that they are a European nation, that they have always had their back to the rest of South America. It was their great error, and is part of their failure. Their habits of wealth made them, profoundly, a colonial people, educated but intellectually null, consumers, parasitic on the culture and technology of others.[11]

It is an impressive list, and the problems which concern him are genuine – dependence, disorder, self-deception, the imported language irrelevant to the society.

Yet one queries the linking together of quite so many countries. Naipaul's thesis is broadening to that point of platitude where it can be applied to virtually the whole world. It is one thing to say that *A House for Mr Biswas* and *The Mimic Men* are, for all their particularity, novels of wide significance; it is another to stretch their meaning to such broad generalisations that the real differences between different places are glossed over. It must have some consequences, for instance, that Trinidad has its writers and that Mauritius does not; that village culture survives in India but not in the United States; that South America is empty but the barracoon overcrowded. Naipaul does not obscure such distinctions, but he gives them less than full weight; and he deserves to be reminded of Kripalsingh's insight that often 'in conditions of chaos the human personality is in fact varied and extended.' One begins, with pardonable malice, to suspect that Naipaul's placelessness, his detachment from three cultures, modulates at times into a private quest, a pilgrimage of horror in search of the ultimate decaying society, ruled by ritual and myth, incapable of inquiry, lacking shared concerns or any link with the land, unable to feed itself or to protect its inhabitants, recently cast adrift and awaiting disaster. Where next will he find such grim satisfaction: Ceylon? Ireland? Paraguay?

If this seems caricature, one thing is clear. For the first time in his career Naipaul has published work which raises no questions about its predecessors.

2

It is with *In a Free State* that Naipaul resumes inquiry: from the 'free man' of *The Mimic Men* we turn to the 'casualties' of the 'free state'. The paradox is as old as *A House for Mr Biswas*, but its application is entirely new. Having filled out historically and geographically the arguments of *The Mimic Men*, Naipaul has produced a book in many ways similar to *Mr Stone and the Knights Companion* – one which, while less than completely satisfying, covers fresh ground in both setting and theme as (one hopes) the necessary preliminary to some larger work. Moreover, although overlapped in time by *The Overcrowded Barracoon*, it contains in the prologue and epilogue pieces of non-fiction which bear so directly on the main stories that concern about the dissipation of his energies seems after all unnecessary.

Something of the 'free man' carries over; once again, there is nothing in the book about writing. No character is working on a book himself, no character complains about language. Not even in 'One Out of Many', an account of the narrator's progress from Bombay to Washington, from a society in which he was 'part of the flow' to a society in which individual self-assessment is part of the culture – not even in Santosh's story is there anything about the literary implications of that shift in sensibility which permits his account to be in the first person. The book as a whole is more direct and unambiguous than for a long time. Paragraphs are shorter, sentences less complex with fewer semi-colons. Themes are heavily underlined: the closing paragraph of 'One Out of Many' is almost too explicit; the narrator of 'Tell Me Who To Kill' speaks the title of his story at the climax. At the same time, Naipaul is again quite clear where his sympathies lie. The main characters are all victims. The shadowy Americans in Washington, the English 'louts' in London, the ominous Africans of the title story, are all people with power. However this simple division is modified, by the recognition that Linda can exploit Bobby and Bobby his houseboy and that it is not always clear 'who to kill', the antithesis between those with power and those without remains the centre of the book.

Yet it is not at all obvious that *In a Free State* can be discussed as a single work. At first sight it seems, like *A Flag on the Island*, to be made up of odds and ends – a short novel, two short stories, and two extracts from Naipaul's journals. Naipaul admits that the book has not worked out as originally planned:

> The whole thing was conceived as a big novel containing all the elements of American involvement with weaker communities, and the way that individuals from them are trapped by bigger powers. The book is properly about power and powerlessness. But then something I find harder and harder to do is the artificial side of making up big narratives – even while, as one becomes older, one becomes more fictitious – and I decided to let the book fall into its component parts. I shouldn't wish the African story to be published independently of the other parts.[12]

There seems little point in worrying about the American angle. The first story is set in Washington. But its America consists of TV commercials and a view of distant fires from the appartment window, and the narrator's only contacts are with Negroes and hippies, people on the fringe. Linda, in the title story, has an American boyfriend who is used to comment on the English-African involvement. There is an American Negro directing traffic at the scene of the King's death, and an American school built to straddle symbolically the King's and President's territories but never used until it becomes the headquarters of the hunt for the King and the scene of Bobby's beating. But such scattered references scarcely even supplement each other, and certainly do not add up to a single unifying framework.

That framework is now provided, literally and thematically, by the Prologue and Epilogue, two brief extracts from Naipaul's journal of separate visits to Egypt. They record fact not fiction, yet the Prologue anticipates so many of the book's concerns and the Epilogue reflects so appropriately on its conclusions, that they seem intentionally emblematic, the details refined to the point of parable. The prologue, for instance, describes a two-day voyage from Piraeus to Alexandria. Naipaul's fellow passengers are a cross-section of nationalities – Italian, Greek, Spanish, Egyptian,

Lebanese, American – and they include an English tramp whose unpleasant behaviour makes him generally disliked and, briefly, persecuted. It seems a simple enough account, yet in it are the seeds of the whole book. Each of the three stories, for instance, deals with a journey – by plane, train, ship, bus, and in the title story by car. The journey is, in fact, the book's central metaphor, a bleaker alternative to Kripalsingh's hotel. Thus, each of the stories deals with people removed from the surroundings which normally sustain them. The mixture of nationalities on the Greek steamer, the two-dimensional relationships, the simplified conversations in several languages, the temporary alliances of strong against weak, look forward to the groupings and relationships in the main stories – to Santosh marrying the *hubshi* woman, to the complicated rivalries of 'Tell Me Who To Kill', to Linda's alliances with Carter and the Colonel against Bobby. Most important of all, in each of the stories there is a victim: Santosh ends waiting for death, the narrator of the second story allows it to be believed he is dead, Bobby is beaten up by the President's soldiers. Their fates are anticipated by the tramp on the steamer, a 'citizen of the world' who is unable to comply with society's mildest demands, an ageing Englishman – such are the shifts of power – who, hunted and beaten, seeks refuge from freedom in a locked cabin.

Something of this same emblematic simplicity carries over into the title story – 'In this country in Africa there was a president and there was also a king'; the tone is that of the moral fable. Yet most readers will recognise the events. The politics of the story are those of Uganda in May 1966 when the Kabaka of Buganda ('King Freddie') was overthrown (though not killed; he escaped by taxi) by the Prime Minister, Milton Obote, who controlled the army. Where Naipaul departs from actual history, is by adding other familiar elements – the details of the oath-taking refer to Kenya and Mau Mau, the disappearance of the President during the mutiny to Dr Nyerere and Tanzania. Bobby's and Linda's journey 'south' is impossible; it begins (according to Naipaul) in Kigale in Ruanda, seems to take in the Kampala-Nairobi highway, and to end in Buganda.[13] Along this route are distributed the names Naipaul has given to his African characters – Mubende-Mbarara are two towns in Uganda ('something like Edinburgh-Cardiff', a Ugandan reviewer scornfully remarked),[14] the Busoga are a tribe straddling the Nairobi road, Gisenye (Kisenyi in the novel) a town on Lac Kivu in Ruanda, across the lake from Zaire – though it is also a Kampala slum. We are presented, in other words, with an African version of Isabella, a 'free state' sufficiently located in recent history to seem real, and sufficiently generalised to seem representative.

'You've been reading too much Conrad', says Bobby at one point in the journey when Linda remarks about 'forest life . . . going on forever'. This brief reference, supplementing that in *The Mimic Men* to the novelist who covered such similar territory, is interesting. Like Conrad in *Heart of Darkness*, Naipaul's concern is less with Africans than with what happens to white men in Africa. Now that power has been restored to the inhabitants, he concentrates not on the President and his undisciplined, overfed army, not even on the deported Asians and their exploited remnants, but on the few Englishmen who, with the retreat of Empire, find themselves stranded, unable to escape or hoping against hope that Africa still has something to offer them. The creations of Empire are in decay; Bobby's and Linda's journey is, in one sense, a tour of the country examining the colonial ruins. They begin in the capital, that 'English-Indian creation' owing 'nothing to African skill', and find the forest dwellers encroaching on the suburbs with a shanty town. They visit the Hunting Lodge where African grooms in jodhpurs and a van-load of beagles are all that remain of its unreal grandeur – the garden a wilderness, the terraces collapsing, the polo pavilion in ruins. They stay the night at the lakeshore resort where the promenade is overgrown, the street lamps smashed, the guard dogs wild and dangerous, the huge villas settled by Africans who recreate within the tall rooms and on verandahs the limited facilities of their bush huts. They drive swiftly through the administrative centre:

> Crooked telegraph poles, sagging wires, the broken edges of the asphalt road, scuffed grass sidewalks, dust, scattered rubbish, African bicycles, broken-down lorries and motor cars outside the bus-station shed.[15]

Only the compound with its high wall and watchman, its bright lights and safe houses on neatly labelled streets, remains alive. The long journey ends in security.

Bobby has no regrets about the decay; the settler ethos is not for him. Yet in a predictable way he remains totally dependent on it as a means of defining his response to Africa, colonial guilt giving him a frame of reference with his constant ironies about 'settler grandeur' and 'wogs' and 'keeping your eye on the natives', and his determination to smile and wave and be un-South African on all occasions. It is this that feeds his liberalism, not a genuine concern for either people or truth, and his words never connect with the violence and terror. He has no sympathy for the middle-aged proprietors of the Hunting Lodge, man and wife in plaster, matching the ruin around them, while the smiling African at the door awaits his opportunity. He is bored and irritated by the Colonel, an old man with an injured hip, shell-shocked in the Great War, a career in Empire behind him, now living on his will, keeping at bay by sheer force of character the Africans who will eventually kill him. They envy Bobby as the 'short contract man' who can pull out when he chooses. But in all but style and sentiment, his situation parallels theirs; he too ends up with a broken wrist with his houseboy laughing.

The word 'exploited' occurs only once in the story. It is used by Bobby not about Africans (he calls them 'oppressed') but about himself in England trying to come to terms with his homosexual nature. At home he is a victim, one 'of Arthur's young queers'; he has even been arrested; he has an eighteen-month nervous breakdown behind him. There seems no reason to doubt the emotion of his claim that 'Africa saved my life'. Liberation for Africans is paralleled by the personal fulfilment he is seeking in the 'free state'. Africa for him is freedom, a place where his impulses do not get him into trouble, where simple adventures and simple relationships can bring the simple satisfactions he requires. He adopts the camouflage of liberal sentiments, making the appropriate – and apparently sincere – noises about being 'here to serve'. Yet his position is deeply ambiguous. There are hints of conspiracy: it is Denis Marshall who brought him to Africa; when Marshall is jealous of

Bobby's affairs with Africans, Bobby gets his contract cancelled by reporting to the minister the false claims for a baggage allowance. When does the exploited become the exploiter? It is significant that the only African Bobby abuses in the story – over the damage to his windscreen at the garage at Esher – belongs to the King's tribe. Bobby, the victim, is on the side of power. The incident looks forward to the conclusion and to Bobby's alternatives:

> Bobby thought: I will have to leave. But the compound was safe; the soldiers guarded the gate. Bobby thought: I will have to sack Luke.[16]

Luke, too, is one of the King's men.

Such a climax is only reached, however, after a steady assault on Bobby's prejudices. The opening incident with the Zulu is a paradigm of what follows – Bobby seeking adventure, sex and sympathy with the oppressed: the Zulu baiting him, paving the way for that insult to the white man which is the only revolution he knows. Once on the road, however, the real attack on Bobby's blindness is mounted by Linda. She has been in Africa for six years; she wants to leave, but the escape routes are closed except those to the South; she is tied to a husband who is too old to make a fresh start and not enough of a fighter to protect their position; her sexual escapades parallel those of Bobby who, after the violence of their quarrel and of the President's soldiers, has a sudden vision of her as another 'for whom so much had gone wrong'. She too is lost; her world has shrunk to the compound. Naipaul is not entirely on her side – she retails too many of the oldest expatriate jokes (about the Africans being 'restless today'; about them being able to strip a Boeing in a week; about car accidents making the compound look like a ski resort) to be wholly acceptable as an interpreter of events. She has all the light arrogance, the artificial brightness, the pretended concern of the worst sort of compound wife, and her inadequacies are not glossed over – they include a readiness to exploit Bobby herself; she only calls at the Hunting Lodge to continue her affair with Carter.

Yet Bobby never disagrees with her without being proved wrong. He rejects as 'last night's ex-patriate gossip' the story about the King's escape in a taxi; they turn out to be following him. He mocks Linda's talk about the oathings; they almost become the victims of conspiracy. He brushes aside Linda's fears about violence at the roadblock; he ends up being beaten by the soldiers. He is angered by Linda's insistence at the hotel that there is someone in his room, and furious – until Linda kicks him under the table – at the Colonel's abuse of Peter; but Peter turns out to have the Volkswagen keys after all, and after the attempt to steal Bobby's car he finds his own keys on the bedroom floor where they have been pushed under the door. Even such tiny details as Linda being right about the clouds piling up, or Linda being right about the 'fat one' being in charge at the roadblock, or Linda being right about the incompetence of the garage attendants, add to the undermining of his position as the man who has decided 'my life is here'.

Bobby has no answer. He dreams:

He was in a car with a woman whose identity he couldn't be sure of. They were quarrelling. Everything she said was accurate; everything was wounding; and though to everything there was a reply, he couldn't explain himself. He had to shout above her shouts; he was screaming; and as they sped along the empty road, dangerously, the wheel jumping in his hands, she wounded him and wounded him more and more deeply; and there was rage and ache in his head, which seemed about to explode. He was no longer in the car. He was standing beside a table in a room full of people and chatter; and his exploding head made him collapse and stretch out right there, before them, on the floor.[17]

His eventual reaction is like Mr Stone's. Provoked beyond endurance by her borrowed phrases, her assumption of the right to judge, he abuses her violently, rehearsing with savage irony all that has angered him on the journey. Yet even here he makes no attempt to refute what she has been saying. He simply denies her right to say it, to claim for herself the superiority from which all such judgements proceed. Linda is implicitly acknowledged to be correct, but Bobby denies her right to make an issue of it – 'I don't know why you think it matters what you think about anything.' It is a powerful attack; but it leaves Bobby no basis for continuing to live in Africa.

When the Israeli instructors come to dine in the lake-shore hotel, they keep to themselves, talking in their own language 'like people under orders not to fraternize, comment or *see*.' The italics are mine, but the word is one of Naipaul's favourites; in this context, it can only be contentious, implying that all who do not agree with his assessment of this 'free state' are refusing to look at what is happening in Africa. There is a good deal in 'In a Free State' that needed saying. Linda's horror at the people who 'hadn't died' in the earthquake and the massacres that 'hadn't happened' across the lake because the countries were not important enough to make news, is obviously very close to Naipaul's concerns in his recent non-fiction. The description of the Colonel, abandoned by Empire, living on his will, is powerful and original; in his set-piece argument with Peter, culminating in his oath made 'under these lights, in the open, before witnesses', he achieves a tragic grandeur unrivalled in Naipaul's work. Which contemporary English writer would have treated him without satire? It is good to read an account of independent Africa which recognises minorities and which is not afraid of appearing prejudiced.

The difficulty is that the whole argument is conducted without any African perspective on events. Naipaul's treatment of the people who actually inhabit this country is very rudimentary. There is little point in objecting to his emphasis on physical unpleasantness; words like 'fat' and 'smell' enter the story as part of Linda's vocabulary and are adopted as Naipaul's from the Hunting Lodge incident onwards; but the same points are made about the Colonel, and Bobby is appalled by Linda's vaginal deodorant. Similarly, the emphasis on their general unfriendliness to expatriates – their blankness, sullenness, readiness for racial revenge – seems legitimate comment. When one reads such an assessment as the following by a local reviewer, one acknowledges the justification for Naipaul's sharpest passages:

Bobby in this confrontation with the army soldiers gets away like a whipped dog with its tail between the legs. To an East

African he is the very picture of the timid Asian who gets whipped all round for his lack of strength of character and for his being prone to panic – which invariably invites a kick on the pants as well as the derisive laughter like what Bobby gets from his servant at the end of the story. In other words, Bobby is an East African Asiatic vaguely disguised as an English ex-patriate.[18]

Nor do recent events in Uganda give much ground for attacking Naipaul's emphasis on anarchy and arbitrary violence.

What fatally undermines the liberal case, however, and makes it impossible for Bobby to build an answer to Linda's attack, is that Naipaul allows to the Africans no similar sense of loss and displacement. The African is simply a 'man of the forest', the 'man flushed out from the bush' to whom, with independence, 'civilisation appeared to have been granted complete.' Whether Africans really do feel like this about the overthrow of their village systems is never questioned. There is no hint in the story that, for all their present confusion, they may once have had a society with shared reverences, links between men and men, a sense of belonging to a particular landscape settled by their ancestors and praised in their myths – all those things whose absence Naipaul regrets in country after country of *The Overcrowded Barracoon*. When one turns to King Freddie's own account of the destruction of his palace, the perspective is very different:

> Among the sad news of who is dead, who is in prison and what is destroyed comes the confirmation that the Royal Drums are burnt. I saw this work begun and feared that it must have been completed. These drums of which there are more than fifty are the heart of Buganda, some of them hundreds of years old, as old as the Kabakaship. To touch them was a terrible offence, to look after them a great honour. A Prince is not a Prince of the Blood but a Prince of the Drum and his status determined by which Drum. They all had separate names and significance and can never be replaced.[19]

Set alongside this, Naipaul's comment that 'now the site had its first true ruin' seems not simply ungracious but trivial.

3

For such a perspective, one must turn to the other stories and to the Epilogue. The narrators of the first two stories are both Indians. In 'One Out Of Many', the point is established immediately; in 'Tell Me Who To Kill', it emerges very slowly from references to *roti* and curry, to 'shameless' short dresses, and the single name Dayo. The contrast is appropriate. Santosh in Washington has a language and a society to look back on; the second narrator, who is never even named, is a man without identity; he arrives in London speaking an English dialect and with imperfectly remembered film scenarios as his only other frame of reference. It is not even explained where he comes from, though his dialect is Trinidadian. Santosh can dream of home, of travelling through villages where 'there would have been welcome, water, food, a fire in the night'; the second narrator wonders about his home only 'how people get to a village like that'.

The title 'One Out Of Many' has again something of the parable, though its meaning is not just that Santosh is one of many examples that could have been chosen. What he loses is his sense of community; he becomes an individual. The stages of his loss are straightforward. In Bombay, where he was the servant of a high official, he was 'so happy'. He lived in a cupboard and slept on the pavement, but he had status, security, friends with whom he talked each evening, and an employer whose own friends complimented him on his cooking. The nightmare plane journey when for the first time his character is unacceptable (his clothes unkempt, his spitting forbidden, his toilet habits filthy) transports him to 'prison' — in the car, the corridor under the 'imitation sky', the elevator, the cupboard, the apartment. Unable to pay his fare home, too poor to enjoy Washington on $3.75 a week, he accepts his new status. He gains his freedom slowly — the word, used briefly of his mornings in Bombay, reappears in the story only when he walks through the burnt-out streets and meets Priya. But already in the apartment he has discovered his appearance and learned to measure it by the TV commercials. He has begun to see his employer as an individual, no longer someone to whom he is attached, but a man of his own age with nervous habits, worried about money, patronised at his own dinner table. The final stage, after he gets his job with Priya and after he has failed to make Priya accept responsibility for him, is his decision to act for himself, to call 'a halt' to a chain of meaningless events:

> I am a simple man who decided to act and see for himself, and it is as though I have had several lives. I do not wish to add to these. Some afternoons I walk to the circle with the fountain. I see the dancers but they are separated from me as by glass. Once, when there were rumours of new burnings, someone scrawled in white paint on the pavement outside my house: *Soul Brother*. I understand the words; but I feel, brother to what or to whom? I was once part of the flow, never thinking of myself as a presence. Then I looked in the mirror and decided to be free. All that my freedom has brought me is the knowledge that I have a face and have a body, that I must feed this body and clothe this body for a certain number of years. Then it will be over.[20]

It is a simple story, but the ironies are acknowledged: Santosh in Bombay is already 'a city man' unfitted for life in the village with his wife and children; in the Washington apartment, he is surrounded by glamorous Indian artefacts which are as alien to him as America; at the roundabout with the fountain, the Negroes chanting sanskrit in praise of Lord Krishna seem to him a doubly lost people; offered friendship with other Indians, he is so burdened by his secrets that he cannot enjoy the contact – even a compliment on his cooking causes fear and suspicion. Even the style of his first-person narrator reflects not Kripalsingh's sense of progress towards the state of thinking which permits this kind of honest self-assessment, but a mock-classical poise, a longing for the past when he had no story to tell.

'Tell Me Who To Kill' is necessarily more diffuse; the dialect does not permit such clarity, and there can be no straightforward contrasts between past and present. 'From small,' the narrator tells us, 'I know I had no life.' He envies the local rich man, but is disillusioned when the desolate concrete house is opened to a wedding party. He admires his educated uncle Stephen who (like Mr

Biswas visiting his brothers) finds the family donkey a joke, and who gives the impression of having escaped. But he grows up to realise that for everyone, the real world is elsewhere, and accessible only by proxy. Stephen lives through the son who goes to study in Montreal, the narrator through his brother Dayo who 'was going to break away; he was going to be a professional man; I was going to see to that.' But even these hopes are poisoned by the rivalry of those who are to remain behind — Stephen patronising his poor relations, his daughters treating Dayo as a yardboy, the narrator's peasant father glad when Stephen's son 'turn foolish' because, by doing nothing and wanting nothing, he 'feel he win'. Long before the narrator follows Dayo to England, his hatred is formed — 'Even today I can hate them, when I should have more cause to hate white people.'

But Dayo, too, cannot do what is required of him. Untalented, confused, unable to pass exams, he can do no more than pick up a style, some impressive words, and expensive habits. The situation which made him the focus of his brother's frustrations has been cruel to him too. Later, the narrator hates him for not helping with the café or appreciating his concern; but Dayo's function was never this — he was to be the success, and he seems as burdened by this responsibility as the narator is by his beauty. The climax of the story is a vision of desolation as powerful as those in *The Mimic Men*:

> The sun shining bright now. The grass green and level and pretty. You can see the edges of the lawn black and rich, like the first time you clear a piece of bush and you know anything will grow: you can feel the damp with your foot when you walk, you can see the seeds coming up, splitting and tiny, growing day after day. The schoolgirls sitting young and indecent on the concrete curb in their very short blue skirts, laughing and talking loud to get people to look at them. The buses come and go. The taxis come and turn, and men and women get out and get in. The whole world going on. And I feel outside it, seeing only my brother and myself in this place, among the pillars, me in my working clothes, he in his suit that is so cheap it can't hold a

crease or a shape, smoking his cigarette. I would like him to smoke the best cigarettes in the world.[21]

Santosh ends by accepting responsibility for his life, making his presence legal by marrying the *hubshi* woman. But Dayo's brother will never know what went wrong or who is to blame. Frank tries to goad him into rebellion. But who is the enemy — is it his family at home, the brother who let him down, the hooligans who ruined his café, the white family into which Dayo is marrying? It seems to him that action will only end, as in his dream, as in *Rebecca* and *Rope*, by his killing the wrong person. It is not just that his situation is complicated; his background has not equipped him to understand the world. All he can do is withdraw, allow Dayo to live his own life, and accept the apparently homosexual relationship with Frank, whose attitude to him parallels his own to Dayo. At home, he allows it to be thought he is dead.

Among the passengers on the Greek steamer of the prologue were a number of Egyptian-Greek refugees. Egypt had won its freedom, and these deported Greeks were 'the casualties of that freedom'. The word is precisely chosen, for the heroes of these stories — Santosh, Dayo's brother, Bobby — are casualties not only in the sense that they suffer but in the deeper sense that there can be no solution for them. They are people for whom nothing can now be done. Mr Biswas gained his house; Kripalsingh found calm and order in writing his memoirs; but Mr Biswas was lucky, and Kripalsingh's was a special case, corresponding to Naipaul's. Not everyone can be a writer — witness Bobby and the Colonel; not every writer will find that the account of his displacement brings release — witness the two narrators. There can be no solution in violence, for it is not even clear who precisely is the enemy. So, Santosh waits for death; Dayo's brother allows it to be believed he is dead; Bobby submits to further exploitation; and the reader of *In a Free State* turns to the Epilogue.

Naipaul has returned to Egypt, by plane to Milan and Cairo and by train to Luxor. Egypt is still free, but the Greeks and Lebanese are in business, discussing fortunes to be made out of Rhodesian tobacco; the peasant soldiers back from Sinai are as disregarded as before the revolution; the imperial resort, the Winter Palace, is overrun by package tourists; in Luxor, in the tombs, Naipaul studies the work of an ancient artist:

> The pleasures of the river, full of fish and birds, the pleasures of food and drink. The land had been studied, everything in it was categorised, exalted into design. It was the special vision of men who knew no other land and saw what they had as rich and complete. The muddy Nile was only water: in the paintings, a blue-green chevron: recognisable, but remote, a river in fairyland.[22]

Freedom and decay, exploiter and exploited, the vision of the past and the vision of the artist: already, in this swift and complex piece of writing, all the book's themes have been touched on. But there is something new. In the rest house, packed with tourists, the Italians toss food to the beggar children in order to film the man with the whip beating them away. Exploiter and exploited, with the tourist taking pictures: it is like the tiger hunt of the prologue, with Naipaul taking notes. But this time he intervenes, shouting, snatching the whip, threatening a report to Cairo. Nothing is achieved. The tourists look blank, the beggar boys are puzzled, the man with the whip is frightened and suddenly powerless; and Naipaul himself, too honest to present his action as victory, feels exposed and futile.

How is the incident to be read? As a statement about the Egyptians, so easily exploited, so quickly cowed, a foretaste of that defeat in the desert in the wars brought by the revolution? As a comment on the proceeding stores, a further proof that nothing can be done? Both interpretations have been put forward.[23] But Naipaul writes as a writer, concerned in this piece of non-fiction with the responsibilities of art. He thinks again of the paintings in the tomb. In *The Mimic Men*, the vision of order was a vision of the past. Now, even with the evidence of ancient art before him, he questions this notion of lost purity and innocence:

> Perhaps that vision of the land, in which the Nile was only water, a blue-green chevron, had always been a fabrication, a cause for yearning, something for the tomb.[24]

But there is a fresh alternative. The epilogue begins in Milan, and the link between events is not just that the tourists are Italians. Wherever Naipaul goes, he comes across the hundred-odd members of the touring Chinese circus. They are small, cool, well dressed, relaxed, self-contained, handsome, healthy – the adjectives pour out in their praise, contrasting absolutely with those used of the Italians who are stout, stiff, jerseyed and chattering. Such enthusiasm from Naipaul is rare. Where else has he seen people like this, so 'silently content with one another'? They are the heralds of another empire, to be built on 'anger and a sense of injustice'.

This is not to predict a Marxist – or Maoist – future for Naipaul. The man who rejected political commitment in his earliest work remains convinced of the irrelevance of those left-wing, right-wing divisions of the world which make further thought unnecessary. But the glimpse of the Chinese is a reminder of what is possible, not in the past but now. Nothing is achieved when Naipaul seizes the camel whip. But the sudden clarity, the sense of outrage, the decision to act – all these are positive in that they define a concern which the writer cannot abrogate. The impulse to act has become the impulse behind his writings. It is not enough to record – so much was said by Kripalsingh; now it is no longer enough to produce a design in which every irony will come full circle, a pattern of metaphor which will exorcise disturbance.

The personal longing remains, for place and society, for stability and adventure. To these, Naipaul adds the insistence that in the free state we all now inhabit the writer must keep alive that responsibility to other people which is the raw material of our humanity.

NOTES

Chapter One
1 V.S. Naipaul, 'Critics & Criticism', *Bim* (Barbados), vol. 10, no 38, p. 76.
2 Ibid.
3 Seepersad Naipaul, 'Peasants' Paradise', *Trinidad Sunday Guardian* (24 Apr 1932).
4 'Liza of Lambeth', *Queens Royal College Chronicle*, vol XXIII, no 11, (1948) 42–3.
5 Ibid.
6 'London', *The Overcrowded Barracoon* (London, 1972) p. 16.
7 *An Area of Darkness* (London, 1964) p. 280.
8 'Without a Place', interview with Ian Hamilton, *Times Literary Supplement* (30 Aug 1971), p. 897.
9 Ibid.
10 Interview with Ewart Rouse, *Trinidad Guardian* (28 Nov 1968).
11 Eric Roach, *Trinidad Guardian* (17 May 1967); John Hearne, *Trinidad Guardian* (3 Feb 1963); Gordon Rohlehr, 'The Ironic Approach', *The Islands in Between*, ed. Louis James (London, 1968) p. 122.
12 *The Middle Passage* (London, 1962) p. 68.
13 George Lamming, *The Pleasures of Exile* (London, 1960) p. 225.
14 William Walsh, *A Manifold Voice* (London, 1970) p. 70.
15 *The Middle Passage*, p. 70.
16 'London', *The Overcrowded Barracoon*, p. 11.
17 *An Area of Darkness*, p. 226.
18 *Observer* (30 Apr 1967).
19 *The Middle Passage*, pp. 116–7.
20 *An Area of Darkness*, pp. 123–4.
21 Anthony Trollope, *The West Indies and the Spanish Main* (1860) pp. 209–10.
22 *The Middle Passage*, p. 199.
23 *An Area of Darkness*, p. 38.
24 Interview with Francis Wyndham, *Sunday Times* (10 Sep 1968).
25 'Speaking of Writing', *The Times* (2 Jan 1964).

Chapter Two
1 Interview with David Bates, *Sunday Times* magazine (26 May 1963).
2 Seepersad Naipaul, 'Confession of Faith', *Trinidad Guardian* (24 June 1933). The story occupies issues 18–25 June 1933.
3 *Trinidad Guardian* (31 Mar 1932).

4 Ibid. (8 Dec 1932).
5 Ibid. (3 Aug 1933); and interview with Frank Winstone, *Sunday Mirror* (Trinidad, 26 Apr 1964).
6 E.g., 'The Perambulator', *Trinidad Guardian* (7 Feb 1935).
7 Seepersad Naipaul, *Gurudeva and Other Indian Tales*, Trinidad Publications (n. d.) pp. 54–5.
8 Ibid., p. 60.
9 *A House for Mr Biswas* (London, 1961) p. 144.
10 *Gurudeva and Other Indian Tales*, pp. 70–1.
11 Ibid., p. 13
12 'Jasmine', *The Overcrowded Barracoon*, pp. 23–9.
13 Ibid., pp. 25–6.
14 *Gurudeva and Other Indian Tales*, pp. 63–4.
15 Ibid., pp. 16–7.
16 *The Middle Passage*, p. 41.
17 Interview with David Bates, *Sunday Times* magazine (26 May 1963).
18 *Miguel Street* (London, 1959) pp. 213–14.
19 The Mighty Wonder, 'Follow me Children' (date unknown).
20 Michael Anthony, *The Games Were Coming* (London, 1963) p. 42.
21 *Miguel Street*, p. 79.
22 Ibid., p. 77.
23 Ibid., pp. 165–6.
24 London, 1965 and 1967.
25 *A House for Mr Biswas*, pp. 250–1.
26 *A Flag on the Island* (London, 1967) p. 77.

Chapter Three
1 Interview with David Bates, *Sunday Times* magazine (26 May 1963).
2 *A Flag on the Island*, pp. 13–4.
3 *The Mystic Masseur* (Penguin ed., 1957) p. 139.
4 Ibid.
5 Ibid., p. 36.
6 Ibid., p. 144.
7 *The Middle Passage*, p. 72.
8 *The Mystic Masseur*, p. 196.
9 *The Middle Passage*, pp. 76–7.
10 *Times Literary Supplement* (31 May 1957).
11 'Speaking of Writing', *The Times* (2 Jan 1964).
12 *The Suffrage of Elvira* (London, 1958) pp. 115–17.
13 Ibid., p. 74.
14 Ibid., p. 19.
15 'London', *The Overcrowded Barracoon*, p. 9.
16 *The Mimic Men* (London, 1967) p. 250.

Chapter Four

1   *A House for Mr Biswas*, pp. 523–4.
2   Ibid., p. 267.
3   Ibid., p. 530.
4   Ibid., p. 7.
5   'Speaking of Writing', *The Times* (2 Jan 1964).
6   *A House for Mr Biswas*, pp. 12–13.
7   Ibid., p. 433.
8   *An Area of Darkness*, p. 32.
9   *A House for Mr Biswas*, p. 291.
10   Ibid., p. 171.
11   Ibid., p. 263.
12   Ibid., p. 100.
13   Ibid., p. 436.
14   *Times Literary Supplement* (29 Sep 1961).
15   *A House for Mr Biswas*, p. 344.
16   Ibid., pp. 501–2.

Chapter Five

1   'London', *The Overcrowded Barracoon*, p. 14.
2   'The Perfect Tenants', *A Flag on the Island*, pp. 107–8.
3   *An Area of Darkness*, pp. 207–8.
4   *Mr Stone and the Knights Companion* (London, 1963) p. 53.
5   Ibid., p. 149.
6   *A Flag on the Island*, p. 194.
7   'A West Indian Culture?', *The Illustrated Weekly of India* (30 May 1965).
8   Interview with Ronald Bryden, B.B.C. Third Programme (1 Feb 1973).
9   *Mr Stone and the Knights Companion*, p. 53.
10   *An Area of Darkness*, pp. 222–3.
11   Interview with David Bates, *Sunday Times* magazine (26 May 1963).
12   'Speaking of Writing', *The Times* (2 Jan 1964).
13   *An Area of Darkness*, p. 161.

Chapter Six

1   Interview with David Bates, *Sunday Times* magazine (26 May 1963).
2   *The Mimic Men*, p. 38.
3   Derek Walcott, 'Crusoe's Journal', lines 53–61, *The Castaway* (London, 1965).
4   *An Area of Darkness*, p. 45.
5   'What's Wrong with Being a Snob', *Saturday Evening Post* (3 June 1967).
6   'The Little More', *The Times* (13 July 1961).
7   *Trinidad Guardian* (27 Aug 1944).

8 *A Flag on the Island*, pp. 49–50.
9 Ibid., p. 35.
10 Interview with Francis Wyndham, *Sunday Times* (10 Sep 1968).
11 *The Mimic Men*, p. 292.
12 J.A. Froude, *The English in the West Indies* (Silver Library ed., 1909) pp. 73, 148–52.
13 Sarah Morton, *John Morton of Trinidad* (Toronto, 1916) pp. 79–80.
14 *The Times* (23, 24, 27 Dec 1963).
15 *The Mimic Men*, p. 230.
16 Karl Miller, *The Listener* (28 Sep 1967) pp. 402–3.
17 *The Mimic Men*, p. 220.
18 Ibid., p. 237.
19 Ibid., p. 151.
20 Ibid., pp. 204–5.
21 Ibid., pp. 282–3.
22 Ibid., p. 300.
23 Interview with Francis Wyndham, *Sunday Times* (10 Sep 1968).
24 *The Mimic Men*, p. 292.
25 *Trinidad Sunday Guardian* (6 Aug 1967).
26 'Violence in Art: The Documentary Heresy', *20th Century* (winter 1964–5) 107–8.
27 *A House for Mr Biswas*, pp. 523–4.

Chapter Seven
1 V.S. Naipaul, 'Without a Dog's Chance', *New York Review of Books* (18 May 1972) p. 31.
2 *The Middle Passage*, p. 29.
3 *The Loss of El Dorado* (London, 1969) p. 319.
4 'Pooter', *The Times* (9 Sep 1968).
5 *The Loss of El Dorado*, pp. 316–17.
6 'Pooter', *The Times* (9 Sep 1968).
7 Interview with Alex Hamilton, *Guardian* (4 Oct 1971).
8 Interview with Ronald Bryden, B.B.C. Third Programme (1 Feb 1973).
9 *The Middle Passage*, p. 5.
10 'The King Over the Water', *Sunday Times* (6 Aug 1972).
11 'A Country Dying on its Feet', *Observer* (10 Feb 1974).
12 Interview with Alex Hamilton, *Guardian* (4 Oct 1971).
13 Ibid.
14 Laban Erapu, review presented to East African English Conference, Nairobi (Feb 1972).
15 *In a Free State* (London, 1971) p. 219
16 Ibid., p. 245.
17 Ibid., p. 205.

18   Laban Erapu, review presented to East African English Conference, Nairobi (Feb 1972).
19   'King Freddie', *Desecration of My Kingdom* (London, 1967) p. 193.
20   *In a Free State*, p. 61.
21   Ibid., p. 100.
22   Ibid., p. 251.
23   Paul Theroux, *V.S. Naipaul: An Introduction to his Work* (London, 1972) p. 124; and William Walsh, *V.S. Naipaul* (Edinburgh, 1973) p. 72.
24   *In a Free State*, pp. 255–6.

INDEX